Alcoholics Anonymous
as a Mutual-Help Movement

This book is part of the International Collaborative Study of Alcoholics Anonymous, carried out in collaboration with the World Health Organization, Regional Office for Europe.

Alcoholics Anonymous as a Mutual-Help Movement

A Study in Eight Societies

Klaus Mäkelä, Ilkka Arminen, Kim Bloomfield,
Irmgard Eisenbach-Stangl, Karin Helmersson Bergmark,
Noriko Kurube, Nicoletta Mariolini,
Hildigunnur Ólafsdóttir, John H. Peterson, Mary Phillips,
Jürgen Rehm, Robin Room, Pia Rosenqvist,
Haydée Rosovsky, Kerstin Stenius, Grażyna Świątkiewicz,
Bohdan Woronowicz, and Antoni Zieliński

The University of Wisconsin Press

The University of Wisconsin Press
114 North Murray Street
Madison, Wisconsin 53715

3 Henrietta Street
London WC2E 8LU, England

Library of Congress Cataloging-in-Publication Data
Alcoholics Anonymous as a mutual-help movement: a study in eight
   societies /
Klaus Mäkelä . . . [et al.].
   322 p.   cm.
   Part of an international study of Alcoholics Anonymous, carried
out in collaboration with the World Health Organization, Regional
Office for Europe.
   Includes bibliographical references and index.
   ISBN 0-299-15000-3 (cloth: alk. paper).
ISBN 0-299-15004-6 (pbk.: alk. paper)
   1. Alcoholics Anonymous.   2. Alcoholics—Rehabilitation—Cross
cultural studies.   3. Twelve-step programs—Cross-cultural studies.
4. Self-help groups—Cross-cultural studies.   I. Mäkelä, Klaus.
II. Alcoholics Anonymous.   III. World Health Organization.
Regional Office for Europe.
HV5278.A756   1996
362.29'286—dc20   95-42146

Contents

Tables

Authors

ILKKA ARMINEN, Department of Sociology, University of York, York (At the time of the study, Ilkka Arminen was affiliated with the Finnish Foundation for Alcohol Studies.)

KIM BLOOMFIELD, Institute for Medical Statistics and Informatics, University Clinic Benjamin Franklin, Free University Berlin, Berlin (In the course of the study, Kim Bloomfield was also affiliated with the Alcohol Research Group, Medical Research Institute, Berkeley, and the Prevention Research Center, Berkeley.)

IRMGARD EISENBACH-STANGL, Ludwig Boltzmann Institute for Addiction Research, Vienna

KARIN HELMERSSON BERGMARK, Department of Sociology, University of Stockholm, Stockholm

NORIKO KURUBE, Department of Social Work, University of Stockholm, Stockholm

NICOLETTA MARIOLINI, Lausanne (At the time of the study, Nicoletta Mariolini was affiliated with the Swiss Institute for the Prevention of Alcohol and Drug Problems, Lausanne.)

KLAUS MÄKELÄ, Finnish Foundation for Alcohol Studies, Helsinki

HILDIGUNNUR ÓLAFSDÓTTIR, Department of Psychiatry, National University Hospital, Reykjavik

JOHN H. PETERSON, Department of Sociology, Anthropology and Social Work, Mississippi State University, Mississippi State (died 1993)

MARY PHILLIPS, Pittsburgh, Pennsylvania (At the time of the study, Mary Phillips was affiliated with the Alcohol Research Group, Medical Research Institute, Berkeley.)

JÜRGEN REHM, Addiction Research Foundation, Toronto (At the time of the study, Jürgen Rehm was affiliated with the Swiss Institute for the Prevention of Alcohol and Drug Problems, Lausanne.)

ROBIN ROOM, Addiction Research Foundation, Toronto (During the first part of the study, Robin Room was affiliated with the Alcohol Research Group, Medical Research Institute, Berkeley.)

PIA ROSENQVIST, Nordic Council for Alcohol and Drug Research, Helsinki

HAYDÉE ROSOVSKY, Mexican Institute of Psychiatry, Mexico City

KERSTIN STENIUS, Nordic Alcohol Studies, Helsinki

GRAŻYNA ŚWIĄTKIEWICZ, Institute of Psychiatry and Neurology, Warsaw

BOHDAN WORONOWICZ, Institute of Psychiatry and Neurology, Warsaw

ANTONI ZIELIŃSKI, Institute of Psychiatry and Neurology, Warsaw

Acknowledgments

We are grateful to numerous members of AA and other mutual-aid organizations who have helped to make this study such a rewarding experience. We also thank the representatives of national service bodies and offices of AA as well as the General Service Office in New York for their generous help with all stages of this project.

David Robinson provided helpful advice in the planning stage of the project. Danuta Dudrak, Eckart Kühlhorn, Patricia Morgan, and Christine Vourakis participated in the beginning of the project and contributed with working papers. Lee Kaskutas joined the project at a later stage and presented valuable comments on the final report.

The project group greatly benefitted from the support of the World Health Organization, Regional Office for Europe, particularly from Cees Goos, coordinator, Alcohol, Drugs and Tobacco Unit, and Jens Hannibal, scientist, programme for the Prevention of Alcohol Abuse (till 1991).

A large number of individuals and organizations in all the participant countries have supported the project with data and advice. The project group remains indebted to participants at the annual conferences of the Kettil Bruun Society for Social and Epidemiological Research on Alcohol who over the years discussed a series of working papers.

Special thanks go to our colleagues who provided critical and helpful comments on the manuscript: Risto Alapuro, Christa Appel, Howard P. Brown, Tom Colthurst, Keith Humphreys, Risto Jaakkola, Jaana Jaatinen, Ernest Kurtz, Harry Levine, Johanna Mäkelä, Kirsti Määttänen, Pirjo Paakkanen, Juha Partanen, Aino Sinnemäki, Jorma Sipilä, Astrid Skretting, Marja-Leena Sorjonen, Jukka-Pekka Takala, Christoffer Tigerstedt, and Matti Virtanen.

The participation of the Ludwig Boltzmann Institute for Addiction Research was supported by a grant from the Austrian Federal Ministry of Science and Research.

The Finnish project group greatly appreciates the help of the following colleagues: Kari Haavisto, Kalervo Koskela, and Tuula Muhonen-Niskanen.

The participation of the National University Hospital's Department of Psychiatry was supported by a grant from the Icelandic Liquor Prevention Council.

The Department of Epidemiological and Social Research of the Mexican Institute of Psychiatry received support from the Mexican Foundation for Social Research and the Mexican Council of Science and Technology.

The participation of the Institute of Psychiatry and Neurology was supported by the Polish Ministry of Health.

The participation of the Department of Sociology. University of Stockholm, was supported by the State Monopoly's Foundation for Alcohol Research (SFA), the Research Foundation of IOGT-NTO, and the Foundation in Commemoration of Lars Hierta.

The participation of the Swiss Institute for the Prevention of Alcohol and Drug Problems was supported by a grant from the Swiss National Science Foundation (Ref. Nr. 32-28658.90). We akcnowledge our gratitude to Sophie Ayer, Jacques Besson, Sabine Girardet, Maja Huber, Harald Klingemann, Kaj Noschis, Steve Vaucher, and Tatjana Vaucher.

Work on U.S. components of the project was partly supported by grants from the U.S. National Institute on Alcohol Abuse and Alcoholism (AA07240, AA05595 and AA06282) to the Alcohol Research Group; to the Prevention Research Center; and to the School of Public Health, University of California, Berkeley; and by the Marin Institute for the Prevention of Alcohol- and Other Drug-Related Problems. We acknowledge the help of many staff members from these institutions, particularly Connie Weisner, Michael Sparks, and Joel Grube.

The Nordic Council for Alcohol and Drug Research provided support to the Nordic participants' attendance at working meetings of the project.

The other authors wish to pay tribute to John H. Peterson, who died in the midst of the project.

Part One
The Research Perspective:
AA as a Mutual-Help Movement

1

Introduction

Alcoholics Anonymous (AA) is one of the great success stories of our century. AA originated in the 1930s in middle-class North America, but in successive stages it has been able to outgrow the cultural milieu of its birth. In 1990, it had an estimated membership of two million worldwide. AA began as a mutual-help movement aiming at inner reform and addressing the existential problems of a small minority. Its organizational principles outline strict limits against any attempts to effect political change or to carry out cultural propaganda. Nevertheless, the end result is that important segments of the general public in North America are deeply affected by the 12-step program.

With the exception of the seminal work of Ernest Kurtz (1991), most studies analyze AA as a treatment modality, either from the perspective of individual members (Denzin, 1987; Robinson, 1979; Rudy, 1986) or from the perspective of treatment professionals (Galanter, 1990; Madsen, 1980; Ogborne, 1989). It is by no means our intention to dispute the relevance of these perspectives. With the growth of professional treatment using the AA program, it becomes increasingly important to evaluate the efficiency of the treatment modality. In this report, however, a complementary perspective is adopted, from which AA is analyzed as a forerunner and a key representative of the new mutual-aid movement of the last few decades.

Unlike traditional organizations, membership in AA is based on individual life experiences and existential identity rather than on one's position in the social structure. As in many so-called new social movements, the focus is on problems of self-definition, and work on one's identity is a central feature in AA. Despite its size and longevity, AA has been able to preserve its internal informal structure and the autonomy of individual groups. AA has successfully carried out large-scale economic activities, such as the production and distribution of millions of

3

pieces of literature, without bureaucratizing the internal structure of the movement. Furthermore, the 12-step program and the organizational principles of AA have been adopted by numerous mutual-aid movements addressing problems other than drinking. It is, therefore, of considerable sociological interest to analyze AA as the prototype of an emerging social form (Room, 1993).

The Study Sites

Most of the previous research on AA has been conducted in North America. In the International Collaborative Study of Alcoholics Anonymous (ICSAA), a broader comparative perspective has been adopted, and our study is based on data from eight countries (for a description of the organization and data base of the project, see appendices A–C). Since AA is mainly a phenomenon of relatively developed countries, the societies participating in the study are by no means a representative selection of the world's countries. It was our goal, however, to include countries with varying social and economic structures, religious traditions, and drinking cultures.

It was obviously important to include the United States because it is the country of origin of AA. Reflecting the data available and as specified in each table, some of the information concerning the United States referes to the country as a whole, some to California, and some to AA in the United States and Canada. Because of important regional differences, AA in California does not necessarily mirror the whole country. As an example of emerging cultural trends, however, California provides a useful base for international comparisons.

Because of the affinity of AA to the Protestant tradition, three Nordic countries were included. Despite their cultural similarity, however, Finland, Iceland, and Sweden represent different experiences with AA. Austria is a Catholic wine country, and Switzerland represents a field laboratory with three linguistic cultures. Poland is a formerly socialist Catholic country with a tradition of spirits drinking and a rapidly expanding AA. Mexico, where AA is very strong, is another Catholic country with a tradition of occasional binge drinking.

Although the study countries exhibit a fairly broad range of AA experiences, the AA world is not evenly represented. We were unsuccessful in our attempts to involve other English-speaking countries besides the United States. We also regret that Spanish-speaking America is represented by only one country, even though Latin America accounts for more than one-third of the world membership of AA.

The Basic Approach of the Study

The purposes of the project are (1) to present an analysis of AA as an international mutual-aid movement and (2) to study how AA activities are adapted to various cultural surroundings.

To accomplish these goals, we propose to discuss AA in three different conceptual frames:

(1) social movement and social network,
(2) belief system, and
(3) system of interaction.

Our discussion of AA as a social organization focuses on the organizational guidelines of AA as an innovative codification of the principles for non-hierarchic and non-bureaucratic social structures. In addition, we will discuss national variations such as structural complexity; relationships to outside society, particularly to professional treatment; and relationships to and the impact on mainstream culture.

According to a common view, mutual-help groups achieve their results through a cluster of social-psychological processes: confession, catharsis, mutual identification, and the removal of stigmatized feelings. Despite its considerable merits, this view neglects the very feature the members take most seriously, namely the belief system of each group (Antze, 1979; Kennedy & Humphreys, 1994). In this book, therefore, we discuss the AA program as a system of beliefs and as a way of looking at the world (Bateson, 1985; Kurtz, 1982). We pay particular attention to the relationships of belief and action in AA, the role of written and oral traditions in the transmission of the beliefs, and the cultural variation in the content of the belief system.

Most program activities are carried out through interaction among members. It is important, therefore, to analyze AA as a system of interaction. In particular, we aim to show that the AA meeting is a very specific type of speech event that can nevertheless be adapted to widely varying cultural traditions.

In each of our three conceptual frames—social movement and social network, belief system, and system of interaction—we will argue that there is no single element that would be peculiar to AA. What makes AA unique is the combination of elements. In order to be able to identify these combinations we should be wary of preconceived theoretical classifications that are usually not sensitive to new combinations of familiar elements. This is why we emphasize the importance of concrete descriptions.

Our project was immediately confronted with the bewildering variety of AA groups. The basic texts of AA are used universally but they allow for significantly diverging interpretations. The structure and tenor of AA meetings vary widely from American professional 12-step treatment centers to Austrian closed meetings, or from the actively religious American South to secular Sweden.

At the very outset, we want to resist the temptation to define a "true AA" and to label divergent forms as adulterations or deviations. Instead, our aim is to illustrate the diversity and to describe some of the main dimensions of variability of AA (Mäkelä, 1993a, 1993b).

Any student of AA is confronted with the dilemma of the degree to which they should adopt the insider's perspective and vocabulary. Professional journals abound with presentations of AA couched in AA's own terminology. Another common procedure is to present functional analyses of AA and to provide translations of what is going on in AA into the vocabularies current in different scientific or therapeutic traditions. The growth of the professional 12-step treatment has also brought about a mixture of inside and outside languages, combining AA vocabulary with psychodynamic theories. The distinction between inside and outside language is further blurred in some countries where segments of the 12-step vocabulary have become part of the common language.

As social scientists, we bring with us our conceptual perspectives. Our aim is, however, to provide a concrete description of AA that is understandable to members and outsiders alike. When we use internal AA language, we try to use it in our analytical frame, which is from outside rather than inside the AA worldview, but we would also like to avoid the opposite danger of squeezing AA into preconceived categories of sociological jargon.

The adoption of an outside perspective makes it difficult to express the transcendental or spiritual nature of AA, a feature that for many members is central to AA. Many members emphasize that to them AA meetings are spiritual events, and even an outside observer can sometimes sense moments of extraordinary intensity at AA meetings. In principle, we do not believe that transcendental experiences are beyond analysis. Spirituality is best conceived as a field of meaning, and fields of meaning are mutually understandable even to people who do not share the same beliefs. We can understand sentences and concepts we do not believe have external referents. Descriptions of inner states are understandable, up to a point, to persons who do not share similar experiences. Although they remain beyond the scope of the present report, we are in no way denying the importance of transcendental experiences in the AA process.

The Structure of the Book

Our book begins with the historical background and organization of AA. In Part I, we present a preliminary analysis of the specificity of AA as a mutual-aid movement in comparison to other related organizations. Part II draws a background sketch of the early history of AA and describes its diffusion and international structure. Part III is devoted to the organizational principles of AA and its present structure, finances, and membership. Part IV analyzes the belief system of AA, AA meetings are speech events, and program activities of individual members. In Part V, we discuss AA in relation to professional treatment and alternative mutual-aid organizations for alcohol problems, and we describe the impact of AA on mainstream culture. Finally, in Part VI, we draw together the main results of our study and discuss their implications for professional practice and research.

This book is an overview of AA as an international mutual-aid movement. National case studies of AA in each particular setting will be presented in a forthcoming companion volume edited by Irmgard Eisenbach-Stangl and Pia Rosenqvist, *Diversity in Unity: Studies of Alcoholics Anonymous in Eight Societies.*

2

The Place of AA among Social Movements

AA's Conference Charter uses the term "AA movement" (*The A.A. Service Manual,* 1988, p. 24), but AA's preferred description of itself is as a "fellowship," a term which carries meanings of companionship, of a community of interest and feeling, of constituting an association, and of the equal status of members of the association (see "fellow" and "fellowship" in Stein, 1967). The term has specific usages in the contexts of religious groups and higher education, but also a more general connotation emphasizing mutuality and collective activity as primary purposes of a voluntary association, rather than as the means for some other purpose.

We recognize the aptness of characterizing AA as a fellowship, and recognize also the significance of AA's choice of this self-characterization. But "fellowship" is not a very restrictive category; it can be used to refer to a wide variety of groupings, from a small prayer-circle to the whole of humankind. In our consideration of AA, we have thought of it in an additional frame as well: as a *mutual-help movement*—a specific kind of social movement.

AA as a Social Movement

Traditionally, for sociologists, the prototype of a social movement was a worker's movement—a class-based movement developed to change society in the interests of its members' class. It has been pointed out, however, that already in the nineteenth century, in addition to such "beneficiary" movements, other movements such as abolitionism and temperance based largely on "conscience" constituencies were prominent, particularly on the American scene (Zald, 1988). In recent years a burgeoning literature on "new social movements" has appeared, bringing into the general analytical framework the ecology movement, the peace movement, and other movements whose members

8

are not acting on behalf of their own class or sectional interest. Drawing its inspiration from a member of theoretical perspectives presented in the 1970s and 1980s (Habermas, 1981; Melucci, 1989; Offe, 1985; Touraine, 1978), the study of new social movements has culminated in rapidly growing comparative investigations and conceptualizations (Dalton & Kuechler, 1990; Eyerman & Jamison, 1991; Klandermans, Kriesi, & Tarrow, 1988; Rucht, 1991; Scott, 1990). In terms of organizational ideals and practices, AA shares several characteristics of these new social movements and could be seen as their forerunner (Bloomfield, 1994).

Most new social movements are aimed at changing the society in which they operate, even if not necessarily in conventional political arenas or at the level of the nation-state. However, AA seeks only personal change among its members, and specifically renounces any ambition to change the surrounding society. But AA should not be dismissed as irrelevant to the study of new social movements and, more generally, of new agents of social change. According to the literature, social movements tend to focus more and more on self-transformation and on problems of self-definition and challenges to dominant lifestyles (Diani, 1992). Cohen (1985) states that new social movements "target the social domain of 'civil society' rather than the economy of the state, raising issues concerned with the democratization of structures of everyday life and focusing on forms of communication and collective identity" (p. 667). Contemporary movements, in this view, "defend spaces for the creation of new identities and solidarities" and "consciously struggle over the power to socially construct new identities, to create democratic spaces for autonomous social action, and to reinterpret norms and reshape institutions" (pp. 689–690). The identity work of AA is more inwardly oriented than that of the movements usually analyzed by students of new social movements, but AA certainly has invented new forms of communication and fosters new types of social relationships.

Analysts of new social movements often put emphasis on the reflexivity of identity work. According to Melucci (1980), contemporary collective actors have become reflexive regarding the social processes of identity formation (Melucci, 1980, 1989). That is, they have become aware of their capacity to create identities. The existential destiny of becoming an alcoholic is not structurally determined, but from an AA perspective it certainly is not a matter of choice. The identity of an AA alcoholic is, however, very much based on self-definition. The reflexivity of identity formation is even more clearly visible in the emerging general 12-step movement. In northern California, joining a 12-step group may be more of a value and lifestyle choice than the only way out of intolerable pain.

An alternative framing of AA is as a religious movement. A number of researchers have noted analogies between the structure, activities, and ideology of AA and those of religious organizations (Bufe, 1991; Fichter, 1976; Galanter, 1990; Gellman, 1964; Greil & Rudy, 1983; R. K. Jones, 1970; Madsen, 1979, 1980; Petrunik, 1972; Thune, 1977; Whitley, 1977; for a critique, see Rudy & Greil, 1989, and Sadler, 1979). The analogies can be formulated in functional or in substantive terms. Functional definitions, which run the danger of being too general, identify the crucial element of religion as the ability to "relate man to the ultimate conditions of his existence" (Yinger, 1970, p. 70). Substantive definitions insist that religion must make reference to the sacred or the superempirical (R. Robertson, 1970, p. 47). Obviously, the AA ideology and way of life provides a meaningful system that enables the members to understand their current and past lives, but this holds for clearly irreligious world views as well.

Many members of AA are religious in the conventional sense, and some even identify AA as a religion (Rudy & Greil, 1989). On the other hand, AA literature and most AA members resolutely deny that it is, and claim that AA is spiritual, not religious. In fact, this ambiguity is an essential feature of AA. AA has developed an ideology in which the religious and its denial exist in a state of dynamic tension. It is not a religion camouflaged as spirituality, since members and the fellowship, as a whole, obstinately cling to this ambiguity both in their internal and external relations. Rudy and Greil (1989) conclude that AA is a quasi-religion and that quasi-religion should be studied as a category of its own.

As an organization, AA does not fit neatly the usual descriptive categories of social science. It began as an organization sui generis, but it has become the prototype of a burgeoning category of mutual-help organizations (Room, 1992).

AA as a Mutual-Help Movement

The main literature in which AA is discussed as a movement is the literature on self-help movements (Katz, 1993). The term "self-help" is normally used only with reference to historical situations where other forms of support are available or politically conceivable. Networks of mutual help in preindustrial societies are usually not considered self-help, and folk medicine becomes self-help only when the alternative of professionally educated experts has emerged. Since self-help is always seen as an alternative to some other option, the term gets variable ideological loadings.

The historical content and nature of self-help varies so widely that any general definition runs the danger of becoming vacuous. Most definitions presented in the literature (Jacobs & Goodman, 1989; Katz, 1981; Katz & Bender, 1976; Lieberman, 1986; Smith & Pillemer, 1983) deal only with the modern self-help groups of the last few decades. According to Smith and Pillemer (1983), a self-help group "is a voluntary group valuing personal interaction and mutual aid as means of altering or ameliorating problems perceived as alterable, pressing, and personal by most of its participants" (pp. 205–206). Katz and Bender (1976) provide a fuller characterization:

> Self-help groups are voluntary, small group structures for mutual aid and the accomplishment of a special purpose. They are usually formed by peers who have come together for mutual assistance in satisfying a common need, overcoming a common handicap or life-disrupting problem, and bringing about desired social and/or personal change. The initiators and members of such groups perceive that their individual needs are not, or cannot be, met by or through existing social institutions. Self-help groups emphasize face-to-face social interactions and the assumption of personal responsibility by members. They often provide material assistance, as well as emotional support; they are frequently "cause"-oriented, and promulgate an ideology or values through which members may attain an enhanced sense of personal identity. (p. 278)

Katz (1981) argues that this characterization is sufficient to distinguish self-help groups from "groupings and agreements among those who exercise political or economic power—such as unions, cartels, corporation boards, 'old boy' networks, and friendship cliques" as well as "from various voluntary membership organizations, such as 'service organizations,' oriented to traditional philanthropy" (p. 136).

The choice of the term itself indicates something about the ideological positioning of the literature: *self*-help is viewed as an adjunct or alternative to *professional* help, with the latter assumed to be the normative response to a health or social problem. The literature is largely aimed at professional audiences, and often has a programmatic and, indeed, a celebratory bent. Against the often unstated skepticism of professionals about avowedly nonprofessional activities in their field of expertise, the literature argues for the usefulness of self-help groups as an adjunct or sequel to professional treatment (Jacobs & Goodman,

1989). Some authors push beyond this to argue that there are things self-help groups can do that professionals cannot do.

The 1970s and 1980s witnessed an upsurge of self-help groups in North America and Western Europe (Barath, 1991; Bender, 1986; Katz, 1981, 1986). One widely accepted interpretation was that self-help groups were a response to the breakdown of traditional informal support systems such as the family and local community. At the same time, self-help groups were seen as empowering the ordinary citizen against professional and bureaucratic machines (Smith & Pillemer, 1983). In the wake of the anti-authoritarian currents of the 1960s and 1970s, the report of the 1980 German Public Health Conference speaks of a growing movement against the power of experts (*Selbstbestimmung in der Offensive, Dokumentation des Gesundheitstages Berlin 1980*, vol. 5, p. 7; cited in Brill, 1987, p. 35).

From early on, however, health professionals took an active interest in self-help (Moeller, 1978), and the World Health Organization envisaged self-help as an integral part of overall public health policies (Badwa & Kickbusch, 1991; Kickbusch & Hatch, 1983; World Health Organization, 1981). Self-help was also seen as a method of curbing the ever-increasing cost of health and welfare services, and attempts were made to increase the linkages among self-help groups and professional health and welfare providers (see, for instance, Borkman, 1990; Katz et al., 1992; Marzahn & Bossong, 1989; Moeller, 1978). In the United States, one important event was the 1987 Workshop on Self-Help and Public Health, sponsored by Surgeon General C. Everett Koop (Borkman, 1990; Riessman & Gardner, 1987). In Germany as well, "help through self-help" has become an important aspect of welfare policies (Brill, 1987).

As the term is commonly used, self-help includes not only self-started and autonomous groups meeting to deal with a common affliction or problem, but also after-care clubs, groups formed and guided by professionals, and advocacy groups working on behalf of the interests of those afflicted. In this broad sense, self-help groups have become a common feature of many developed societies. A recent guide to "mutual-aid self-help groups" for disabilities and stressful life situations lists more than 600 national movements and model groups in the United States (White & Madara, 1992). Table 2.1 shows in rough terms their distribution by type of problem addressed. Most of the pages in the guide are taken up by groups dealing with disabilities and problems of physical health. Groups addressing parental and family problems are another common category. The list of movements dealing with addictions and dependencies is no more than 8 percent, but in terms of

Table 2.1   Mutual-Aid Self-Help Groups in the United
States, by Type of Problem Addressed

	Pages in national directory, % (N = 126)
Addictions/dependencies	8
Bereavement	4
Disabilities	11
Physical health	41
Mental health	7
Parental/family	11
Physical/emotional abuse	4
	14
Other/miscellaneous	—
	100

Source: Calculated from White & Madara, 1992

membership strength they are considerably more prominent. For example, of all self-help or mutual-help groups in 1984 in New Jersey, 46
percent were AA groups (Maton et al., 1990).

To characterize AA, however, we have chosen the term "mutual-
help movement," rather than "self-help movement." This choice of
term conveys two signals: we are classing AA in a more specific
subcategory of self-help movements, and we are also using a term with
a more descriptive connotation. The ideology of AA is explicitly one
of *mutual* help, and many elements of its program emphasize social
and group interaction, while the term self-help carries an inappropriate connotation of the individual acting by him- or herself. "Mutual-
help movement," furthermore, is intended to exclude groups led by
professionals or others who do not share the defining affliction of the
movement, and to exclude advocacy groups. In our usage, then, a
mutual-help movement is an association or aggregate of groups whose
members meet on an egalitarian basis to counteract through mutual
interaction a common affliction or problem in their lives.

For a historical understanding of the new mutual-help movement,
it is useful to identify the key dimensions distinguishing new mutual-
help groups from their nineteenth-century precedents. The proto-
types of classic mutual help are the institutions developed by the English working class to cope with the disruptive effects of the market
economy. The mutual-help groups in nineteenth-century England
originated as systems of mutual insurance and support funds for unem-
ployment, sickness, and burial expenses. In the next stage, resources
were pulled together for future investments (e.g., building societies).

Nineteenth-century mutual help was economic in nature, although it included important aspects of self-improvement such as self-education and temperance.

For the new mutual-help groups, the main problems are less related to economic survival than to existential issues: how to be a woman, how to face approaching blindness, or the loss of a family member. Solving personal problems guides most mutual-help group members to inner change, but a number among them also engage in political advocacy (Smith & Pillemer, 1983; Steinman & Traustein, 1976; Suler, 1984).

Identity work is central when existential problems are being dealt with, but economic cooperation also affects the selfhood of participants. The friendly societies provided economic security, but they also offered conviviality and modified the worldview of their members (Garrard, 1991; Thompson, 1979). Solving existential problems has corresponding practical aspects. Support groups for persons with deteriorating eyesight help their members to adjust to a blind existence, but they also give practical advice about available services.

Arguably, AA has the longest history of any mutual-help movement in addressing existential problems, and has served as the prototype or seedbed for a variety of other movements. With more than 92,000 groups in 1990, AA also is the largest mutual-help movement in today's world. The significance of AA lies not only in its longevity and influence on other mutual-help and self-help movements, but also in the large size of its membership.

Antecedents of AA

Two clear antecedents of AA are usually cited. One is a direct organizational link: as a movement, AA grew out of the Oxford Group movement, an evangelical Protestant offshoot of the Young Men's Christian Association, which sought religious conversions with methods developed in missionary work in China (Kurtz, 1991; Peterson, 1992). Though the early connection with the Oxford Group movement has always been acknowledged by AA, the eventual development of the Oxford Group movement into a politicized movement with some fascist sympathies (eventually renamed Moral Rearmament) has led AA to de-emphasize its early connection with the movement.

The other antecedent is a historical parallel: the Washingtonian movement of the 1840s in the United States (Lender & Martin, 1982, pp. 74–79). This movement of reformed drunkards, arising in the wake of the temperance movement's first great surge in the 1830s, swept from one American city to another, carried by the enthusiasm of audiences for speeches by "experience lecturers" about their former disgrace and present redemption. Even though a few more self-reform movements emerged (Baumohl, 1986), by 1850 the Washington enthusiasm had subsided, giving way to organized temperance fraternities with memberships dominated by lifelong abstainers. It is doubtful that the founders of AA knew of the Washingtonians in the 1930s, but by the late 1940s the historical parallel was well recognized (Maxwell, 1950). In *Alcoholics Anonymous Comes of Age* (1986, pp. 124–125), the political conflicts within the Washington movement and its rapid decay were explicitly used to support the principle that AA should take no stands on outside issues (Tradition Ten).

In hindsight, a continuity can be discerned between the old temperance movements and AA. Thus Blocker (1989) has recently interpreted the founding of AA as the first sign of a fifth cycle of temperance reform in America that has not yet crested. The founders of AA would have rejected the idea of such a continuity, however, and would have been horrified at the idea of AA as a neo-temperance manifestation. The founding generation of AA was drawn from the vanguard cohort of youth generations, which took up heavy drinking as a symbol of rebellion against the Victorian bourgeois moral order, including the temperance movement (Room, 1989). In banding together to find a way out of the trouble drinking had caused in their life, early AA members were at pains to insist they were not against other people drinking, and to distinguish themselves from the temperance movement.

The temperance movement against which early AA members were reacting was, however, a highly politicized movement of the turn of the century, a movement focused on political action to control others' drinking by prohibiting alcohol beverages to all. But there was another side to temperance thinking, with which AA had a much greater continuity. The temperance movement had started from men's concern about their own drinking, and the theme of alcohol as the potential enslaver, as the great cause of the disgrace and ruin, had become deeply entrenched in American culture. This concern about self-control, and about alcohol as an externalized cause of loss of self-control, carried over into AA's conception of alcoholism as a disease (Jellinek, 1952; Levine, 1978). AA adopted, intact, the argument of doctors and others in the temperance era that the only cure for inebriety or alcoholism was to stop drinking forever. The important conceptual shift that differentiated AA from temperance thinking was that it was only a special class of people, alcoholics with an in-built predisposition or allergy, who must abstain from drinking.

Besides the parallels in thinking between AA and the temperance movement, there are clear temperance antecedents in terms of mutual-help organizations. In its polycephalous structure of groups focused on mutual help, AA bears some resemblance to the groups of craftsmen and professionals in the early temperance movement who met to support each other in their pledge to abstain from spirits. These resemblances, however, are mostly a matter of two independent adaptations of general patterns of voluntary organization.

Much of AA practice and organizational structure was borrowed or reinvented from older forms in the culture. The Quaker meeting offers a model of a non-hierarchical meeting composed of personal testimonies—and of a decision rule of substantial consensus rather than majority voting. Several liberal Protestant denominations offer examples of acephalous organization, with anyone allowed to set up a new congregation. Fraternal organizations such as the Masons and the Oddfellows offer models of mutual-interest groups with a strong emphasis on regular meetings and fellowship, and in some cases on secretiveness with respect to the outside world.

In its period of gestation in the United States during the late 1930s and early 1940s, AA's ideology and organizational structure were not distinctively new. What was new was the combination of elements, as the founders and early members of AA drew together themes and principles from diverse traditions.

Part Two
Early Years and the Diffusion of AA

3
The Early Years of AA in the United States and Canada

The history of Alcoholics Anonymous in the United States has been well and often told (Kurtz, 1991), and it would be superfluous to recount it here. Instead we give as a background to our analysis a basic outline of AA's early development in the United States and Canada (Table 3.1). This movement served as the rootstock from which other national movements were transplanted, and has continued to exercise a strong influence on the fellowship as a whole.

The Beginning

The beginning of AA can be traced to the meeting of two people with severe drinking-related problems—William Griffith Wilson (Bill W. by his AA name), a stock company investigator living in New York, and Robert Holbrook Smith (Dr. Bob), a physician living in Akron, Ohio, an industrial city in the American Midwest. Alone on a business trip in Akron, Bill W. felt that he had to talk to another alcoholic in order not to drink again. Some weeks after their encounter, on June 10, 1935, Dr. Bob took his last drink. This is regarded as the founding site of Alcoholics Anonymous.

Both founders had experience in the Oxford Group movement, an evangelical Protestant movement of spiritual renewal. During the months following June 1935, Bill W. met with Dr. Bob in Akron, and the two developed the basic ideals and program of Alcoholics Anonymous, adapting the principles and practices of the Oxford Groups to the specific problem of the inability to control drinking. The new program consisted of helping, talking to, or otherwise maintaining contact with other drunkards and engaging in some kind of spiritual activity—which in the early days meant attending local Oxford Group meetings. Both activities were seen as crucial to maintaining one's own sobriety.

Table 3.1   Milestones in the History of AA in the United States and Canada

1935	12 May. Bill W. meets Dr. Bob, in Akron, Ohio.
1935	10 June. Dr. Bob has his last drink, AA's official starting point.
1938	May. Alcoholics Foundation formed to raise funds. Works Publishing, Inc., formed to publish a book describing AA.
1938	December. Twelve Steps written.
1939	April. *Alcoholics Anonymous* published.
1939	October. Akron AAs separate from Oxford Group. AA is now independent of other organizations.
1940	First World Service Office for AA, New York.
1941	March. *Saturday Evening Post* article gives AA national publicity. Membership grows from 2,000 to 8,000 in the last 10 months of 1941.
1944	Formation of the National Committee for Education on Alcoholism (later called the National Council on Alcoholism).
1944	First publication of *A.A. Grapevine*.
1946	Publication of first version of the Twelve Traditions in *A.A. Grapevine*.
1946-1949	Memoranda from Bill W. to trustees; trustees opposed to creating a conference or even an advisory council.
1950	First International Convention in Cleveland. Adoption of the Twelve Traditions and the Third Legacy (Service) proposal establishing a five-year experimental General Service Conference (United States and Canada) to meet annually.
1950	Conference plan approved by trustees.
1950	Death of Dr. Bob.
1951	First General Service Conference in New York begins a five-year experimental period.
1951	Publication of the *Third Legacy Manual*, later called the *A.A. Service Manual*, describing the principles of conference organization for the United States and Canada.
1953	Publication of *Twelve Steps and Twelve Traditions*.
1954	Alcoholics Foundation renamed General Service Board of Alcoholics Anonymous. The majority of the trustees remain non-alcoholic.
1955	Fifth General Service Conference takes over the leadership of AA: adoption of the General Conference Charter (North America) establishing a representative service structure linking the membership to the General Service Board.
1955	Works Publishing, Inc., becomes A.A. Publishing, Inc. Publication of the second edition of *Alcoholics Anonymous* with unchanged text but a section of new stories.
1959	A.A. Publishing Inc., becomes A.A. World Services, Inc.
1962	"Twelve Concepts for World Service" adopted by the 12th General Service Conference.
1966	Change in the General Service Board (United States and Canada) to provide that two-thirds of the board be composed of alcoholic members.
1971	Death of Bill W.

The circle of recovering alcoholics grew slowly both in Akron and New York, to which Bill W. had returned. By 1937 there were forty members, and the nameless fellowship had begun to take on an existence of its own. In that year, the New York fellowship, with a more secularized and cosmopolitan membership, separated from the Oxford Group movement, while the Akron group remained in close cooperation for another two years. Traces of the differences in orientation to religion between the Akron and the New York traditions in AA can be noticed even today. These variations were accompanied by nuances of difference in the way the AA program was actually pursued. In Akron, for instance, joining AA usually meant first being hospitalized, then kneeling and praying in the presence of the group for help with one's problem and one's life. In New York, kneeling was not customary, and there was a strong emphasis on not "preaching" when talking to another alcoholic. As the AA program evolved, it was gradually adapted to be acceptable to those from a broad range of religious traditions. For instance, the public confessions in the Akron group were switched to the private disclosure now found in the movement's Fifth Step when it was found that Catholic recruits saw the public procedure as uncomfortably Protestant. Despite the differences in practice, the emerging movement had enough common ground to remain together. Certainly the unique and deep friendship between the two founders contributed to maintaining this unity.

By 1939, the movement had reached one hundred members. Led by Bill W., the members had taken on the project of writing down the movement's program and their experiences as an inspiration and guide for others, and these were published in 1939 under the title *Alcoholics Anonymous*. The book's title became the movement's name. In the succeeding months, a spate of national publicity brought a flood of new members, and AA became a truly national and rapidly growing movement.

The Basic Program

The basic program of AA is outlined in the Twelve Steps (see Appendix D), published in the 1939 book (known in the movement as the *Big Book*). The Steps were written by Bill W. during 1938 and 1939, but they were widely debated among members and the wording reflects these collective discussions.

Organizational Structure

The creation of an organizational structure for Alcoholics Anonymous began in 1938 with the formation of the Alcoholic Foundation, comprised primarily of non-member supporters to raise funds for the movement, and with the setting up of a company to publish the *Big Book*. A headquarters office for AA, later called the service office, was set up in New York in connection with the publication of this book.

There were a lot of unanticipated problems in the growing movement during the 1940s, and no role models to follow. Issues such as ownership of property, anonymity, methods of selecting leaders, and the propriety of taking jobs in the alcohol field and public relations came up and were dealt with differently in different places.

Following the publication of the *Big Book*, a growing correspondence was directed to the New York office. Bill W. became the key person in the evolving relationship between different AA groups, as well as with the general public. In 1946, in AA's periodical, *A.A. Grapevine*, Bill W. published his views on the successful methods AA groups had used to deal with organizational problems. These were called the Twelve Traditions. In the same year, the *Grapevine* published what is now called the *Preamble* (see Appendix D), conveying one of the most important organizational principles—that AA is not an organization but a fellowship. Two other principles had been chiseled out by the middle of the 1940s—the principle of anonymity and the principle of non-alignment with outside views. The Twelve Traditions were discussed among members and finalized in 1950 (see Appendix D). With the adoption of the Traditions, the group became clearly identified as the base unit of AA.

In the late 1940s and early 1950s the founders of AA, especially Bill W., engaged in numerous discussions and several plans to develop the organizational structure of AA. In 1950, at the first International Convention of AA in Cleveland, the Twelve Traditions, known as the Second Legacy (the first being the Twelve Steps), were adopted. At the same convention a proposal (published in a pamphlet called the *Third Legacy*) was made on how to arrange the organizational structure in the future. It included plans for a representational conference made up of AA members. The composition of the trustees of the Foundation and their relations to the AA members and the movement were among the main issues. The majority of the trustees of the foundation were non-alcoholics. While they were a self-perpetuating board chosen from within a circle of friends of AA, no consideration was given to what the membership-at-large thought. With the growth of the membership from around 2,000 in 1941 to 15,000 in 1945, the role of the trustees as fundraisers was not important anymore. However, they still played a major role in mediating between AA and the general public.

From 1951, delegates of AA groups from different parts of the United States and Canada started to meet at yearly conferences according to a plan drafted mostly by Bill W. and adopted by the trustees. During the same year the principles of the conference organization were published as the *Third Legacy Manual* (later called the *Service Manual*). After a five-year experimental period, at the Fifth General Service Conference in 1955, the national leadership of AA was turned over to the conference, which adopted the General Conference Charter. The conference thereby assumed responsibility for diverse functions of the movement—among them the service office and the publishing company. It also took over responsibility for a separate corporation, established to publish the periodical *A.A. Grapevine*. The conference, to which the participants were elected in a representative manner from different parts of the United States and Canada, became the body electing the trustees. In 1954 the foundation was renamed the General Service Board, but the majority of the members remained non-alcoholic. Provisions stating that two-thirds of the board members should be alcoholics were not made until 1966.

Hence, by the 1960s, AA had created a representative structure, with yearly conferences of delegates choosing the General Service Board. As in the United States and Canada, AA in other countries had adopted the custom of calling its representative structure "the service structure." The choice of term is an expression of the democratic ideals of the movement: according to Tradition Two, "Our leaders are but trusted servants; they do not govern."

Literature

In the early years, personal contact between members was seen as crucial for the success of the AA program. Later developments have focused more attention on the written word of AA and its importance for recruiting new members as well as sustaining older ones. By far the best-known AA book is the *Big Book*. It was an attempt to sum up the experiences of those who had been with the movement in the early years; it consisted of the personal stories of a number of members and presented the 12-step recovery program. The stories comprise more than half of the text. In the two later editions only the story section has been changed.

The first issue of *A.A. Grapevine* was published in 1944, originally for members in the New York area and for those serving in the armed forces, but starting in 1945 it became the national organ of the fellowship. Most of the texts that later became building blocks for the AA corpus of literature as well as material for everyday reading were first published in this periodical. A collection of Bill W.'s *Grapevine* writings was later published as *The Language of the Heart* (1988). Another collection of Bill W.'s texts had been published earlier in *As Bill Sees It* (1967).

Twelve Steps and Twelve Traditions (*12 + 12*, 1986, originally published in 1953) constitutes a second standard text of AA along with the *Big Book*. It consists of Bill W.'s essays on the content and meaning of these two sets of principles.

Alcoholics Anonymous Comes of Age was published in 1957 and could be considered the third basic text of AA. It describes and records the events of the fellowship's 1955 convention, from which it took its name. It also includes the speech given by Bill W. on the history of AA.

The A.A. Service Manual and *Twelve Concepts for World Service* were published in one volume in 1962 and lay out a detailed description of the organizational structure of AA (*The A.A. Service Manual*, 1988). The introduction states that the Twelve Concepts are "an interpretation of A.A.'s world service structure," but in concrete terms they refer to the structure of AA in the United States and Canada.

In monograph form, AA also has published the biographies of the two co-founders (*Dr. Bob and the Good Oldtimers,* 1980, and *Pass It On,* 1984), a collection of members' writings (*Came To Believe,* 1973), and a discussion of practical methods used by AA members for not drinking (*Living Sober,* 1975).

Since 1959, most AA books and pamphlets are anonymous, and all are checked and approved by the General Service Conference and published by AA's own publishing company, called A.A. World Services, Inc. The texts are protected by copyright law and are called "conference-approved literature."

Finally, mention should be made of the Serenity Prayer (see Appendix D), adopted by AA in the early 1940s. Although not part of AA literature in the formal sense, its significance is shown by its being printed on the back cover of each issue of *A.A. Grapevine*.

4

The International Diffusion and Structure of AA

Worldwide Growth of AA

The growth of AA during the last four decades has been impressive (Table 4.1). From 1953 to 1990, there was an eighteen-fold increase in world membership. Another important feature is that the proportion of members outside the United States and Canada has been growing steadily.

Table 4.2 presents average annual growth rates for the United States and Canada and the rest of the world for ten-year periods. Although the early growth of AA in the United States and Canada was spectacular, the rate of growth slackened in the 1950s and 1960s. The increase in membership was considerably steeper in the 1970s and 1980s, most likely because of the growing symbiosis between AA and the professional treatment system, with the influx of new members through rehabilitation centers. Throughout the study period, membership growth has been faster in the rest of the world than in the United States and Canada. Because of the nature of the data, it is hazardous to draw any strong conclusions concerning trends in rates of growth. Annual rates are slightly lower for the last decade, but AA continues to grow at an amazing rate, and even for North America there are no signs of its approaching a saturation point. The steady growth of AA should be emphasized, since there are probably few other social movements that would show a similar continuous expansion over such a long period.

The 1980s have been described as a period of dramatic expansion of self-help in Europe (Barath, 1991). In the Federal Republic of Germany, the number of known self-help groups doubled during the first half of the 1980s from 30,000 to 60,000 (Vilmar & Runge, 1986). By the end of the decade, however, the number of groups had stabilized at around 45,000 (Braun & Greiwe, 1989). The continuing growth of AA

25

Table 4.1   AA Membership, United States/Canada and Worldwide, 1953–1990

	Groups	Groups outside U.S. and Canada, %	Members	Members outside U.S. and Canada, %
1953	5,000	7.1	111,000	8.4
1960	7,800	14.2	137,000	12.9
1970	14,800	24.1	260,000	25.7
1980	39,800	35.2	839,000	43.3
1990	92,300	44.2	1,994,000	44.8

Note: Tables 4.1–3 use data provided by the General Service Office in New York. Data for North America are available from 1941 onward. Uniform and comprehensive series are available from 1953 onward. The figures are based on reports from groups to various national bodies, which transmit them to G.S.O. in New York. Not all groups are listed with their national offices, and membership criteria may vary from one group to another or from one country to the next.

The statistical series on members and groups in the United States, Canada, and the rest of the world are not based on the same principles. For the United States, but not for other regions, institutional and other members and groups are reported separately. At its highest, the share of United States institutional members of the world membership was 19 percent in 1963. It is evident that these series are particularly inaccurate and show inexplicable leaps and drops. It is likely that statistics for other countries include some institutional groups and members, but their number is unknown. There is no good solution to this problem, but it seemed wise to disregard United States institutional data in the analysis. In the membership statistics, the so-called loners and internationals are not included in any regional figures. Their share of the world membership has always been less than .5 percent. In order to make regional percentages add to 100 percent of the world total, loners and internationals have been omitted from the tables.

Particularly, the series on the rest of the world contains sudden leaps that do not accurately reflect the true annual growth, but may be connected with special efforts to collect up-to-date data from all countries. At least in the late 1980s, rough estimates of the number of groups and members in countries that did not respond to G.S.O.'s enquiry were added to the world figures. For 1991 on, only the countries reporting back to G.S.O. were included in the statistics.

Table 4.3 is based on a more detailed breakdown of members and groups by country. The breakdown is not available after 1988. In 1988, the figures for the United States and Canada are the same as in the data used for tables 4.1–2, but the time series data report 25 percent more groups and 20 percent more members in the rest of the world than does the breakdown by country. The difference is probably due to the estimation procedure described above.

in the 1980s is thus extraordinary even in the context of the general self-help boom.

International Diffusion of AA

By looking at the diffusion of AA we can shed light on what is essential in AA, as opposed to those features that are merely accidental reflec-

Table 4.2   Percentage of Average Annual Growth of Number of AA Groups and Members, 1954–1990

	Groups			Members		
	U.S. and Canada	Rest of the world	Entire period	U.S. and Canada	Rest of the world	Entire period
1954–1960	5.4	18.1	6.6	2.3	10.1	3.0
1961–1970	5.3	12.4	6.6	4.9	14.4	6.6
1971–1980	8.8	15.8	10.6	9.6	23.0	13.0
1981–1990	7.2	11.5	8.8	8.8	9.7	9.1
Total	6.8	14.2	8.3	6.7	14.6	8.3

Note: See note to Table 4.1.

tions of its time and birthplace. The cultural specificity of AA has been formulated on many different levels, in terms of American middle-class values (Trice & Roman, 1970b), in terms of the white male Anglo-Saxon experience (Denzin, 1987, pp. 164–165), and in terms of temperance cultures (Levine, 1992). However, none of these formulations convey an accurate sense of the cultural adaptability of AA. Jilek-Aall's (1978) study of the AA among Coast Salish Indians in the Upper Fraser Valley of British Columbia, Canada, in the 1970s is a detailed example of how the AA program has been adapted to a cultural tradition that is quite different from the movement's origins in the American middle class. Sutro (1989) similarly presents a concrete picture of how an AA meeting is adapted to rural Mexican culture. AA is an American middle-class invention, but "American middle-class values and ideas may be superficial factors that can easily be changed in the spread of the basic A.A. methods" (Peterson, 1992, p. 54).

Since the original literature was written in English, it is natural that AA first spread to Anglo-Saxon countries. These countries, in addition, also happened to be highly developed economically with strong Protestant traditions and close contact with the United States. The significance of cultural ties also becomes clear from looking at former colonial countries that gained independence after the Second World War. Of 33 countries with a British colonial background, 15 reported having at least one AA group in 1986, in comparison to 24 countries with a French colonial background, which had none. The difference cannot totally be explained by internal social differences between former French and British colonies, however (Mäkelä, 1991).

The prospects of AA also seem to be influenced by alcohol-specific factors. If the level of alcohol consumption in a given culture is very low, there may be no need for AA. Patterns of drinking may also be significant. AA may be more attractive in countries where alcohol problems are mainly connected to disruptive drinking, as they are in many liquor-drinking countries, than if most alcohol-dependent persons are not socially visible and deviant, as is the case in traditional wine-drinking countries.

Levine (1992) discusses AA as a continuation of temperance traditions characteristic of English-speaking and Nordic countries. In these countries, distilled liquor was historically the dominant alcoholic beverage and Protestantism the dominant religion. The combination of disruptive drinking and Protestantism led to an obsessive concern about alcohol problems and to enduring and powerful temperance movements. AA is a continuation of the same concern about alcohol in a new historical situation. The distribution of AA groups in the world by linguistic and cultural region (Table 4.3) provides partial support to Levine's interpretation. Levine's temperance cultures accounted for 65 percent of the membership of AA in 1988. The main trends visible in Table 4.3, however, point in a different direction. The proportion of all active AA groups that are in English-speaking and Scandinavian Protestant countries clearly diminished from 1965 to 1988, and the share of central and southern European countries and, particularly, Latin America was substantially increased. In 1988, Latin America accounted for almost one-third of the world membership of AA. This shows that the movement has spread well beyond the range of traditional temperance countries.

Table 4.4 provides an overall picture of the linguistic diffusion of AA by presenting the years of first publication of the *Big Book* in different languages. Table 4.5 presents another way of looking at the international diffusion of AA by listing the countries where AA has been strong enough to establish an operating general service board and/or a literature distribution center. By comparing the two tables, we may note that during the last few years the General Service Office in New York has begun to sponsor translations even before local AA activities become consolidated.

The diffusion of AA has definitely moved beyond the cultural confines of the Anglo-Saxon and Protestant world. By 1986, long-lasting AA activities had typically been established in all wealthy non-Communist, non-Islamic countries (Mäkelä, 1991). After the upheavals in Eastern Europe, AA has spread throughout Europe. The fellowship also has established bridgeheads in some industrialized Asian countries.

From 1965 to 1986, an interesting change occurred in the relationships of AA to social and cultural background factors (Mäkelä, 1991).

Table 4.3   Percentage, by Linguistic and Cultural Region, of AA Groups and Members in the World, 1965 and 1988

	Groups		Members
	1965	1988	1988
U.S. and Canada	81.1	59.9	59.1
Other English-speaking countries	8.3	6.1	5.0
Scandinavia	2.0	1.4	1.3
Other European countries	2.3	5.2	5.0
Latin America	5.7	26.8	29.1
Other countries	0.6	0.6	0.5
Total	100.0	100.0	100.0

Note: See note to Table 4.1.

In 1965, but not in 1986, the strength of AA corresponded to the percentage of Protestants in the population. Recently the rate of growth of AA has actually been higher in Roman Catholic countries.

AA tends to have fewer groups in traditional wine-drinking countries, but the level of beer consumption is correlative to the strength of AA (Mäkelä, 1991). Spirits consumption is not related to the cross-sectional strength of AA, but the rate of growth of AA has been higher in countries with high levels of spirits consumption.

The first wave of diffusion brought AA to the Anglo-Saxon and Protestant world. The second wave covered American and European Catholic countries. It is still too early to judge whether we are observing the beginnings of a third wave during which AA will spread throughout the industrialized world.

Mechanisms of Diffusion of AA

American culture has often been actively exported or promoted by centralized organizations. In contrast, there are no military, political, commercial, or even national cultural interests connected to the spread of AA.

Table 4.6 presents a summary of the influences on the early beginnings of AA in the study countries. The diffusion of AA has mainly been based on the efforts of individual members, often with a middle-class background, in connection with their regular work and everyday activities (diplomatic or military missions, commercial or professional travel, tourism). It is worth pointing out that direct influence by American residents or visitors has been significant in only three among the

Table 4.4 Year of First Publication of the *Big Book* of Alcoholics Anonymous in Different Languages

Year	Language	Country
1939	English	United States
1956	Spanish	United States
1956	French	Canada
1962	Finnish	Finland
1963	French	France
1963	German	United States
1965	Spanish	Colombia and United States
1969	Portuguese	Brazil
1974	Swedish	Sweden
1974	German	West Germany
1976	Icelandic	Iceland
1979	Japanese	Japan
1979	Norwegian	Norway
1980	Italian	Italy
1981	Spanish	Spain
1982	Flemish	Belgium
1983	Dutch	Netherlands
1984	Afrikaans	South Africa
1985	Korean	South Korea
1987	Tagalog	Philippines
1989	Polish	Poland
1989	Hebrew	Israel (chapter 5 only)
1989	Russian	United States
1989	Czech	United States
1990	Hungarian	United States
1990	Arabic	United States
1991	Marathi	India
1991	Lithuanian	United States
1991	Turkish	United States
1992	Cebuana-Binisaya	Philippines
1992	Danish	Denmark
1992	Swahili	United States
1993	Portuguese	Portugal

Note: In some languages, the printing history of the *Big Book* is quite complex. For example, translations exist in several local versions of Spanish that have been published in a number of countries. Listed in the table are the first editions of the *Big Book* in each language. When the first edition was published in North America, the first editions published outside North America and outside the Americas are also included. Local editions of the English version are not listed. The information for the table was provided in May 1993 by the General Service Office in New York.

Table 4.5   Countries Where AA Has Established an Operating General
Service Board and/or a Literature Distribution Center, 1992

Argentina
Australia
Belgium (Flemish-speaking)
Belgium (French-speaking)
Bolivia
Brazil
Chile
Colombia
Costa Rica
Denmark
Ecuador
El Salvador
Finland
France
Germany
Great Britain
Guatemala
Honduras
Iceland
India
Ireland
Italy
Japan
Mexico
Netherlands
New Zealand
Nicaragua
Norway
Paraguay
Peru
Poland
South Africa
Spain
Sweden
Switzerland (German-speaking)
Switzerland (French- and Italian-speaking)
Trinidad/Tobago
United States/Canada
Uruguay
Venezuela

Source: List of General Service Offices and Literature Distributions
Centers (1/13/93)

Table 4.6 Influences on Early Beginnings of AA in Study Countries

	Austria	Finland	Iceland	Mexico	Poland	Sweden	French-speaking Switzerland	German-speaking Switzerland
Significant influence of locals having emigrated to the U.S.	–	+	+	+	+	–	–	–
Significant influence of locals having visited the U.S.	–	–	+	+	+	+	–	–
Significant influence of U.S. residents								
members of AA	–	–	–	+	–	–	–	–
treatment professionals	–	–	–	–	–	–	+	–
Significant influence of U.S. visitors								
members of AA	–	–	–	+	+	–	–	–
treatment professionals	–	–	–	–	+	–	–	–
Significant influence of visitors from other countries								
members of AA	+	–	–	–	+	–	+	+
treatment professionals	–	–	–	+	+	–	+	+
Professionals playing important role as initiators of first few groups								
medical doctors	–	–	–	+	–	–	+	–
psychiatrists	–	–	–	–	+	–	–	+
social workers	–	+	–	–	–	–	+	–
Professionals playing important supporting role for first few groups								
medical doctors	+	–	–	+	–	–	+	+
psychiatrists	–	–	–	+	+	–	+	+
social workers	–	–	–	–	–	–	+	–
Direct financial support from G.S.O. in New York	–	–	–	+	–	+	–	–
Direct financial support from AA in other countries	–	–	–	–	+	–	–	–

study countries. In the 1950s Austria, for instance, local people attended AA meetings organized by personnel of the American occupation army, but this did not lead to permanent AA activities; the first Austrian group was established by two women in 1960 (Eisenbach-Stangl, 1992a). Direct contacts with the United States are nevertheless important, since in five countries key roles have been played by locals who had visited the United States or emigrated there.

Professional conferences and networks usually play a decisive part in the diffusion of health technologies and techniques. Until recently, this mechanism of diffusion had not been of great significance to AA, although alcohol professionals have played an important role in the early stages of AA in many countries (Eisenbach-Stangl, 1992a; Mäkelä, in press; Rehm et al., 1992). Lately, institutional treatment systems based on the AA program also have been important for the diffusion of AA in, at least, Iceland, Sweden, and Switzerland (Mariolini, 1992; Stenius, 1991). In Poland, the support from treatment professionals has been significantly greater and more systematic than in countries that received AA at an earlier stage (Świątkiewicz, 1992a).

Unlike religious groups, AA does not have paid employees for missionary work, although the General Service Office in New York since early on has provided centralized advice and occasional assistance regarding, for example, translations of the literature. Individual members sometimes have carried out energetic campaigns to strengthen AA in some region. In 1958, an AA veteran from the United States, Gordon M., traveled to the Caribbean on what was later known as the "Caribbean crusade," his objectives being "the development, integration and strengthening of AA in the area" (Ramirez, 1987). In the 1980s, a group of Finns went to Poland each year to visit Polish AA groups in various cities. Finnish AA members also have made informal trips to Estonia and to St. Petersburg on a regular basis, and fledgling groups in former East Germany received considerable support from Swiss and West German visitors.

In the late 1980s, a certain kind of AA diplomacy emerged, notably with respect to the Soviet Union. Private foundations closely related to AA supported several North American AA delegations visiting the Soviet Union (Don P., 1989; *Final Report of the Thirty-Ninth . . . General Service Conference,* 1989; Zink, 1990).

Until quite recently, AA has for the most part spread from drunkard to drunkard as an authentic grass-roots movement. This is in clear contrast to many other innovations bearing the imprint of American culture, such as the new religious movements of the last decades. The implantation in Europe of the Unification Church, Scientology, Transcendental Meditation, and other such cults has been directed from the United States (Beckford & Levasseur, 1986).

Regional and Bilateral Collaboration

Frequent contacts among AA members across national borders also take place. Members continue to go to meetings while abroad on business or on holiday and, thereby, learn about AA customs and rituals in different cultures. There are also formal structures for contact and collaboration within and between linguistic regions (Tables 4.7 and 4.8). Every five years, the International Convention of AA draws thousands of participants from around the world. Many conventions and conferences are explicitly open to all members speaking the same language, such as the annual German convention or the annual French conference in Delémont. Conventions are mostly occasions for social contacts but there also are regular service structures that are supranational. Belgium, France, Luxembourg, and the French-speaking part of Switzerland each have four representatives on the Committee for French-Speaking Europe (Comité Francophone Européen), and service representatives of the Nordic countries meet formally each year in connection with the Nordic convention. Latin America has a system of international sponsorship through which countries formally sponsor other countries (*Memorias de la VI Reunion Iberoamericana de AA*, 1989). German support to Austria and Switzerland provides examples of similar mechanisms (Eisenbach-Stangl, 1992a, 1992b; Rehm et al., 1992).

Bilateral financial support is extended across borders. The Colombian General Service office has sent literature to Panama, Ecuador, Peru, Chile, and Bolivia, and the Finnish AA has provided money for printing the *Big Book* in Polish.

In a world of nation-states, AA is an interesting movement in that although it is usually organized by country, linguistic groupings may override political borders. The collaboration between Francophone groups in France, Belgium, and Switzerland is closer than in the case of many other organizations, and German-speaking groups have established strong links across political borders. The interplay of linguistic divisions and political borders can be quite complex. In the Finnish service structure, Swedish-speaking groups in Finland and Finnish-speaking groups in Sweden constitute two areas of their own. Finland is bilingual, and because for a long time AA in Finland was stronger than in Sweden, Finnish AA also published literature for the Swedish-speaking minority. Moreover, the Swedish groups in Finland have always belonged to the Finnish service structure. There are quite a few groups among Finnish immigrants in Sweden, but these groups also belong to the Finnish and not the Swedish service structure.

Issues connected to the relationship of the AA service structure to political and linguistic divisions may occasionally cause some friction. In Sweden, there have been disagreements concerning whether Finnish-speaking groups should be listed in Swedish directories, since they pay their contributions to Finland. At the General Service Conference of the German AA, a proposal for a new structure was presented in 1991 (*Bericht der 11. Gemeinsamen Dienst-Konferenz,* 1991) and adopted one year later. Since that reform, Austria and the German-speaking part of Switzerland no longer have general service conferences of their own but have become a part of the German conference (Appel, 1992). The proposal brought about heated discussions in all countries concerned. In Switzerland, for instance, any kind of integration into larger units tends to animate the population, and the debate continued even after the adoption of the new structure.

Relationships between the North American and the International Service Structure

Compared to most international organizations, AA is exceptional in not having any international bodies entitled to make decisions in the name of the international movement. To understand this peculiarity, an historical overview is required.

In the beginning, the co-founders acted as leaders and advisers for the fellowship worldwide. In 1955, the responsibility for the leadership of the fellowship was taken over by the General Service Conference (United States and Canada). At that time, groups were already meeting in a number of countries and languages, and in Bill W.'s vision AA was to spread around the globe. The original version of the North American conference charter also foresaw that "other Sections of the Conference may sometimes be created in foreign lands as the need arises out of language or geographical consideration" (*The A.A. Service Manual,* 1986, p. 24). The charter also envisaged a formal procedure by which worldwide joint actions could be taken up on a two-thirds vote of the combined sections. No other sections of the conference have been established, however.

In 1957, the first General Service Board outside the United States and Canada was created in Great Britain and Ireland, and other countries soon followed the example (Table 4.5). As national AA movements grew stronger, they also became interested in taking part in the general service structure. As an expression of this interest, countries like Fin-

Table 4.7   Important Dates in the History of the International Service Structure
of AA

1950	First International Convention
1957	Creation of first overseas General Service Board in Great Britain and Ireland
1959	AA Publishing becomes AA World Services
1962	Twelve Concepts for World Service adopted by the 12th Annual General Service Conference
1964	Membership outside of United States and Canada exceeds 20% of total membership
1969	First World Service Meeting in New York
1974	Third World Service Meeting in London (first World Service Meeting held outside the United States)
1979	Membership outside of United States and Canada exceeds 40% of total membership
1979	First Ibero-American Service Meeting
1981	First European Service Meeting
1990	11th World Service Meeting in Munich, Germany

land sent observers to the North American General Service Conference as early as the 1960s (Kolumbus, no date).

The First World Service Meeting was held in New York City in 1969. Twelve countries that had developed central headquarters were represented. At the Eleventh World Service Meeting, held in Munich in 1990, twenty-one countries were represented. The World Service Meeting represents the international voice of the fellowship, but it has no power to make decisions in the name of the world's AA groups. There are members who would like to change this situation: "The present World Service Meeting structure was a failure from the very beginning. The meeting was created when countries like Finland wanted to have their voice heard. At the World Service Meeting their voice is heard alright but it is of no consequence" (Finnish field interview). Occasionally, delegates may also feel that more account should be taken of the cultural variability of the world in planning World Service Meeting discussions. One of the agenda items of the 1988 World Service Meeting was stated as follows: "Discuss instances where the original literature does not reflect local conditions, e.g., 'too American.' " Some concern was expressed with respect to the cultural specificity of the content, but

Table 4.8   Internationally Significant AA Conferences and Meetings, 1990

	First year held	Frequency
General Service Conference/U.S. and Canada	1951	Annually
International Convention	1950	Every 5 years
World Service Meeting	1969	Biannually
Ibero-American Service Meeting	1979	Biannually
European Service Meeting	1981	Biannually
German-Speaking Convention	1968	Annually
Meeting of the Committee for French-speaking Europe	1975	Annually
Nordic Meeting	1973	Annually

the discussion was mainly restricted to purely linguistic matters and to whether other English-speaking countries would need local idiomatic expressions instead of the original American formulations (Finnish field interview; Report of the Literature/Publishing Committee, 10th World Service Meeting, no date). English continues to be the main language of the World Service Meeting, but from 1982 on simultaneous translation in Spanish has been provided (History and Recommendations of the World Service Meeting 1969–1988, 1990).

An increasing number of countries have established national service conferences (Table 4.5), and regional forms of collaboration have emerged (Table 4.8). Regional conferences are, however, only vehicles for exchanging experiences and do not have the character of a conference section. In a revision adopted in 1987, the reference to future "other Sections of the Conference" was deleted from the North American conference charter, and the present version only refers to the World Service Meeting and speaks of encouraging consultation between national service conferences (*The A.A. Service Manual,* 1988, p. S29).

It is likely that, within a few years, less than half of all AA members will be living in the United States or Canada, but the North American General Service Conference will continue to carry more weight than the World Service Meeting. It may be symptomatic that Kurtz's (1991) comprehensive history of AA contains next to nothing on international issues. Interestingly enough, the topic of AA diplomacy with respect to the Soviet Union, the second superpower at the time, was one of the few international topics referred to. The World Service Meeting is not even mentioned in the index.

So far, the somewhat ambiguous international structure of AA has not caused real conflict. In matters of international service, the key role is played by the General Service Office in New York. If divisions occur within national movements, it still is up to the office in New York to determine which fraction is the official one. In Mexico, there are two parallel service structures, known as Central Mexicana and Sección México. Both publish translations of American AA literature, but only Central Mexicana has been granted legal copyright by the General Service Office in New York. The loose and unbureaucratic structure of AA makes it understandable that legal aspects of AA activities have been recurrent topics at World Service Meetings, where representatives of the General Service Office have encouraged national delegates to pay attention to the legal protection of AA logos and literature.

The moral authority of the North American General Service Conference as representative of the legacy of the co-founders and of the early experiences of the fellowship, probably suffices to explain how this situation has not caused conflict. Financial factors may also contribute. The majority of groups outside North America function in relatively poor countries. Through the General Service Office, North American groups continue to support international service activities financially, including a considerable part of the expenses connected to the World Service Meeting. The World Service Meeting is, however, on its way to financial self-support. Of the expenses of the Ninth World Service Meeting (1986), 52 percent were covered by delegate fees and contributions and 48 percent by the General Service Board of the United States and Canada (*Final report of the 9th World Service Meeting,* 1987). In 1992, delegate fees and contributions already covered 73 percent of the expenses of the meeting (*Final Report of the 12th World Service Meeting,* 1993).

The very nature of AA means that issues of international service structure are of little concern. In most organizations, ordinary members show little interest in organizational matters, and in AA this is accentuated by the total autonomy of individual groups. National AA movements also function very independently, and the power of the General Service Office in New York is strictly limited. As time goes on, a national elite of old-timers who work at various levels of the service structure develops. Yet, there is little growing ground for a diplomatic elite that would feel the vocation to pursue their cultural perspectives on an international level. World service representatives are usually regular members and not employees of AA. The principle of rotation also means that few delegates have time to learn the craft of international meetings.

It is not probable that AA will in the future establish any supranational bodies with power to represent the conscience of the fellowship.

It may be symbolically significant, however, that, based on floor action, the Eleventh World Service Meeting (1990) decided to establish a fund for promoting AA literature worldwide (*Final Report of the 11th World Service Meeting,* 1991). This fund is the first over which the World Service Meeting has some direct control.

Part Three
AA as a Social Organization

5
Organizational Principles of AA

AA was developed by strong personalities, and personal charisma continues to be an important ingredient in the dynamics of the movement. Conversely, the most convincing feature of the structural organization of AA may be that it has enabled the movement to survive its charismatic leaders. In this chapter we present an overview of the organizational principles of AA (Room, 1993). Tensions around and deviations from the principles are discussed in subsequent chapters.

The primary written locus of AA's organizational principles is the Twelve Traditions, but there are principles of AA's organization that cannot be found anywhere in the Twelve Traditions, nor otherwise spelled out in writing. Our discussion of the organizational principles is, therefore, not organized according to the Twelve Traditions, although they are cross-referenced when appropriate.

1. *Openness of membership* (Tradition Three). "The only requirement for A.A. membership is a desire to stop drinking." The organization has none of the usual means for maintaining a boundary between membership and non-membership: there is no membership roster to sign, and there are no membership dues. An important corollary of this is that there are no procedures for excommunicating or being excluded from membership; AA is open to all.

This is an unusual organizational characteristic. Most political, religious, or other voluntary organizations have a well-defined boundary between membership and non-membership. Bans on property and on professionalism help make AA's open membership structure feasible: there are no tangible assets for the members to share or quarrel over, and the AA group is not financially burdened with maintaining professionals (a burden which tends to force a definition of membership in religious congregations, for instance). The lack of any procedure for exclusion from membership has probably helped in avoiding splits of AA as a movement, by removing the possibility of permanent victory in any internal faction fights. The openness of membership and the freedom to come and go also distinguish AA from religious cults.

On the other hand, openness of membership and attendance at meetings does sometimes create problems in their management. While AA meetings generally show a substantial tolerance for deviations from decorum, it is not unknown for obnoxious participants, and particularly drunken participants, to be physically ejected from meetings (H. C. Johnson, 1987, p. 245; Mäkelä, 1992a; and see chapter 11).

2. *The group as the autonomous organizational base* (Tradition Four). The fundamental organizational unit of AA is the group. A group is defined in terms of those who meet face-to-face at meetings scheduled for a particular place and time or times of the week. Each group is "autonomous, except in matters affecting another group of AA as a whole" (Tradition Four). In principle, the group makes its own decisions on most matters. Just as there is no exclusion rule for individuals, there is no exclusion rule for groups.

The primacy and autonomy of the group is reinforced by several specific organizational principles:

(a) *The group as self-governing, subject to no external authority or super-structure* (Tradition Nine). AA has an elaborate structure of service boards and committees, elected directly or indirectly by AA groups, but power is firmly defined as lying at the base rather than in the structure. Accordingly, a headquarters communication to a group will be worded in the form of suggestions: "Of course, you are at perfect liberty to handle this matter any way you please. But the majority experience in A.A. does seem to suggest . . ." (*12 + 12*, 1986, pp. 173–174).

(b) *No exclusive territories or franchises.* No existing AA group can hinder a new AA group from forming, even if it is appealing to the same population as the existing group. This is a fairly unusual provision for a multicelled organization. In many religious denominations, the existing congregation has exclusive jurisdiction in a parish or locality; chapters of fraternal organizations usually have an exclusive franchise for some defined population.

The lack of exclusive jurisdictions might be regarded as a corollary of the autonomy of the group, extended to new as well as existing groups. But the wording of Tradition Four ("each group should be autonomous except in matters affecting other groups . . .") would have lent itself to an alternative interpretation, since the formation of a new group might well adversely affect the status of an existing group.

The lack of exclusive territories or franchises provides both a safety valve for internal conflicts and a mechanism for organizational growth. As an AA proverb puts it, "all you need to start your own AA meeting is a resentment and a coffeepot" (Pittman, 1988b, p. 236), reflecting that a new group often starts as the resolution of a conflict between members of an existing group. From an organizational perspective, the lack of any inhibition on forming new groups turns resentments and conflicts, which might otherwise threaten group continuance, into an instrument of organizational growth.

(c) *The group as self-supporting* (Tradition Seven). Each group is required to be "fully self-supporting, declining outside contributions." The expenses of the group are met from "passing the hat" during the meeting. Normally, these expenses would include rent, refreshments, literature purchases, and contributions to activities at the intergroup and general service levels.

3. *No affiliations or distractions.* The principle that groups should be self-supporting obviously supports the maintenance of a bottom-up organization, where no group is financially dependent on another or on AA superstructures. However, AA texts place at least equal emphasis on the importance of refusing fiscal support from outside AA. The principle of self-support is also one of several measures designed to ensure that AA maintains a singleness of purpose (Tradition Five) and a central focus on the egalitarian fellowship of the AA meeting. Likewise, the idea of external anonymity, discussed below, among its other functions, helps keep AA free of imputed affiliations by breaking the link between the external commitments of individual AA members and their AA membership. Other organizational guidelines aimed at avoiding affiliations or distractions include:

(a) *Prohibition on external affiliations and endorsements* (Traditions Six and Ten). The prohibition on affiliations goes in both directions: AA groups should not affiliate with any other organization, and neither will AA allow any other groups to affiliate with it. There is a de facto partial exception to the latter for Al-Anon, which is indeed separately organized but has long had a special relationship with AA. However, with other 12-step groups, AA's relationship is fully at arm's length.

While AA has remained true to its prohibition on organizational affiliation with alcohol-treatment programs, this may well seem to be a fine distinction to a client enrolled in a "12-step-based" treatment program. In the numerous 12-step-based treatment agencies, therapists and counselors will often be members of AA themselves, and AA-like or AA meetings in the institutional setting will form an essential part of the treatment program.

(b) *Prohibition on property ownership* (Tradition Six). Individual AA groups, and AA as a whole, are enjoined from owning any real property, "lest problems of money, property and prestige divert us from our primary purpose." This principle is the most radical departure from usual organizational practice: the greatest aspiration of a new congregation or fraternal club is normally to own its own building, and most voluntary associations would jump at such a chance. This rule recognizes that property issues, on the other hand, are often sources of collective and individual strife in voluntary associations. In the longer form of the Traditions, the potential utility of property to AA is recognized, but a clear organizational separation from AA itself is insisted upon: "any considerable property of genuine use to A.A. should be separately incorporated and managed, thus dividing the material from the spiritual. . . . Secondary aids to A.A., such as clubs or hospitals . . . ought to be incorporated and so set apart that, if necessary, they can be freely discarded by the groups" (*12 + 12*, 1986, p. 190).

The most extensive exception to the prohibition on property ownership is the copyrights maintained on AA publications and the registered trademarks on AA symbols. The publishing effort of AA is an intrinsic part of the organizational program and a substantial source of revenue, which has long been used to support the costs of the AA structure (service worker wages, travel, etc.) above the group level. As will be discussed in chapter 8, in North America and some other industrial countries, literature sales account for as much as half of the revenue of national service structures.

4. *Internal equality and democracy.* Again, AA texts emphasize the equal status of AA members, an equality symbolized by the expectation that each member should take on a common status identification, traditionally heavily derogated in the world at large: "My name is X, and I'm an alcoholic." In discussing leadership in the context of Tradition Two, *Twelve Steps and Twelve Traditions* acknowledges that old-timers in the movement often play a role of moral leadership, but it distinguishes between "bleeding deacons" and "elder statesmen," with the latter subordinating their personal judgement to the group decisions of the "group conscience." In line with this discussion, seniority in the movement does play a considerable part in who ends up in what position in the structure, and groups often impose a minimum length of sobriety as a prerequisite for election to office, but the formal equality of AA members carries much more substantive weight than the formal equality of members in many other organizations. A number of principles and procedures weigh against the build-up of hierarchy or oligarchy within AA.

(a) *No professional relationships* (Tradition Eight) "Alcoholics Anonymous will never have a professional class," begins the discussion of Tradition Eight in *Twelve Steps and Twelve Traditions* (1986, p. 166). Although mutual help between members is at the heart of AA's practice, such help (12th-step work) within the context of AA must not be remunerated for, but must be freely given. This principle, of course, radically distinguishes AA from 12-step-based treatment agencies, in which recovered alcoholics are routinely employed as counselors. Since the 1950s and the rise of 12-step-based treatment institutions, the complex and often blurred roles of the AA member who is also a professional alcoholism therapist, have been a continuing issue for concern and discussion within the AA movement. *Twelve Steps and Twelve Traditions* tends to emphasize the lure and distraction of money in discussing the rationale for Tradition Eight, but perhaps more important is its role in excluding the status relationship of professional versus client from AA's process. Such a status relationship would fundamentally compromise the principle of equality of members.

(b) *Elected and rotating leadership.* The discussion of Tradition Two in *Twelve Steps and Twelve Traditions* clearly favors elections as the method for choosing group leadership, although, in line with the principle of group autonomy, elections are not mandated. *The A.A. Service Manual* (1988) lays out a suggested method for the election of representatives that is to be used by group delegates, involving successive ballots to seek an absolute majority, with a drawing of lots in case of a tie. Rotation of representation and leadership is mandated in the service structure, and is recommended to groups concerning their own leadership (*12 + 12*, 1986, p. 191).

The principle of elections, of course, reinforces the ideology of a bottom-up structure, and the principle of rotation helps keep the leadership structure open and relatively free of oligarchy. That voting is implicitly open to all members, no matter how new, supports the ideology of equality of status of members.

(c) *Decisions by consensus.* The only formulation concerning processes for group decision-making offered in *Twelve Steps and Twelve Traditions* is in Tradition Two: "Four our group purpose there is but one ultimate authority—a loving God as He may express Himself in our group conscience." "Group conscience" in AA terminology has come to mean decision-making by consensus. This does not necessarily mean complete unanimity, but neither does it mean decisions by majority vote. Instead, it entails a frequently lengthy discussion in search of common denominators before the group decision is taken.

Although reference to the Higher Power is constant throughout the Steps, this is its only appearance in the Traditions. Thus, while other elements of the organizational principles are worded and justified in rational terms, the process of group decision-making is associated with the sacred and the mysterious. This is no accident; as discussed elsewhere in this volume, Bill W. saw "self-will run riot" as the central vice of the alcoholic, and, consequently, would have seen the subordination of the individual ego to collective interests as the stresspoint in making the organization work.

When AA in Finland wanted to revise the linguistically rather inadequate translation of the Twelve Steps at the end of the 1960s, this resulted in an animated debate. Since the Twelve Steps had shown the way to a new life, every word had tremendous emotional charge. And the rule of consensus meant that even minor and obvious improvements had to be argued through one by one to consensus.

Mäkelä, 1989

As noted above, elections of officers and delegates are excluded from the principle of decision-making by consensus, although here, too, the widest possible consent is sought. Otherwise, the consensus principle is almost universally applied. The limits of the consensus principle will receive further discussion in the next chapter.

The official translation of the Twelve Steps in Icelandic is not quite accurate. The Eighth Step, for instance, reads "made a list of our wrongdoings" instead of "made a list of all persons we had harmed." The inaccuracies have never been changed. People have learned each Step in a particular wording and don't want to change them. In addition to the official translation, three other translations are available.

(d) *Internal openness—no secrecy of process, partial anonymity.* Although, as discussed below, anonymity with respect to the outside world is a fixed principle, information, including names, is relatively freely available within AA. This is partly a matter of convenience or necessity: AA groups often circulate a list of members' names and addresses to their members, as an aid to 12th-step work and to organizational maintenance. Worldwide listings of AA groups and meetings facilitate visiting and networking by traveling members. But the transparency of AA as an organization and the availability of information to members is also an important means of limiting oligarchic tendencies and subordinating the service structure to members' governance.

(e) *External anonymity* (Traditions Eleven and Twelve). The principle of external anonymity invoked in the organization's name is justified on several grounds. It facilitates AA's policy of "attraction rather than promotion" in public relations. As noted above, it reinforces the practice of avoiding affiliations and distractions. But it also is a crucial element in maintaining equality and democracy. It is a common experience of social movements with a democratic style and a collective leadership that these tenets are inexorably undermined by the results of media attention to the movement. Reporters and authorities want to deal with leaders, preferably as few as possible, and a spokesperson for the movement soon becomes a celebrity. The enhanced status in the outside society tends to be reflected back into the organization's internal processes. Hence, an oligarchic leadership for the movement may be created not by internal but by external processes. Again, the ideological emphasis on individual egoism as a main problem for alcoholics may have tended to underline the special importance of anonymity in an organization of alcoholics.

Anonymity plays a much more central role in AA than simply serving as part of the organization's name. Three stages of development in the anonymity principle can be discerned in the history of AA's early days. The first was the recognition of the importance of the promise of anonymity as an inducement to recruits. Along with the avoidance of aggressive and public evangelism, this promise of anonymity was one of the fundamental points of separation between AA and its forerunner, the Oxford Group movement (*Alcoholics Anonymous Comes of Age,* 1986, p. 74).

The principle of anonymity originated in the practical experience of alcoholics working with other alcoholics. It helped to attract new members, while protecting the group from the inevitable slips and erratic behavior of these newcomers and sometimes of old-timers. But anonymity is mentioned in only two places in the first edition of *Alcoholics Anonymous (Big Book,* 1955, pp. xiii, 19). It seems that at least through the publication of the first edition in 1939, anonymity was so unquestioned among recovering alcoholics that it was not even necessary to mention it as part of the personal recovery program.

The publication of the statement on anonymity in *Alcoholics Anonymous* in 1939 began a second stage in which the principle of anonymity was questioned, and then reaffirmed and expanded. In the fourteen years after 1939, AA in the United States grew from a handful of individual groups and a personal recovery program to a structured movement with a central organization and groups in most larger towns. During this period, the movement experienced a host of problems in dealing with the larger society. The difficulties that AA experienced with this are reflected in the fact that four of the Twelve Traditions deal with the relationship of AA and AA members to non-AA organizations and people; three of these (Six, Eleven, Twelve) may be seen as involving the issue of anonymity.

The third stage began with the publication of the expanded statement of the principle in *Twelve Steps and Twelve Traditions*. This stage has involved the testing of anonymity in a time of continuing organizational success and growth, and in an era in which having triumphed over alcoholism might be seen in some cultural situations as a positive rather than a negative entry on a resumé (*The Language of the Heart*, 1988, pp. 209–218). The internal arguments against anonymity—that anonymity is out-of-date and prevents a more effective passing on of the message—have tended to remain the same, although the situation in which they are put forward has grown more complex.

The de facto anonymity of socially prominent AA members has always been problematic in small towns or small societies. In some societies, AA has had a larger social presence in recent years, and membership is a potential source of cachet rather than disgrace. As a result, the membership of public figures in AA (e.g., politicians and show-business personalities) is sometimes general knowledge. In other societies included in our study (e.g., Finland, Austria, Switzerland) such compromising of the anonymity principle remains unthinkable.

5. *Organizational unity* (Tradition One). "The unity of Alcoholics Anonymous is the most cherished quality our Society has. Our lives, the lives of all to come, depend squarely upon it. We stay whole, or AA dies" (*12 + 12*, 1986, p. 129). Kurtz (1991, p. 146) notes that Bill W. saw AA's unity linked to its singleness of purpose—the fact that AA was concerned only with alcoholism. Until the 1970s in the United States, and up to the present in many countries, another aspect of AA's unity was the insistence that all members were alike in their affliction, so that separate meetings for different kinds of alcoholics were out of the question. Since the 1970s, this aspect of unity has been abandoned in the United States. Separate meetings for different demographic segments are an increasing reality in the larger metropolitan areas.

The original AA groups were in two very different milieus, New York and Akron, and maintaining unity between the disparate circumstances of these two settings required considerable diplomacy. Kurtz notes that Bill W. took on the role of "the man in the middle . . . mediating between different understandings of Alcoholics Anonymous by those who *were* Alcoholics Anonymous" (Kurtz, 1991, p. 63). As we have noted, the freedom to form new groups within the movement served as a safety valve in cases where resentments or personality conflicts resulted in splits within individual groups. For the movement as a whole, however, unity has been maintained in the United States and in most other national or linguistic AA movements. Mexico, the exception among the countries in our study, will be discussed in chapter 7.

Unity, which has been the rule in the AA movement, should by no means be taken for granted in mutual-help movements. Kurube has chronicled the complicated history of fissions and fusions in the Links movement in Sweden, which is presently divided into seven separate splinter groups (Kurube, 1992a). Even in newer 12-step movements, a diversity of movements dealing with a particular life problem is not uncommon.

6

The Local Structure of AA and
AA as a Social Network

For professionals advising AA to their clients and for individual new-comers alike, AA meetings are readily available. Even students of AA seldom pay attention to the fact that organizing regular meetings requires people, money, and work.

AA consists of two interrelated but analytically distinct structures. First, AA has a formal structure of groups, intergroups, and answering services, and of local, regional, and national service meetings and boards. The prototypical description of this type of structure is the organization chart. Second, AA is a network of individuals interacting with each other both in and outside of meetings. This network is concentrated at the local level, but it has regional, national, and international ramifications. By joining AA, the member is inducted into a wide-ranging social network, offering not only mutual support in sobriety but also friendships, and, for that matter, a variety of other potential relationships—business, romantic, and professional.

As a social network, AA and its group and service structure are closely interconnected. The network looks quite different if there is just one large AA group in the community than if there are several smaller groups. On the other hand, the service and group structure is kept alive by individuals interacting with each other. Any structural aspect of AA can be analyzed either in terms of groups and service structure or in terms of AA as a network.

AA as a Fellowship Based on Mutual Trust

In pre-modern societies, friendships were embedded in community and kinship. In modern times, friendship and trust are individual projects of mutual cultivation by way of intimate disclosures between individuals. An emphasis on personal relationships, friends, or lovers, is a way of looking for something or someone to trust, a trust not "naturally" found in society (Giddens, 1990). Alcoholics Anonymous combines features of pre-modern and modern relations. It is not based on pre-existing networks like pre-modern ties of intimacy. At the same time its exclusiveness, in that only alcoholics are members, reminds us of pre-modern kinship ties, dividing the world into AA members and non-members.

An important feature of AA is that members usually enter AA as individual atoms cut off from their social matrix. A person's social position affects the linkages that may lead him or her to AA. The newcomer's social background, at least initially, determines which groups feel attractive. The crucial thing, however, is that a person does not bring his or her social position to the AA meeting. Since children of alcoholics often become heavy drinkers, it is not uncommon for two generations of the same family to be members of AA. Usually, however, children prefer to attend different meetings from their parents in order to avoid mixing family ties with AA ties. In a similar fashion, one of the first women's-only groups in the United States and one of the few Finnish women's groups were started by wives who felt uncomfortable attending the same meeting as their husbands (H. C. Johnson, 1987; Rosenqvist, 1992b). Professional and AA relationships also do not always mix smoothly. This is one of the reasons why members who have become professional counselors tend to reduce their meeting attendance. On Samoa, the traditional system of deference remains so strong that at some AA meetings, members reportedly speak in order of rank bestowed to them in outside society (American field interview). Special studies would be needed to show whether this represents a successful adaptation of AA to pre-modern social structure or a deviation from what is essential in AA.

Since members enter AA as individuals, it seems that *individuation* is the particular aspect of modernity that is a precondition of AA. Individuation here refers to the process by which individual persons become the basic units of social action (Turner, 1986), superseding the family, the household, the kinship group, the work team, and the village community.

Members of the Finnish General Service Board are paid in cash for their travel expenses, based on their own report, and without receipts. The general service office employee responsible for the payments once carried 7,200 U.S. dollars in his wallet. Evidently other organizations could save a lot of administrative expenses if they could have the same faith in people presenting travel bills.

Researchers have tried to capture the special nature of AA by comparing it to an ethnic group (Madsen, 1980, p. 157), describing it as a clan-like formation in a modern society (Trevino, 1992), or by analyzing the use of "leveling devices" that put all members on an equal status, thereby fostering homogeneity (Sadler, 1979). Membership is sometimes seen as "us against the rest of the world," and outside people are sometimes referred to as "civilians," "normies," or "earth people." Among members, there is an assumption of mutual and automatic trust stemming from the simple identification of being an alcoholic.

The Basic Unit of AA

Groups and meetings are the basic units of AA. One indication of this is the system of record-keeping. Most groups and meetings are listed in local and national directories. In contrast, the movement keeps no membership records, although individual groups may list their members for internal purposes such as keeping track of sobriety anniversaries.

The names of most groups are geographical and refer to the meeting place (and sometimes the time of the meeting), but some names refer to aspects of the AA program or commemorate important people, places, or dates in the history of the movement. Programmatic and commemorative names, such as New Sunrise, Freedom and Action, Living Sober, Akron, Sister Ignacia, and June 10th, are particularly common in Mexico.

A new group is given loosely defined official status once it is listed in the AA directory. In some localities, there are some forms of recognition or non-recognition of AA groups. In southern California, the local service office sends out a delegate to observe procedures in a new group, "to see that the group is not violating the Traditions," before listing it in the area directory of groups and meetings (H. C. Johnson, 1987, pp. 427–431). Listing in the area directory is an important means of recruitment, often by referral, so that denial of a directory listing may affect the continuation or growth of the group. But there is nothing to stop an unlisted group continuing and considering itself to be an AA group. Certainly failure to participate in and support AA's service structure does not hinder recognition.

Some groups do not register at a higher level of AA. This may reflect a radical grass-roots ideology, or it may stem from members' fear of the loss of their anonymity if their group were to be listed and open to everybody. In Mexico, with its two competing service structures, groups may avoid registration simply because they resent having to choose between two sides.

The central activity of a group is to arrange regular meetings. The connection between the group and its meeting is so close that in some countries, such as Austria, Iceland, and the German-speaking part of Switzerland, there is no clear distinction between the two. In these countries groups usually sponsor one weekly meeting (Table 6.1). In other countries, it is more common that groups have more than one meeting each week, even several daily meetings.

Alcoholics Anonymous groups vary widely in size from a handful of members to several hundred. Small groups foster intimacy, whereas large groups provide a platform for star speakers as well as an opportunity for members of the local AA community to see each other. Groups in Austria and the German-speaking part of Switzerland tend to be smaller than in other countries, whereas large groups are considerably more common in California than in the rest of our study sites (Table 6.1).

For a group to function, a number of service positions have to be filled. According to an AA pamphlet (*The A.A. Group,* 1990, pp. 22–23), it is through the work of group members and its officers that:

- A meeting place is provided and maintained.
- Programs are arranged for meetings.
- Literature is on hand, and refreshments are available.
- Donations are collected and properly spent.
- Alcoholics in the area learn that AA is available and how to find it.
- Calls for help are answered.
- Group problems are aired and resolved.
- Contact is made with the rest of AA.

As is characteristic of AA literature, the suggestions of the pamphlet are presented as loose guidelines with a lot of openness: "Individual groups have many ways of making sure the necessary services are performed with a minimum of organization" (*The A.A. Group,* 1990, pp. 23–24). "Experience suggests" that chairpersons "should have been sober for awhile, at least a year; and ideally, they have held other offices first" (*The A.A. Group,* 1990, p. 24).

According to the ICSAA group survey (Appendix C), the following officers are the most common: chairperson or secretary, treasurer, coffee person, clean-up person, greeter, general service representative, literature person, and liaison officers to treatment institutions, hospi-

Table 6.1 Sizes of AA Groups in Study Countries

	Austria	Finland	Iceland	Mexico	Poland	Sweden	German-speaking Switzerland	California
Proportion of groups with fewer than 20 members, %[a]	87	66	53	70	75	60	80	14
Proportion of groups with more than 50 members, %	0	8	9	3	3	7	0	26
Proportion of groups having more than one meeting per week is more than 20 percent.[b]	–	+	–	+	–	+	–	+

Source: California figures are based on data collected in connection to the membership survey in Contra Costa county (Appendix B). Data for the other countries come from ICSAA group surveys (Appendix B).

[a]*Question wording*: Approximately how many men and how many women belong to your group?

[b]*Question wording*: How many weekly meetings does your group hold?

tals, and prisons. Many groups restrict themselves to choosing a chairperson or secretary and a treasurer, and distribute the remaining tasks on an ad hoc basis among the participants of each meeting. At the other extreme, the largest group in Helsinki designates thirteen different persons as responsible for specific tasks (Haavisto, 1992, pp. 73–75).

The chairperson or secretary coordinates group activities both during the meetings and outside the meetings. The treasurer is responsible for the finances of the group, and the general service representative connects the group to the AA movement as a whole.

Keeping the meetings going requires considerable commitment and attention to practical details, and there are few external rewards for this service. Since there are more outward-oriented service tasks, groups may take turns in staffing AA answering services, organizing meetings at treatment institutions and prisons, and taking on different sub-tasks in organizing joint local AA events. Group surveys carried out in Finland, Iceland, Mexico, and Sweden indicate that between one-fourth and one-third of the membership participate in service tasks at the group level. Although these figures are quite impressive in comparison to most informal and voluntary organizations, there is usually little competition for service positions. In most groups, the selection of officers is informal and regular elections are an exception.

Rapid expansion could intensify the shortage of people to fill service functions within the group. In Marin County in northern California, where the number of AA meetings had grown from 56 to 90 in four years, groups were having increasing trouble recruiting volunteers for coffee-making and setting up, among other tasks, particularly in the affluent southern part of the county, where attending AA meetings had become "hip, slicking cool" (Kaskutas, 1989a, pp. 31–33).

Because of the informality of the selection process and the lack of competition for service positions, most AA groups are run by a smaller inner circle, often dominated by one or two strong personalities who are prepared to spend a lot of their time and energy on group activities (cf. Gellman, 1964, p. 61). It is clear that the principle of regular rotation of leaders is not in effect in all AA groups. In a survey of AA groups in the German-speaking part of Switzerland, 68 percent reported a chairperson having been in office for more than three years (Rehm et al., 1992). In one large Finnish AA group, the same person chaired the weekly open meeting for almost ten years in the 1970s and 1980s (Haavisto, 1992, p. 33).

On the other hand, newcomers are encouraged to participate is service tasks quite early on, since taking responsibility in the group is seen as an important part of the recovery program. The doctrine of AA declares that all tasks are of equal value. It is not unusual for experienced members to take on the tasks of preparing coffee and cleaning up after the meeting, and there are groups that encourage newcomers to serve as group or meeting chairpersons after quite short periods of sobriety, both because this is felt to be good for them and because they often are eager and have time to take on responsibilities.

"For the newcomers, understanding service helps them realize that if somebody doesn't unlock the door, set up the chairs, and make the coffee, there will be no meeting to keep any of us sober. For the old-timers, service is a reminder that we must give it away in order to keep it."

Joan T., 1992

In ICSAA membership surveys (Appendix C), between 40 and 70 percent of all members in the study countries had taken part in household tasks in connection with AA meetings during the last four weeks, and between 60 and 80 percent during the last twelve months. In this respect, there were no notable differences between newcomers and experienced members. Nevertheless, there is a clear hierarchy among offices, and the main influence usually remains with the old-timers in the group. In a study of the atmosphere of four AA groups in a southwestern city in the United States using a modified version of the Group Environment Scale (Moos, 1986), members rated all groups as discouraging innovation (Montgomery, Miller, & Tonigan, 1993). Particularly offices at higher levels of the service structure are reserved for longtime members.

"I'm a pliable member of AA. For the first three years, I did the cleanup, filling my throat full of dust. Then other newcomers began to show up, and since dust is bad for my health I thought that cleaning is good for other people too, it makes one humble."

Finnish female AA member, Aune, 1991

Groups vary a lot in regard to the extent that they tolerate disagreements and how they interpret the consensus principle. Majority voting is rarely used as a means of decision-making, but there are exceptions. Decisions about whether a meeting is to be a smoking or a non-smoking meeting sometimes comes down to majority voting. H. C. Johnson

(1987, p. 443) observed two majority votes on smoking at successive meetings of a group, in a situation complete with meeting-stacking and other manipulations reminiscent of party politics. From time to time, issues more directly related to divergent interpretations of the AA program, such as whether to end the meeting with the Lord's Prayer, may also be decided by majority vote (Barbara N., 1994).

The importance of charismatic individuals and their idiosyncracies further contributes to the variation among groups. It also prepares the ground for personality clashes and rivalry. Personal power struggles occasionally threaten the functioning of a group, but discontented members always have the option of moving to another group or of starting a group of their own.

Variations in Density of the AA Network within Individual Groups

The AA networks vary along several dimensions. First, in some groups, members are linked together in a cohesive but closed network, whereas in other groups newcomers are quickly integrated. A second dimension is the role of family members in AA. Networks may be limited to individual members or they may include whole families. A third aspect is the relative significance of special-interest networks within AA.

"My wife and I attend two open meetings and my wife goes to one or two Al-Anon meetings every week. My daughter has attended Alateen meetings for more than one year. I think it is necessary that the family understands what an alcoholic is going through—and I feel the family should speak the same language."

Icelandic field interview (M, 51, 3)*

Participation in additional social activities varies from group to group. In Poland, some groups focus their activities almost exclusively on the meetings that are perceived, like church, as a special ritual hour, which does not include wider social activities. There are Finnish groups where contacts outside meetings are kept to a minimum, and anonymity is so strictly respected that members do not know each others' last names after years of going to the same meeting. In other groups, members see each other regularly.

---

* In this and other extracts from field interviews (see Appendix B), the information in brackets indicates the sex, age, and years of sobriety of the respondent.

Table 6.2 provides a picture of cross-cultural variations in members' joint activities between meetings at the level of individual groups. There are clear differences in the intensity of social contact between meetings. There are a lot of contacts in Finland, Iceland, and Poland and fewer contacts in Austria, Sweden, and Switzerland, with Mexico falling in between.

Many groups and some members in all groups restrict their AA participation primarily to meeting attendance. But an established pattern of social activities is part of the AA way of life, available to members who choose to participate. This also means that members changing residence can use the AA network as a way of getting entrance to a new community. There are few subcultures, professional networks, or fraternal organizations that can provide as immediate and pervasive access to a new community as AA.

A Swedish woman in her early thirties followed her husband on a one-year business assignment to the American Midwest. After nine months she became a member of AA. "Through the AA network, we got acquainted with the whole community. During the last three months we went to twice as many dinners as before."

Swedish field interview (F, 36, 3)

The Dynamics of Establishment of New Groups

In the early phase of AA in particular areas, groups are mainly founded by people who have had little or no previous experience with the organization. Later on, most new groups come into existence through the participation of persons who are already members of other AA groups. Very commonly, a new group grows out of an existing larger one. The moving of an AA member to a community where no AA group exists is another way in which new groups are established. New groups also arise from personality clashes and conflicts about practical issues.

Another type of offshoot is due to ideological differences or changes in the tone of the old group. In Helsinki in the 1950s, for instance, groups split because of disagreements about the role of religion in AA. In a women's-only group in the San Francisco Bay Area, when younger members started to use terms from popular psychology more frequently than those from the 12-step vocabulary, some of the

Table 6.2 Members' Joint Activities between Meetings, and Collaborative Projects with Other Groups in Study Countries

	Austria	Finland	Iceland	Mexico	Poland	Sweden	German-speaking Switzerland
Percentage of groups putting on special activities (e.g., meals, meditation weekends, summer camps)[a]	5	15	26	9	67	12	7
Percentage of groups reporting joint activities outside AA meetings[b]							
have family meetings	0	41	29	27	54	6	9
have coffee together	16	56	60	49	62	30	31
spend weekends together	10	36	46	11	41	15	8
Percentage of groups having worked on a project together with other AA groups during the last three years[c]	42	53	77	65	51	18	36

Source: ICSAA group surveys (Appendix B)

[a]*Question wording:* Does your group put on special activities (e.g., meals, meditation weekends, summer camp)? If yes, what are the activities and how often or on what days of the year do they occur?

[b]*Question wording:*
What kinds of activities do members engage in outside of AA meetings? (*check all that apply*)

( ) Family meetings
( ) Have coffee together
( ) Have dinner (or another meal) together
( ) Practice sports together
( ) Spend weekends together
( ) Other activities, please describe

[c]*Question wording:* Over the last three years, has your group worked on a project together with other AA groups (e.g., holiday celebrations, regional conference or sharing a hotline)?

long-term members left the group; they started a women's Step group, to focus on traditional AA and the Twelve Steps (Vourakis, 1989). A final reason for starting a new group, particularly in the United States, is to serve some category of members such as young people, women, or gays and lesbians.

Groups may also decline, for instance because of internal conflicts, because key members of the group move to another community or resume drinking, or because the group cannot attract new members to replace old-timers who are dying or dropping out.

The birth and mortality rates for any mutual-help groups vary in time and place. In 1984 in New Jersey, for example, the annual birth rate of AA groups was 13 percent. The growth rate of other mutual-help groups was considerably higher, 21 percent. AA groups had, however, a distinctly low mortality rate, 2 percent against 12 percent for all other mutual-help groups. The annual growth of the number of AA groups was thus 11 percent against 9 percent for all other mutual-help groups.

Maton et al., 1990

An interview study of founders of seventy-three Polish groups (Zieliński, 1992) shows how the dynamics of the movement vary according to its phase of development. In Poland, the role of treatment professionals was quite important in the early expansion of AA. The number of AA groups in Poland increased from 6 in 1980 to 390 in 1990. Non-alcoholics were among the initiators of 38 percent of the groups, and in 53 percent of the groups non-alcoholics participated in the first meetings. Most of the non-alcoholics were treatment professionals, but priests were also represented. In 68 percent of the groups, at least one of the founders had previous experience with AA. The role of experienced members increased over time. Only half of the groups founded up to 1986 had experienced AA members among the initiators, whereas the corresponding percentage for groups established from 1987 to 1990 was 82 percent. In the early groups, almost all had newcomers to AA among their founders, whereas one-third of the more recent groups were split-offs from existing groups and were established by experienced members without the participation of newcomers.

As a result of the branching out of groups, there is considerable diversity within AA, and members often move between different groups. In rural areas, where AA groups are less plentiful, the individual has few choices. In urban and suburban areas, there is usually a larger number of groups to match diverse preferences.

Outsiders often believe that all AA groups are virtually the same and that members attend any groups that are available. It is, indeed, a part of AA rhetoric for members to regard all meetings as valuable irrespective of the demographic composition, tenor, and ideology of the group. Members do, however, prefer certain groups over others, and their preferences frequently change over time (H. C. Johnson, 1987; Maxwell, 1984; Vourakis, 1989).

Most members select one group as their "home group," which they attend on a regular basis and to which they feel a special allegiance (Leach & Norris, 1977). Geographical proximity is often the decisive criterion: members choose a group that is close to their home or workplace. In other cases, people choose a group in another part of town in order to safeguard their anonymity. Reflecting the demographic composition of their neighborhood, many groups are socially and ethnically homogenous, but the nature of AA also encourages the crossing of boundaries of class and ethnicity. Mixture of age and life experiences is often mentioned as adding to the attractiveness of a group.

On the other hand, many members are attracted to people they can identify with, "someone like me" (Vourakis, 1989). For example, Hispanics in Los Angeles tend to cluster in different AA groups by nationality, level of education, and length of residence in the United States (F. Hoffman, 1994). The criteria for similarity are, however, highly variable. The tenor of meetings and interpretations of AA's belief system quite often are as important as social position in determining the individual's choice of groups. The process of continuous and flexible self-selection is an important part of the functioning of AA as a mutual-aid movement, and serves as an informal and self-directed form of "treatment matching," which probably is beyond the reach of any professional treatment program.

"I often meet my friends who are drivers or workers. Earlier I thought that these kinds of people were not good company for me since I am a highly educated medical doctor. In AA I discovered that every alcoholic can teach me something."

Polish life-story interview (M, 46, 5)

Special Groups

In principle, all AA groups should be open to everyone. In reality, however, there are special groups based on gender, age, and sexual identity. Despite the explicit requirement put forward in official AA literature (*The A.A. Group,* 1990, pp. 17–18), not all of them are open to people who do not meet the special criteria.

Most common are women-only groups. Although they exist, men-only groups are less common, probably because of the male dominance in AA in general. Female members report that women's groups are more intimate than mixed-sex groups and more open to talk about feelings, family relationships, and sexual problems (Hornik, 1977; Stafford, 1979; Vourakis, 1989). There has been considerable resistance against same-sex groups since they cannot be open to all members. Some groups attempt to solve the ideological dilemma by escorting potential newcomers of the opposite gender to some other group meeting being held at the same time. As same-sex meetings become more common, however, it is accepted that their membership is restricted.

In 1990, certain areas in the German-speaking part of Switzerland refused to include women-only groups in the official AA directory.

In the United States and, more recently, elsewhere, there are special groups for gay and lesbian members. Many gay and lesbian members see the availability of special groups as of crucial importance to their entering AA. In some communities, these groups are an integral part of the gay and lesbian subculture.

If a female newcomer turns up at a meeting of a men's group in Helsinki, one of the participants takes her to another meeting.

If a man appears at the door during a meeting of Wednesday Women, all talk stops and the women turn and stare at the man. Someone will say, "This is a women's meeting. You can't come in." It is not until the man is out of sight that the meeting continues.

H. C. Johnson, 1987, p. 530

Young people's groups are meant to attract newcomers who would not feel at home in groups dominated by older people. In the United States, they also have served the purpose of protecting more traditional groups from the influx of young drug users and their lifestyles.

Newcomers' groups seem to be restricted to the United States. They are a response to the large influx of beginners, many pressured to come by the courts, as a condition of probation, or by a 12-step treatment program. This trend threatens to change the nature of traditional groups. Since beginners' groups are open to everybody, they are not against AA principles, but they are another sign of the diversification of AA.

In the United States, the name of some groups includes an ethnic label, such as "Native America" or "Latino." Again, these groups usually are formally open to any members.

No official groups for specific professions exist in AA. There are, however, "dim-light" groups for some professions who want to stay more anonymous than is possible in normal AA meetings. Dim-light groups protect professions such as airline pilots who must adhere to strict rules on drinking, and whose known attendance at AA might cause problems with an employer. These groups do not appear in AA directories. There also are organizations such as Lawyers for Sobriety that promote AA within a given profession. This is not an AA group, however, but a network of lawyers providing information about alcohol problems and AA to their colleagues.

"A few of the old-timers who had stopped smoking sat in the smoking section anyway. They told me that was where most of the newcomers sat and they wanted to be there with them."
Bernie B., 1992

Smoking during meetings has become an increasingly passionate issue within AA. In many meeting facilities smoking is prohibited by the landlord, but heated conflicts often surround the issue in cases where the decision is up to the group. Smoke-free groups are not special groups, since they are open to everybody. In addition to personal convenience, however, ideological issues are involved in the sense that prohibiting smoking may raise the threshold for some newcomers.

Looking at the occurrence of special groups in our study countries (Table 6.3), it seems that they are more common where the AA movement is large and long-established. Women-only groups exist in all

Table 6.3 Special Interest Groups in Study Countries, 1990

	Austria	Finland	Iceland	Mexico	Poland	Sweden	French-speaking Switzerland	German-speaking Switzerland	California[a]
Young people's	–	–	+	+	–	+	–	–	+
Women-only	–	+	+	–[c]	+	+	–	–	+
Men-only	–	+	–	–	–	–[d]	–	–	+
Newcomers	–	–	–	+	–	–	–	–	+
Gay/lesbian	+[b]	+	–	+	–	+	–	+	+
Occupation	–	–	–	+	–	–	–	–[e]	+[f]

[a]Contra Costa County, California
[b]One group listed as "also for homosexual alcoholics." The group also has straight members.
[c]In Mexico, there are no women-only groups, but women-only meetings exist.
[d]In 1992, but not in 1990, there was a men-only group in Sweden.
[e]There are rumors about a dim-light (unlisted) meeting for professional pilots.
[f]Dim-light (unlisted) groups only

study countries except Austria and Switzerland. The lack of women's groups in Austria and Switzerland reflects both a strong opposition to special groups and the high proportion of women at all AA meetings. Only Finland and the United States have men-only groups. Special groups for young people exist in Iceland, Mexico, Sweden, and the United States. Iceland and Poland are the only study countries not having at least one AA group designated for gays and lesbians. In most countries, however, the number of special interest groups is very low, and only in some regions in the United States do they have any quantitative significance. In three counties in northern California, 11 percent of all groups were listed as special groups in 1988 (Morgan, Bloomfield & Phillips, 1989).

Interrelations among Groups and Local Intergroups

Each AA group is autonomous, but AA is not an amorphous collection of groups. On the contrary, most groups participate in collaborative projects (Table 6.2). As a general rule, collaboration between groups seems to be more pervasive in countries where members of one group have a lot of mutual contacts between meetings.

Joint activities and reciprocal visits bind the various groups together to form a complex network. Many members regularly go to several groups, and AA birthdays and group anniversaries intensify this pattern. "Birthdays," the anniversaries of a person's sobriety, are often celebrated by special recognition at a meeting. Birthday meetings are usually open to the family, and members attempt to attend the birthdays of friends in neighboring groups. Anniversaries are a specially important affair in Finnish AA, celebrated with cakes and congratulatory cards. Customarily, AA banners and fifth anniversary pins are also awarded (Mäkelä, 1989). In Mexico, the celebration of an anniversary at the end of the meeting may develop into a real fiesta with food, soft drinks, a cake with candles and sometimes even live music and dancing (Rosovsky, 1991). Many groups also celebrate their own anniversary.

The local founding of AA is also often celebrated. Groups also schedule special events at religious and national holidays, especially holidays associated with drinking and family gatherings, such as Christmas, New Year's Eve, Independence Day, and Labor Day.

In the Swedish city of Sundsvall, AA members and their families meet every Saturday for coffee at a cafeteria close to the marketplace. On any Saturday morning, the AA crowd amounts to some fifty people in one section of the cafeteria.

Local groups also organize joint activities, either based on informal collaboration or through intergroups. Intergroups are committees composed of representatives of collaborating groups. Intergroup committees may operate local service offices and telephone answering services, offer referral services, handle public information, literature procurement, and distribution, publish meeting directories and newsletters, and sponsor special activities involving more than one group. Larger local service offices may have administrative personnel and paid employees.

Intergroups are financially dependent on support from the local groups and on funds raised from the special activities sponsored by the intergroup, but they are not part of the formal hierarchical organization of AA. Often there is tension between the need to support the formal AA structure and the need to support intergroups.

Fellowships and clubhouses are mainly restricted to the United States and Mexico. Often they are rented or owned by AA members to provide meeting facilities and safe havens. Once a facility is established, it becomes a common social area for members in general, not just a location for meetings. Many are open for long hours to provide a place for AA members to congregate. Clubhouses often involve ownership of furniture and sometimes the building itself. Therefore, their operation is officially not part of AA at all. The name AA is not supposed to appear in connection with the clubhouses but is reserved for regular AA meetings held there. Nevertheless, the organization, operating, and financing of clubhouses can take considerable effort on the part of AA members.

In the United States, it has become increasingly popular to flaunt one's membership in AA by bumper sticks, sweaters, and jewelry displaying AA slogans.

In Finland, over the years, newer representatives on the General Service Board have repeatedly proposed that an AA pin or some similar symbol should be adopted so that members could easily recognize each other. The initiative has always been defeated by more experienced members.

Because of the autonomy of individual groups, their style and ideology vary considerably. It is a peculiar feature of AA that the existence of idiosyncratic and eccentric groups is accepted and, indeed, taken for granted. At the same time, visits by one group to another tend to level out differences in style and program interpretation. Where autocratic leaders cut off the contacts of their group to the wider AA network, one possible outcome is that dissident members start a new group. Dissidents in the deviant groups may also receive active support from their neighbors. Since AA groups that are part of the wider network recruit a greater variety of members, and since variety is important in attracting and maintaining newcomers, it is probable that the new group will survive.

The Economic Relevance of AA Networks

To emphasize that the main purpose of the fellowship is to maintain sobriety, official AA literature explicitly declares that AA does not provide vocational counseling or jobs, yet members informally receive such help. How to get along at work is a frequent topic at discussion meetings, and members speak about problems they have with co-workers and superiors and with job-hunting. After the meeting, members often exchange information about job openings and persons to contact for work. AA also offers a network for possible business relationships, and members may provide employment for each other (Rosovsky, 1992).

Where AA groups are small and personal, mutual support extends to the full range of social and economic ties through which people relate to each other. Even in anonymous urban scenes, mutual assistance can develop. Urban AA clubhouses in working-class areas in the United States provide a place for unemployed members to hang out and to locate temporary work.

AA networks reach across continents. A young bricklayer from rural Florida obtained his job on a construction site in Angola through various contacts with AA members leading from Miami to New York and eventually Angola.

In the United States, professionals may advertise as "A Friend of Bill W." or use other language to indicate their AA membership.

A building contractor in a small Finnish town uses as his business emblem a triangle surrounded by a circle, a symbol from the AA logo recognizable to all members.

The demographic composition of the groups varies, but groups tend toward internal homogeneity. All groups are, however, open to all members and visits between groups are frequent. The AA network has ramifications at all levels of society. As a Finnish member put it: to visit different groups in Helsinki is to make a study trip into Finnish society as seen through liquor. This means that a member can choose both his dentist and plumber from among AA members. Few other informal social networks can offer the same.

In the 1990s, a new type of advertisement started to appear in the Swedish AA newsletter: ". . . driver with taxi license requested for summer job."

Bulletinen, 1990, no. 2, p. 26

AA members at trade or professional meetings seek each other. In AA parlance, this is to remind each other that while they may be members of a professional association, they wouldn't have a job if they forgot they are alcoholics and members of AA. At the same time, however, these contacts may be very instrumental in producing professional opportunities.

Mutual trust based on similar existential experiences promotes economic exchange between AA members, but mixing existential and economic ties can also cause problems. If an employer and his workers attend the same meetings, hierarchical work relationships may threaten the basic symmetry of relationships between members.

Jarkko is an AA member in his late forties and the owner of a mail-order company in Helsinki. Fifteen out of twenty-five employees are AA members, and three have had a relapse during the last year. Jarkko does not pay attention to social background or drinking history but from experience he refuses to hire persons with a history of violence. Jarkko's main problem is that his employees go to the same meetings he does. "It is an extra burden to always take into account that some of the participants are dependent on you. From time to time I go to the movies just to get rid of being responsible for others."

Finnish field interview (M, 47, 10)

Challenges to the Nature of AA as a Fellowship

One key difference between AA and self-help groups of an economic nature has to do with the criteria for membership and their relation to independently existing social networks. In nineteenth-century England, self-help was a direct outgrowth of established social relationships, and members brought with them all their social ties. The inhabitants of the same village or the workers from the same factory went together to the same pub, discussed their economic problems and at the same time enjoyed conviviality and community. In AA, membership is based on individual life experiences that are not direct reflections of social position, and members enter the groups as individual entities. Individual existential experience replaces collective social destiny. Therefore, AA represents a special type of social network. Its networks are not based on mutually beneficial payoffs in the same way as are, for example, formal and informal professional networks. They also differ from networks based on family ties or ethnicity. They are based on individual life experiences transgressing kin, work, and ethnicity. At the same time, they are part of the everyday life of the members in a way that distinguishes them from professional group therapy.

Another unusual thing about AA is that it is an *open* network. Whereas in most such networks access to membership is quite tightly controlled, membership in AA is open to anyone who professes a desire to stop drinking, and there is no mechanism for excluding anyone from membership.

Most AA members may never stray from their home groups and meetings. They may even cease to attend meetings. But many of the non-active members continue to consider themselves alcoholics and know that AA meetings and support networks are available to them around the world. Further, they assume that they will feel at home and be accepted at an AA meeting anywhere.

"In my experience, people juggling several programs are honest to none, committed to none. . . . [P]eople using AA as group therapy simply learn the zip words and actions and become bored, drifting off to another new solution."

Jack G., 1993, p. 18

While the membership of AA is growing worldwide, there are two elements that potentially weaken this assumption of a mutual and automatic trust, both emerging in the United States where AA has been established longest. The first is the development of special-interest groups in AA and the understanding that attendance should be reserved for certain classes of AA members. A second challenge is the development of a 12-step movement in which people participate in more than one program. In terms of the present chapter, the fundamental question relates to the social networks in which AA members participate. If special-interest social networks within AA result in exclusive interaction within special-interest groups, then to that extent the AA subculture will be divided. To the extent that interaction of AA members with members of other 12-step groups becomes pervasive, AA subculture may be absorbed in the wider 12-step subculture.

7
Regional and National
Service Structure

The service structure ties individual groups into an orderly movement without forsaking AA's grass-roots principles. This requires mechanisms that are compatible with the legal requirements of outside society and the internal principles expressed in the Twelve Traditions.

Because of legal requirements and imperatives of economic efficiency, AA has established legal corporations. In most countries, only publishing activities are organized to conform with prevailing legislation on incorporation, and the general service board is run informally and guided solely by internal principles of AA. In the United States and Mexico, the general service board is organized as a legal corporation. Despite these legal structures, AA has managed to outlive its charismatic founders without resorting to a centralized bureaucracy.

The autonomy of the groups is in many ways reflected in the organizational structure of AA. In Switzerland, the groups "have organized themselves into districts that are appropriate in terms of geography and ideals" (*Die Struktur der Gemeinschaft . . .*, 1986). The formulation puts emphasis on the right of groups to choose their district. In the Finnish AA as well, geographic divisions are flexible, since it is up to individual groups to decide to which district or area they belong, and not all groups belong to any district or area (Mäkelä, in press).

The main life of AA is in the groups, and it is a recurrent lament that most members have little interest in what happens above the group level. Usually though, there are enough members who are interested in a career at higher levels of the service structure. Case descriptions presented in this chapter show that service issues can stir up passionate disputes. The overall rate of participation at national service conferences is often quite high. Forty-one percent of all Finnish groups sent a representative to the annual meeting of the Finnish AA Publishing Association in 1988 (Mäkelä, in press). Despite financial distress, 43 percent of the groups in Poland attended the national meeting of group representatives in 1990 (Świątkiewicz, 1991).

Levels of Organization in the United States and Canada

In the United States and Canada, the service structure is quite complex, and *The A.A. Service Manual* (1988) provides detailed descriptions and instructions for each level. The service structure starts in the individual group "that lets its feelings—approval or disapproval, for or against change—be known to the GSR (general service representative) whom the group has elected" (*The A.A. Service Manual,* 1988, p. S22).

Districts are the next level of organization of AA then the area level, which is key, because the delegates elected at area assemblies constitute two-thirds of the participants to the General Service Conference.

The General Service Conference consists of area delegates, the trustees of the General Service Board, directors of AA World Services and *A.A. Grapevine,* staff members of *A.A. Grapevine,* and the General Service Office. The conference approves the financial and policy reports of the General Service Board and its related corporate services. It gives advice and directions to the General Service Board on all matters affecting AA as a whole. Furthermore, it considers appropriate action concerning "serious deviations from AA tradition" and "harmful misuse" of the name "Alcoholics Anonymous" (*The A.A. Service Manual,* 1988, p. S32). Finally, the General Service Conference plays a key role in approving AA literature.

The General Service Board is the highest executive body of AA. The General Service Office, located in New York City, functions as an overall office for AA in the United States and Canada. Among its tasks, the office is the center for the various committees appointed to handle AA matters. Besides this, the office staff prepares the annual conference, takes care of public information, and has an important function in publishing and distributing AA literature. The staff is mostly made up of AA members. An interesting feature is that staff members rotate between office departments.

The regulation of the relationships between the General Service Conference and the General Service Board is a key example of how the organizational principles of AA are adjusted to the legal requirements of the outside world. The General Service Board of Alcoholics Anonymous, Inc., is an incorporated trusteeship. Its membership consists of trustees who elect their own successors. Each trustee becomes a member upon being elected, and ceases automatically to be a member upon ceasing to be a trustee. The sole reason for constituting trustees as members is in order to comply with the laws of New York State. In legal terms, the board is absolutely autonomous and self-perpetuating. The Conference Charter (*The A.A. Service Manual*, 1988, pp. S29–S32) stipulates, however, that regardless of the legal prerogatives of the board, the nominees for trustees selected by the General Service Conference will be elected to the General Service Board, the trustees being obligated by tradition to do so. The Charter further makes it clear that, as a matter of tradition, a majority vote by the Conference shall be a suggestion to the General Service Board, but a two-thirds vote shall be absolutely binding upon the board, regardless of legal considerations.

The Complexity of the Service Structure

There are differences in the complexity of the service structure (Table 7.1). In Austria, Iceland, Poland, Sweden, and Switzerland, service meetings are held at two levels above the group level, whereas the number of levels in the service structure is four in Finland and five in Mexico and the United States. Another indicator of organizational complexity is the number of subcommittees of the national service board, which varies from none in Austria to eleven in the United States and thirteen in Mexico.

The number of levels does not give a full picture of how much direct control individual groups have of what happens at the national level. In the United States, Canada, Mexico, and Sweden, the control is mediated in the sense that the delegates to the general service conference are chosen by indirect elections, whereas in the rest of the study countries all groups can send their representatives directly to the national meeting.

The Role of Non-Alcoholics

In the beginning, a majority of non-alcoholics were appointed as trustees of the Alcoholic Foundation (which later was transformed into the General Service Board of AA). Only in 1966, after a prolonged struggle, did Bill W. succeed in changing the composition of the General Service Board to have a two-thirds majority of alcoholics (Kurtz, 1991, p. 142).

Table 7.1 Service Structure of AA in Study Countries, 1990

	Austria	Finland	Iceland[a]	Mexico	Poland	Sweden[b]	French-speaking Switzerland	German-speaking Switzerland	U.S. and Canada
Number of levels above group level at which service meetings are held	2	4	2	5	2	2	2	2	5
Types of national service bodies									
service conference	–	+	+	+	+	–	+	+	+
service board	+	+	+	+	+	+	+	+	+
publishing board	–	+	+	+	+	–	–	–	–[c]
Number of AA members on national service board	14	44	3	17	7	21	17	15	19
Number of non-AA members on national service board	1	0	3	5	0	0	1	0	8
Number of national service board committees[d]	0	4	3	14	9	3	1	0	11

[a]Information for Iceland refers to 1989.

[b]The Swedish service structure was thoroughly reorganized in 1991–1993.

[c]A.A. *Grapevine* has its own publishing board as a separate incorporated entity, but they only publish the newsletter, one or two special books, and cartoon collections.

[d]A committee should have at least two members, i.e., one person having some specific responsibility is not a committee.

When the American AA delegation to the Soviet Union stopped over in Helsinki in the fall of 1988, the Finnish AA members were surprised to hear that they presented themselves by their full names. When it was explained that such is the custom in America, and that one member of the delegation was a non-alcoholic trustee, some Finns felt quite annoyed at the idea of non-alcoholics representing AA.

The proportion of non-alcoholic members on the National Service Board in various countries seems to reflect different ideological perspectives rather than organizational maturity (Table 7.1). Countries refraining from having non-alcoholic members in service bodies often do so in order to safeguard the autonomy of the movement. Countries having non-alcoholic trustees feel that they provide important links to professional communities and to the outside world.

In Finland, all members of service bodies are members of AA. In the very beginning, three non-alcoholics were elected members of the Council of Finnish AA Clubs, but they did not participate in council meetings. Subsequently there have been no non-alcoholic trustees. The lack of non-alcoholic trustees accentuates the self-reliance of the AA movement in Finland. Poland, Sweden, and the German-speaking part of Switzerland also did not have non-alcoholic board members in 1990. Austria and the French- and Italian-speaking parts of Switzerland had just one non-alcoholic trustee, whereas Mexico and Iceland follow the American model with a rather high ratio of non-alcoholic trustees. During the first twenty-four years of AA in Iceland, all members of service bodies were alcoholics, but reorganization of the movement in the late 1970s brought non-alcoholic members to the National Service Board. The decision to appoint non-alcoholic members did not originate from any special need. It was rather a symbolic gesture indicating the willingness to follow the American model. After prolonged discussions, Swedish AA also decided in 1991 to elect two non-alcoholics to its National Board of Trustees.

The formal position of non-alcoholics in the service structure does not always reflect their true influence in the movement. For example, outside experts play an important role in the Polish AA, although they cannot be elected members of the service board.

Organization of Publishing Activities

Since AA publishes and distributes literature, the organization must adapt itself to comply with local laws. In Sweden and Iceland, publishing activities are separate from the general service structure of AA. The publishing companies are run as non-profit corporations and are administered by a board elected by the National Service Conference.

The Finnish AA Publishing Association is a legal body under the Finnish Association Law. The pamphlet representing the service structure describes the AA Publishing Association as "our legal link to organized society" (*Tervetuloa palvelemaan*, 1989, p. 5). The association has six members only, who at the same time serve as the board of the association. Every year two new members are elected by the annual meeting of general service representatives of AA groups to serve for a three-year period. On their election, the new members sign an agreement to resign their membership in the association when their term ends.

In Switzerland, the legal corporation AA-Verein Literaturvertrieb Schweiz is the means by which the financial system of AA is organized in order to conform to Swiss legislation (*Die Struktur der Gemeinschaft . . .*, 1986). The corporation has a formal membership with fees, and non-alcoholic persons are allowed to become members. AA tries to stay in line with its own organizational principles by putting the corporation under the control of the Chairmen's Conference and the financial officer of the General Service Board.

The unit responsible for publishing is AA's link to the juridical society with its rules, boards, accounts, and auditors. Although the members of an AA publishing committee have considerable influence, the publishing unit has not become an independent center of power, and it has not influenced the inner structure of the movement.

Switzerland: Two Linguistic Service Structures

In Switzerland, there are two service structures: one for the German-speaking region, and the other for the French- and Italian-speaking regions together (Rehm & Mariolini, in press). The two structures are roughly parallel in organization, although there are cultural differences in their style of functioning. As of 1990, the 112 groups in the German-speaking part of Switzerland were organized into six districts, with each group having one vote at the district conference. Each district elects a delegate to the General Service Board for the German-speaking part of Switzerland. The main decision-making body for the German-speaking region is the Chairman's Conference, which is composed of the chairpersons of all AA groups and meets twice a year. The agenda for the Chairman's Conference, which includes decisions about financial resources, is prepared by the General Service Board, which is composed of the six district delegates and nine officers selected by the Chairmen's Conference. The General Service Board also serves as the executive body.

The groups in French- and Italian-speaking AA (fifty-three groups in 1990) are organized into six French districts and one Italian district. The equivalent to the German-speaking Chairmen's Conference is the General Service Conference of group chairpersons, but it meets only once a year. The General Service Board, which meets four times a year, is composed of the district delegates and ten other officers.

The German-speaking conference meets more frequently and has a stronger role than its counterpart in the French- and Italian-speaking structure, where the General Service Board is more influential. The most striking difference is the very strong role of "grey eminences" in the French- and Italian-speaking region. Here, longtime members of AA, who often were also the founding fathers of AA groups, exert power that cannot be fully detected in the official organizational structures. Though there are fewer AA groups in the French- and Italian-speaking service structure, they are organized more in terms of representative democracy, with a strong role for charismatic leaders, while the German-speaking service structure is organized more in terms of direct grass-roots democracy. In its organization and functioning, the AA structure seems to take on some specific characteristics of its cultural setting.

Mexico: Two Competing Service Structures

In Mexico, there are actually several movements calling themselves Alcoholics Anonymous (Rosovsky, in press). "The 24-hour movement" was formed in 1975. Although this movement regards itself as part of AA, it has become more like a therapeutic community movement and will be discussed in chapter 15, which considers various alternatives to AA.

Regular AA groups in Mexico are divided between two parallel service structures, known as "Central Mexicana" and "Sección México," both of which claim to be the legitimate Mexican AA (Rosovsky, Casanova, Perez-Lopez, & Narvaez, 1992). The former, which established its General Service Office in 1969, is the only grouping recognized by the General Service Office in New York and authorized to publish conference-approved AA literature. Sección México emerged as a dissident group in 1985 as a result of internal strife. It has adopted a similar organizational structure and publishes its own literature, competing with lower prices. Both service structures have a large following. At the level of principles and the recovery program, there are no differences between groups belonging to the two organizations, and members often do not know to which AA they belong, or that there are two movements.

Regional and National Conferences and Arrangements Supporting Wider AA Networks

The primary purpose of regional and national conferences is to discuss and to come to a decision on financial and organizational issues above the local level. Usually, however, business meetings represent just a small part of all activities in connection with a conference, and regional and national meetings are well attended by many AA members that are not official delegates. Larger and smaller AA meetings are held almost around-the-clock, special categories of AA members and members of Al-Anon have meetings of their own, and there are public information meetings and social events such as dinners and dances. A substantial proportion of members have attended AA assemblies, conferences, or roundups in the past twelve months (Table 7.2). In this way, regional and national meetings provide a platform for prominent members and strengthen the social network at all levels of the membership.

The complexity of arrangements supporting AA networks is related to the size and life span of the AA community in each country (Table 7.3). The network arrangements are most developed in the United States and in Mexico, where AA is large and well-established, whereas the small AA community in Austria has few institutionalized arrangements supporting AA networks.

The general extent of AA activities at the national level in North America may be surmised from a look at the "Calendar of Events" given in *Box 459,* a newsletter published by the General Service Office of AA. The first weekend in October 1989 is typical, with nineteen events, including two area conferences, five state conferences, five regional conferences and roundups, two conferences identified by initials only, and five other special events including a Women's Workshop, an Intertribal (American Indian Tribes) Roundup, and a Bilingual Convention (in Montreal). The examples above are only a few of the nationally visible events among a vast number of social activities sponsored by local and regional organizations.

An AA Conference in Poland as a Mirror of AA in a Specific Cultural Setting

While the General Assembly is the highest authority in the Polish AA, it meets only every second year. In a country undergoing rapid change,

Table 7.2   Percentage of Members Having Attended AA Assemblies, Conferences, and Roundups

	Iceland	Mexico	Poland	Sweden	German-speaking Switzerland	California
			All members			
In past 12 months	51	29	17	56	55	47
Ever	68	54	25	62	83	64
		All members with at least one year of sobriety				
In past 12 months	62	30	34	75	72	57
Ever	81	62	55	85	100	81

Source: ICSAA membership surveys (Appendix B)
Question wording:
  How recently did you engage in the following AA activities?
  Attended any AA assemblies, conferences, roundups
    In past 4 weeks
    In past 12 months
    Earlier
    Never

where AA is relatively young but growing at an amazing pace, two years is a very long period between formal decision-making sessions. Hence, the conferences that are held twice a year have become a very important integrating institution and legislative body. The conferences are open to attendance not only by voting representatives of all Polish AA groups but also by members with no voting rights. The group representatives at the conference consider and adopt, among other matters, guiding principles for the movement, plan the publishing policy, and fix the rules for the election of the seven-person Board of Trustees (called the Group of Seven) of the Polish AA.

The conference held in early 1990 was attended by representatives of some 150 of a total of 350 groups in Poland. In all, there were more than 400 persons attending. The business meeting was held in the local town hall, rent-free, over a two-day period. The opening ceremony began with the Serenity Prayer, followed by speeches by the chair of the Group of Seven, the mayor, and the local priest. The mayor and priest, besides expressing their approval of the ideas underlying the AA movement, declared their willingness to assist AA members in their area. After a break, the delegates took their places at long tables, before a dais occupied by representatives of the Group of Seven. The agenda included such matters as the financial problems of the movement and amendments to election procedures. Discussions were occasionally very heated, especially when it came to financial matters.

Almost all proposals concerning the agenda and almost all matters voted on were submitted by longstanding AA members, while other participants remained a bit confused. The discussions were openly controlled and directed by the presiding board. Participation in the debates was not easy for delegates because of a full agenda and uncomfortable physical conditions—the conference room was overcrowded and there was almost no place to relax. Outside the conference room, the corridor was also jammed with participants, along with tables exhibiting AA literature for sale. During the opening ceremony, many participants opted for behind-the-scenes conversations in the corridor.

The headquarters both for socializing and for AA meetings was the parish church and adjacent buildings, at quite a distance from the town hall. In the church and parish building, AA, Al-Anon and Alateen meetings took place around-the-clock in candle-lit rooms throughout the conference. In these meetings the atmosphere was quite different from that in the conference room. People listened attentively, and although as many as fifty people were at the meeting, the principles usually observed in much smaller meetings were rigorously kept. Long-term members predominated among the speakers, and the speeches were shorter than at other large meetings. There was a clear, tacit understanding to give a speaking opportunity to the largest possible number of people. Some speakers told about their recent problems, while others narrated stories of their drinking and sobering up. Some statements were very general and did not touch on personal and intimate problems, but intimate statements were no less common than they would be in small-group meetings.

The environment of the meetings was a scene of controlled chaos. Those who found no seats around the tables sat on the floor or stood. Many moved from one room to another in search of friends and acquaintances. But the incessant movement to and fro did not disrupt the meetings; people came and left quietly, without slamming doors or making noise.

The conference ended with a special mass said by the priest who regularly cooperates with AA in the area, and attended by about half of those still present. Such a special mass has become a traditional event both at AA conferences and at other large assemblies. In his sermon, the priest referred both to universal Christian values and to those specific to the AA movement. The mass was intended as an act of penance by those attending. They knelt for most of the service, and expressed contrition for the wrongs done to their wives, husbands, children, and

Table 7.3 Arrangements Supporting AA Networks in Study Countries

	Austria	Sweden	Iceland	French-speaking Switzerland	German-speaking Switzerland	Finland	Poland	Mexico	U.S. and Canada
Annual national meeting or regional conferences	−	+	+	+	+	+	+	+	+
AA retreats/weekends exist	−	−	+a	+	+	+	−	+	+
AA speaker a recognized vocation (expenses paid)	−	−	−	−	−	−	+	+	+
Regular special-interest conferences (gay/lesbian, women, etc.)	−	−	−	−	−	−	−	−	+

aThe distinction between national meetings and retreats is unclear in Iceland. Something called a "national meeting" is held annually but the format is close to a weekend retreat.

other persons during their drinking years. The mass included a special element termed the testimony. From the pulpit, a fifty-year-old AA woman told the story of her life, expressing thanks to the priests and to God for having found her way to an AA group where she had started her life anew. Another testimony took the form of a song of thanks to the Virgin Mary, sung by a man about thirty years old. The text of the song was a kind of prayer in which the AA movement was described as the road to salvation indicated by God.

For all its specific objectives and the official disavowal of interest in politics, the conference mirrored the problems and changes that mark the Polish society as a whole: ubiquitous financial troubles, a group of confused people who cannot comprehend what is taking place, and, finally, the omnipresent Roman Catholic Church.

Anarchy in the Anthill

The relative lack of a bureaucratic apparatus in AA does not lead to chaos, though the segmented structure brings some overlapping in the division of responsibility. Division of work within AA is both vague and flexible. To an outsider accustomed to bureaucratic organizations, it seems almost a miracle that AA can arrange large national conferences, or that the AA answering service is regularly staffed. Many members of AA employed by the business community, municipalities, and other bureaucracies are well aware of the differences between the organizational principles of these bureaucracies and of AA. A Finnish member compared AA to an anthill, in which everybody carries his straw in a different but right direction so that everything always gets done.

8
The Finances of AA

There are two main sources of income at AA, literature profits and voluntary contributions from members. Fledgling national movements occasionally receive support from AA groups abroad. In Poland, donations from members who have emigrated to the United States are of some importance. Dances, holiday celebrations, and other social events organized by AA also bring in income, mainly at the local level. In addition to internal funding, national movements sometimes receive direct or indirect support from the outside.

Outside Funding and the Principle of Self-Support

Achieving financial self-sufficiency has not always been an easy task, particularly in the early stages of national AA movements. In the early days of the Finnish AA, many groups were established as legal associations and received support from social authorities. Over the years, bitter conflicts evolved between those who accepted legal organization and outside support and those who insisted on an informal structure and self-support. The dispute culminated in a court struggle about who was entitled to use the name of AA. The conflict was finally resolved in 1961 with the decision that no outside contributions would be accepted in the future (Mäkelä, in press).

In the German-speaking part of Switzerland, an outside association called "The Friends of AA" (Freunde der AA), composed of both non-alcoholics and AA members, provided support for purchasing literature until the late 1960s (Rehm et al., 1992). Cantonal reports in Switzerland indicate that about one-third of the cantonal governments at one time or another between 1963 and 1988 supported AA as part of their prevention programs (Mariolini & Rehm, in press; Régie fédérale des alcools, 1963–1988). The funding was most substantial in Zurich and Geneva, the home cantons of the general service offices of the

German-speaking and French- and Italian-speaking AA in Switzerland, and here the support was given to "the friends of the AA movement" or towards "general expenses of AA." The reports of other cantons indicate that the funds were allocated at the group level.

A less direct form of public support has also been in use in Switzerland (Mariolini & Rehm, in press). It is common practice in Switzerland for public authorities to step in when recognized social organizations preparing a large conference need a guarantee to cover possible deficits. This option has been used by AA. If for any reason deficits occur, indirect financing could easily become direct financing.

Another type of public support is exemplified by two large AA groups in Finland that run clubhouses with meeting facilities and a few beds. The clubhouses, as well as paint and furniture, were given to the groups for free or token prices by the local municipality.

In many countries, meeting facilities are made available to AA without charge or for nominal prices. In the Scandinavian countries, for instance, municipal meeting facilities have been available free-of-change to all kinds of voluntary organizations. Indeed, if it were not for the respect of AA traditions, neither AA as tenant nor the proprietor of the premises would think of charging rent for the meeting space.

In the United States, some universities take AA literature as token compensation for the use of rooms for AA meetings, or allow AA to use the facilities of 12-step treatment institutions in exchange for services, such as open meetings for patients, or for AA literature. Many groups have traditionally met in church basements and rooms, rented for a relatively small charge. In hard times and with the growth of 12-step groups, however, rents have tended to rise as churches come to view them as a significant source of income.

Borderline issues remain but, for the most part, AA has achieved a high degree of financial self-support in most of our study countries. Only in Poland did outside support still play an important role in the 1980s and early 1990s. For a long time, there was a certain symbiosis between Abstainers' Clubs and AA, which in many places used the same facilities and were not always distinguishable to the members (Worono-wicz, 1992). This meant that the substantial funding of the clubs by the state indirectly provided resources to AA (Świątkiewicz, 1992b). The main financial burden of publishing AA literature in Polish has also been carried out by public authorities, and the Institute for Psychiatry and Neurology has been selling literature to AA much below the production cost. The general economic crisis and the shift to a market economy has aggravated the financial problems of AA. Until recently, rent-free meeting space was available to AA at treatment institutions and other publicly funded facilities. Now the situation is changing, and it is uncertain whether all groups will be able to cover the increasing expenses for meeting space. Achieving self-support has been given high priority within Polish AA, but it is likely that it will take considerable time before this goal is attained (Świątkiewicz & Zieliński, in press).

Membership Contributions

Contributions are mainly collected at regular meetings but also at meetings of service bodies and at special events such as conferences and conventions. In Iceland, for example, the 1990 financial report shows that 79 percent of the contributions came from groups, 10 percent from the general service conference and 11 percent from a special annual meeting of Icelandic AA.

Individual donations may also be sent directly to regional or national service bodies. In order to avoid becoming financially dependent on wealthy individuals, limits have been set on the annual amount of individual contributions allowed, as well as on bequests from the wills of individual members. In some countries, this practice causes legal predicaments. In the United Kingdom, a bill had to be passed by parliament in 1986 to allow AA to have registered charity status and still be able to set limits to the size of contributions it would accept.

The "hat collection" at meetings is genuinely voluntary. Members of the national research teams who attended meetings observed that there was no pressure to contribute, however indirect. Nevertheless, in most countries it is customary to contribute a standard amount, although individual participants are free to give more or nothing at all. One indication of there being a standard contribution is that participants quite frequently put in a larger bill and take back the change they are due out of the hat. In 1990, the value of the most common standard contribution, in U.S. dollars, was as follows:

Austria	$1.50
Finland	$2.50
Iceland	$1.80
Mexico	$0.60
Sweden	$1.50
French- and Italian- speaking parts of Switzerland	$3.75
German-speaking part of Switzerland	$3.00

Table 8.1   Percentage of Monthly Expenses, by Type, of Austrian, Finnish, Mexican, and Swedish AA Groups

	Austria	Finland	Mexico	Sweden
Rent	36	18	56	41
Coffee, food, and accessory supplies	22	36	26	10
Literature	28	16	6	13
Contributions to answering services and local and national service offices	14	26	9	37
Other expenses	–	4	4	–
Total	100	100	101	101

Source: ICSAA group surveys (Appendix B). Expenses reported by individual groups have been rounded off and added together. The percentages refer to the aggregate group budget.

The standard contribution is somewhat but not closely related to the country's general level of affluence. The standard sum is lowest in Mexico and highest in Switzerland, but the Finnish figure is higher than that in equally prosperous Austria, Iceland, and Sweden.

The expenses of individual groups vary widely. Refreshment expenses may be paid for by members separately, rental costs vary greatly, and the net literature expense may be small. Table 8.1 presents a breakdown of the expenses of AA groups in four of our study countries. The table reveals large differences between countries in the proportion of the hat collection that is sent to high-level service functions.

The person in charge of making coffee in a group in Helsinki had a relapse. Having in his possession the key to the meeting room, he broke into the cabinet containing the cashbox and took the money. He told the group by phone what he had done. A note was placed in the cabinet welcoming him back to a meeting.

The chairperson of another group in Helsinki had a relapse and took the funds (about U.S.$ 250) and the keys of the group. The secretary threatened to press charges (the chairperson was on parole) unless he returned the keys, but made no mention of the money.

Various methods are used to encourage groups to support high-level service structures. Following the North American example, general service conferences may put down ideal norms for how the hat collection should be spent. In Switzerland, the "rule of thirds" requests that one-third of the hat collection should go to the group's own expenses, one-third to the intermediate level (contact lists, answering services, regional meetings, etc.), and one-third to the General Service Office. In Iceland, each group is expected to pay a sum corresponding to at least U.S.$ 65 a year to the General Service Office. The rule is relatively new and seldom respected in practice. The Finnish group handbook (*Ryhmäkäsikirja,* 1983) suggests a division of 60 percent of the group's surplus to the national service office and 40 percent to the area committee (where there is no local service office), but very few people are aware of the suggestion, and at any rate few area committees undertake any activity. In general, AA groups pay their contributions mostly either to the local AA ansering service (AA hotline) or to the General Service Office. Special accounts are opened for locally organized activities or events, and local groups are expected to contribute. Funds tend to be allocated flexibly to service activities or levels in financial need and, as the AA in Finland is relatively well-off, conflicts related to financial aspects tend to be resolved smoothly.

Because of the fierce autonomy of individual groups, pleas for support to the national service structure tend to have a limited effect. In 1986, an appeal to groups for greater contribution support for the General Service Office in New York sparked several rejections for, among other things, the "slickness" of the kit supporting it (Kurtz, 1991, p. 281). In Finland a different technique of encouraging support from below is used, whereby contributions and purchases of literature are reported monthly in the AA newsletter, group by group. At one time in the 1980s this practice was felt to encourage unhealthy competition and was discontinued. This resulted in an alarming decrease in income, however, and the old practice was re-established. In the German-speaking part of Switzerland, the General Service Conference has considered publishing the names of groups that have not been contributing to the national services.

In 1988, 45 percent of the 45,000 registered groups in the United States and Canada were unwilling to support AA's central services. The resulting deficit was financed by literature sales, representing a "renewed dependence on publishing incomes [that] might compromise the spirit of the Seventh Tradition" (Anonymous, 1989c).

Insufficient group revenues are by no means unique to North America. According to the Swedish AA newsletter (*Bulletinen,* 1990, no.

2, p. 26), there "are about 300 groups in Sweden of which about 100 are new [and not expected to contribute to the higher level service structure]. Of the remaining 200, 62 groups contributed to the national service board last year." In 1991, less than two out of five Polish AA groups contributed to the maintenance of the national service structure (Świątkiewicz & Zieliński, in press). The report of the German General Service Conference complains that some groups unnecessarily "hoard money in savings accounts to have reserves at their disposal for emergencies" instead of sending their contributions to the national structure (*Bericht der 11. Gemeinsamen Dienst-Konferenz*, 1991).

Most AA members identify with their home group and possibly with local service activities, and the national service structure is sometimes viewed as representing bureaucratic power. As a consequence, the central service structures have to do their utmost to gain the confidence and support of the grass roots. In Finland, a conflict among elder statesmen about the service structure led to a drop in membership contributions, and it has been argued that it was this signal that compelled the combatants to settle their disagreements (Mäkelä, in press). Membership contributions provide a means of effective grass-roots control of higher levels of organization in AA. On the other hand, insufficient contributions may lead to a temptation to increase the prices of literature to compensate for diminishing resources at the national level. "If the percentage of income from contributions continues to decline while income from literature sales increase, then the groups are giving up control and relinquishing responsibility" (Anonymous, 1986).

Income from Literature Sales

The issue of whether and how much AA's superstructure should depend on profits from literature sales has been a source of recurrent discussion. "The challenge was to make GSO's service work self-supporting through contributions of the membership and to sell literature at cost to everyone" (*The A.A. Service Manual*, 1988, p. 122). As shown in Table 8.2, countries vary markedly in how close they follow this ideal. In Iceland and Sweden, publishing activities are run separately, and no income from literature sale goes directly to the national service budget. In all other countries, the service budget is to a considerable extent based on income from literature. In Sweden as well, the service office shares personnel and office space with the publishing company, and the expenses are paid from literature sales income.

If most of the literature is bought by AA members, literature sales and membership contributions can be seen as alternative forms of self-

Table 8.2 Percentage of National-Level Operating Budget, by Source, of National AA in Study Countries, around 1990

	Finland	Iceland	Mexico	Poland	Sweden	French-speaking Switzerland	U.S. and Canada
Member contributions including donations	40	92	25	25	100	38	51
Gross profits from literature	60	–	60 ⎫	75	–	52	49
Donations from emigrants to the United States	–	–	– ⎬	N.A.*	–	–	–
Income from investments	0.4	8	15	N.A.*	N.A.*	N.A.*	0.3

Source: Annual reports on finances of AA in each country. Efforts have been made to calculate comparable figures. Because of differences in accounting systems, all figures are not exactly comparable. The income structure also fluctuates from year to year.

*N.A. = Not available.

financing. The situation is different when large quantities of literature are sold for profit to outside agencies. In the United States and Canada, the share of literature sales outside AA had increased from less than 5 percent in 1977 to about 50 percent by the end of the 1980s, with one large treatment agency accounting for two-thirds of that figure (Kurtz, 1991, p. 281).

Collaboration in publishing between countries often involves financial issues. The German-language publications committee includes Swiss and Austrian representation. The service structure in German-speaking Switzerland receives a part of the net income from publications, and Austrian groups receive discounts on the books and pamphlets they order. The French-speaking Swiss have sought a similar status with respect to AA publications in French, but all profits continue to go to the country having the French-language copyright for each publication, which may be Belgium, Canada, or France.

Most of the profit made on literature usually goes to the National Service Office, although local service offices may receive discounts that provide a profit margin for distributing the books. The division of income from literature between different levels of service bodies often becomes an issue. The discount given to the regional service office in Helsinki for its role in the distribution is a recurrent bone of contention, as service representatives from other parts of the country feel that this amounts to subsidizing the metropolitan region. The counterargument is that any local service offices will receive the same discount if they take on the task of distributing literature.

The split in the Mexican service structure in 1985 was to a large extent caused by a power struggle over the control of income from literature (Rosovsky, in press). The number of groups and members was increasing at a spectacular pace. Literature sales brought in large amounts of income, and there were disagreements about how the money was invested and spent. Central Mexicana continues to have the sole right to sell AA books and pamphlets in Mexico, but Sección Mexico ignores the copyright and sells the literature at lower prices. The two movements are presently involved in a lawsuit over the copyrights to the *Big Books* and other publications.

Sales of AA Paraphernalia

The flourishing market for AA trinkets, particularly in the United States, has caused a prolonged debate in the movement along several dimensions (Anonymous, 1989b; Anonymous, 1993). Does AA paraphernalia vulgarize the program? Is it a breach of anonymity to wear

AA symbols publicly? Should the General Service Office in New York sue enterprises making illegal use of the symbols? Wouldn't it make sense for AA to make some income from the market for recovery items?

An important reinforcement for continuous sobriety is the careful count that most AA members keep of exactly how long it has been since their most recent drink. In principle, any slip, even just a single drink, means that one's personal sobriety clock must be started again. In the United States, it is quite common for groups to award members with a plastic or metal "chip" celebrating a particular sobriety anniversary. These tokens are often highly prized by the members. The chips, with Arabic numerals for months and Roman numerals for years of sobriety, are regularly purchased by AA groups from specialized mail vendors.

In 1955, AA's main symbol, a triangle inside a circle, was registered as a trademark, and since then it has been widely used by various AA entities. By the mid-1980s, it had also begun to be used by outside organizations such as novelty manufacturers, publishers, and treatment facilities. In 1986, the World Services Board began to contact outside entities that were using the triangle and circle in an unauthorized manner, and lawsuits were filed against recalcitrant businesses. Those opposing the policy regarded it as a break with the Traditions and argued that AA's trademark lawsuits demonstrated "the uncontrollable problems that often result from property ownership. Why does AA own a trademark? Lawsuits and public controversy? That's not How It Works" (Sue W., 1991, p. 3). The lawsuits threatened the livelihood of, among others, AA members who produced AA novelties or owned "recovery stores" (Hulac, 1991). In addition, it had become a widespread custom to give out sobriety tokens and anniversary medallions for periods of sobriety from 90 days upward. The medallion business reportedly totals six to eight million U.S. dollars annually, in comparison to the four million dollars of group contributions to the national service structure (D. E., 1993). The 1993 General Service Conference passed a recommendation that the use of sobriety medallions is a matter of local autonomy and not one on which the conference should record a definite position. At the same time, it was concluded that it is not appropriate for AA World Services or the *A.A. Grapevine* to produce or license the production of sobriety medallions. After the 1993 Conference, the General Service Board decided to discontinue protecting the circle and triangle symbol as one of AA's registered trademarks. Commercially produced AA paraphernalia will thus continue to be available. In order to avoid the suggestion of association or affiliation with outside goods and services, AA decided to phase out its own official use of the circle and triangle. The debate ended in AA giving up its own symbol rather than either entering the profitable trinket market or getting involved in legal conflicts (where the other party in many cases would have been a member of AA).

Cost of AA to Individual Members

For individual members, the cost of membership in AA can range from cheap to rather costly. A newcomer with no or little income can participate in meetings for a long time without paying anything, and inner-city meetings occasionally are attended by people who come mainly for the refreshments. For a regular member going to several weekly meetings, the voluntary contributions may well add up to more than the membership fee of most voluntary organizations, and in addition to this there may be expenditures on literature and travel costs to AA conferences. Compared to the role AA plays in members' lives, however, membership is inexpensive indeed. Going to an AA meeting is radically less expensive than any form of professional group therapy, and quite cheap compared to alternative leisure activities such as spectator sports or going to the movies, not to mention drinking.

Money and Power in AA

As everywhere, disputes about money are an important cause of conflict in AA. At business meetings of AA groups, passionate disagreements arise about the use of surplus collection money, and a good deal of time at national service conferences is spent on discussing prices of literature, the division of profits from literature sales, and the overall way the national service board has spent its income.

AA groups and service offices continue to receive occasional outside support. With the exception of Poland, however, outside support is wholly marginal, and a high degree of self-support has been achieved. The principle of self-support is a living reality, and any borderline cases are the subject of intense internal debate. An obvious example is the

American decision not to protect the circle and triangle symbol as a trademark, despite the service structure's strained finances and the fact that presenting sobriety medallions is a regular program activity in a large number of AA groups.

The refusal of outside contributions supports the independent position of AA, but it also prevents individual members from achieving a powerful position in the group or in the movement through their economic contacts. The limits set for individual contributions and bequests have a similar effect. The fact that AA's traditions do not allow it to own any buildings or other property also obviates a major reason for a formal and hierarchic organization.

As sources of power and influence, contributions from members and income from literature sales play radically different roles. Publishing sales are managed nationally, and profits are a centralized resource. The inflow of contributions is a very sensitive indicator of the morale and commitment of the membership and of how happy individual groups are with the management of national affairs. Consequently, membership contributions function as a means of continuous control from below. The increased dependence on sales of literature to the outside, particularly to 12-step treatment institutions, therefore, constitutes the most pressing challenge to AA's principle of self-support.

9
The Membership of AA

Who Is a Member of AA?

Alcoholics Anonymous has no membership records in the usual sense of the word. Membership statistics presented by AA are based on estimates sent by groups to local and national service offices, and the criteria used in the estimates may vary considerably. General population surveys from the United States indicate that the number of people having visited an AA meeting for an alcohol problem of their own during the last twelve months greatly exceeds the membership figure as reported by the General Service Office in New York (Room & Greenfield, 1993).

Membership in AA is based on self-identification, and meeting attendance does not necessarily entail self-defined membership. On the other hand, self-defined membership does not always imply regular meeting attendance. Many people with more than five or ten years of sobriety may attend meetings only once a year or even less frequently, but continue to see themselves as AA members.

"For about ten years I have gone to AA meetings when I have wanted to cut down on my drinking, but I never intended to become a regular member."

Swedish field interview (M, 44, 0)

"Some people come to AA just for a holiday from drinking, and then they leave."

Mexican field interview (M, 55, 8)

AA life stories collected for this study (Appendix B) clearly indicate how affiliation with AA often is the end result of a complex and prolonged process, which may include scattered visits to AA meetings at treatment institutions and elsewhere many years before regular membership.

Early attrition is quite considerable and relapses are not exceptional among more experienced members. Many go back and forth between drinking and AA several times. At a Finnish meeting, one speaker described himself as holding the AA world record with his five one-year sobriety anniversaries.

For Whom Is AA?

AA's answer to this question is simple: The only requirement for membership is the desire to stop drinking (Tradition Three). In actual practice, only a fraction of those making an initial contact with AA stay in the movement. From AA's own survey of membership in the United States and Canada, it has been calculated that about half of those coming to AA for the first time drop out in the first three months (*Comments . . .*, no date). Numerous attempts have been made to find out the characteristics that increase the likelihood of affiliation (Bradley, 1988; Glaser & Ogborne, 1982; Emrick, 1987, 1989; Emrick et al., 1993; Ogborne & Glaser, 1981), but most studies lack adequate research design. It is worth emphasizing that four-fifths of the studies included in a recent comprehensive meta-analysis (Emrick et al., 1993) were based on inpatient or outpatient treatment samples, and most of them were retrospective. Because of selection bias, retrospective studies of clinical populations are particularly ill-suited for an analysis of factors affecting the likelihood of affiliation with AA. Clinical populations consist of people with current drinking problems, and patients who have had previous contacts with AA are a selection of members who have failed.

Of the randomized studies of affiliation with AA reported to date, the first two suffer from the limitation that subjects were mainly or wholly selected from populations of court offenders who were coerced into treatment (Brandsma et al., 1977, 1980; Ditman et al., 1967). The other two randomized prospective studies (Keso, 1988; Walsh et al., 1991) use subjects recruited from employee assistance programs. None of the studies analyze differences in the affiliation rate by demographic groups.

In addition to inadequate research design, more basic issues contribute to the difficulty of identifying variables predicting affiliation with AA. Membership composition is a complex outcome of the recruitment process and personal identification, with the composition of the membership varying widely from one community and country to another. It is no wonder, then, that empirical studies often report conflicting results with respect to factors associated with AA membership (Emrick, 1987, 1989; Emrick et al., 1993; Ogborne & Glaser, 1981). Unfortunately, most studies do not discuss their reported correlations as historically contingent. In our view, the best way out of this confusion is to complement statistical meta-analysis with an analysis of the concrete cultural and social context of each statistical relationship. In order to understand the processes by which membership composition comes to vary widely from one community or country to the next, it is crucial to analyze alternative pathways to AA in terms of their relationships with existing social networks and institutions outside of AA.

Pathways to AA

Becoming an AA member is often the outcome of a complex process, which may involve varying combinations of social pressure, professional advice, and personal discomfort or despair. Members also have often had a series of preliminary contacts before actually joining the movement. Classifying individuals in terms of how they came to AA is, therefore, a complicated issue. From an international perspective, the crucial dimensions distinguishing between pathways to AA are the amount of personal initiative required from the newcomer, the role of direct links between AA members and prospective newcomers, and the role of professional treatment providers.

First, a newcomer may call an AA answering service or go to a meeting on his or her own initiative. If contact is made by telephone, prospective newcomers may be given the telephone numbers of AA members they may call about attending their first meeting.

Second, members of AA personally bring newcomers to their first meeting. The escorting member may be known in advance to the prospective newcomer (e.g., a former drinking companion), or may be previously unknown.

Third, institutional treatment may provide the setting for contact with AA, either allowing meetings to be organized on the premises or actively requiring visits to AA meetings as part of the treatment program.

Professional advice or institutional treatment can be combined with personal contacts with AA members. Professionals referring patients to AA may suggest members whom potential newcomers can call and talk to before going to a meeting, and treatment center counselors may occasionally arrange an AA contact person close to the patient's home prior to the release from treatment. In many countries, the role of personal links in the recruitment process seems to be diminishing.

An additional pathway to AA, used only in the United States, is the court system. As one facet of the increasing role of coercion in alcohol treatment (Fillmore & Kelso, 1987), courts in many American jurisdictions routinely refer persons charged with alcohol-related crimes to mandatory attendance at AA meetings (Speiglman, 1994).

In the United States, institutional 12-step treatment has had an important impact on membership recruitment (see chapter 4). As shown in Table 9.1, the percentage of AA members who check an existing AA member as a factor most responsible for their coming to AA decreased from 55 in 1968 to 34 in 1989. In contrast, the percentage checking a counseling agency and/or a treatment facility increased from 19 in 1977 to 40 in 1989.

There is a wide variation between study countries in the role of professional treatment as a recruitment channel to AA (Table 9.2). In Mexico and in the German-speaking part of Switzerland, only a few members have made their first contact with AA as part of a treatment program. The role of professional treatment is more important in Poland, and in Sweden and Iceland the percentage of members coming to AA through institutional treatment is even higher than in the United States.

Existential Identity and Identification

AA's own answer to the question, "Why doesn't A.A. seem to work for some people?" runs as follows: "A.A. will work only for those who admit that they are alcoholics, who honestly want to stop drinking" (*44 Questions*, 1990, p. 31). In all its circularity, the formulation accentuates the importance of existential self-definition as an alcoholic for those who would continue to be members.

Members of AA are encouraged to admit that they are powerless over alcohol and unable to control their drinking. The admission of powerlessness is often accompanied by a subjective experience of "hitting bottom." This experience may be the end result of repeated failures to control one's drinking but it may also come as a sudden revelation precipitated by a dramatic incident.

Identification with regular members is an important aspect of the affiliation process, and it is easier to identify with "people like me" (Vourakis, 1989). The role of identification is shown in a follow-up study of patients treated at substance abuse agencies in Michigan (Hum-

Table 9.1   The Role of Existing Members and Professional Treatment among Factors Most Responsible for U.S. and Canadian AA Members Coming to Their First Meeting, by Percentage

	1968	1971	1974	1977	1980	1983	1986	1989
AA members	55	52	52	44	41	38	36	34
Counseling agency and/or treatment facility	N.A.*	N.A.*	N.A.*	19	26	31	36	40

Source: AA's own unpublished membership surveys conducted by the General Service Office in New York

Question wording in surveys 1977–1989 (15 response options):
   Check no more than *two* of the following that you feel were most responsible for your coming to your first A.A. meeting:

Newspaper or magazine	Family
Radio or television	Doctor
A.A. literature	Member of clergy
A.A. member	Counseling agency
Al-Anon or Alateen member	Treatment facility
Non-A.A. friend or neighbor	Correction facility
Employer or fellow worker	Other (please specify)
On my own	

Question wording in surveys collected in 1968, 1971 and 1974 (12 response options):
   Which *two* of the following do you feel were most responsible for your coming to your first A.A. meeting? (*please check two*)

Newspaper	Doctor
Magazine	Clergyman
Radio	Employer
Television	A.A. member
A.A. Literature	Counselling agency
Family	Other, please specify

Despite differences in response alternatives, the percentage checking "AA member" can be used for comparisons across the entire period covered by the surveys. No comparisons concerning the role played by treatment agencies can be made between the early and the more recent surveys.
*N.A. = Not available

phreys & Woods, 1993). Whites in predominantly white areas and blacks in predominantly black areas were more likely to attend a 12-step group one year after treatment than individuals who were minorities within their community.

According to AA ideals, an attempt should be made to ensure that potential newcomers will attend an AA meeting where they share some common background with the regular members, thereby increasing the chance of identification. When newcomers are present, AA ideals require that the focus of the meeting turns to the newcomers, and in smaller meetings this often happens in reality. The chair suggests as a

Table 9.2   The Role of Existing Members and Professional Treatment among Factors Contributing to AA Members in Study Countries Coming to Their First Meeting, by Percentage

	Iceland	Mexico	Poland	Sweden	German-speaking Switzerland
Part of treatment program	77	5	33	50	12
Other AA members	25	55	42	19	24

Source: ICSAA membership surveys (Appendix B)
Question wording:
   How did it happen that you ended up at your first AA meeting? (*check all that apply*)
    ( )   It was my own idea
    ( )   Pressure from my spouse
    ( )   As part of an institutional treatment program
    ( )   Suggestion from an AA member
    ( )   Through the courts
    ( )   Through a friend
    ( )   Nowhere else to go; last resort
    ( )   Other, please specify

topic Step One, with each person telling how they came to AA and what has happened as a result of their attending AA. This provides a range of personal stories and increases the chance of newcomers finding persons with whom they can identify.

> The reception of newcomers is one of the most important tasks of a group. The Swiss life-story interviews provide vivid descriptions of how crucial the first reception was for the decision to stay in AA. In French a special term has been coined to designate the group where a newcomer is first welcomed and introduced to AA: "le groupe d'accueil." In Mexico AA members use the formulation "I was born in that group."

The cell structure of AA facilitates the task of reaching different population groups. In large communities there is a great variety of groups for the newcomer to choose from, enabling him or her to join a group that corresponds to his or her social background, ideology, and personality. Newcomers are commonly given the advice to visit as many different groups as possible in order to find one that best suits their temperament. Contrasts between meetings are also used to help newcomers identify with the movement. A Finnish businessman recalls how he was taken aback when his mentor first brought him to a meeting attended by homeless alcoholics: "This bunch most certainly is nothing for me." The emotional shock, however, made it easier for him to identify with other participants when he was taken to a middle-class meeting later in the same day.

Demographic Composition of the Membership

Gender

The most striking differences between countries in the composition of the membership of AA relate to gender. The proportion of women among members of AA varies from 10 percent in Mexico to 40 percent in the German-speaking part of Switzerland and 44 percent in Austria (Table 9.3.). The proportion is likely to be even higher in the French-speaking part of Switzerland, although exact figures are not available.

The large differences across countries in the proportion of female membership cannot be explained by the social position of women nor the amount of female drinking in the society. Rather, they should be related to historical contingencies and internal differences in the national movements. Both in Austria and in Switzerland, key roles in launching the AA movement were played by women (Eisenbach-Stangl, 1992a; Mariolini et al., 1993; Rehm et al., 1992).

In North America and the United Kingdom, the share of women among the membership has grown considerably. In the United States and Canada, the percentage of women increased from 22 percent in 1968 to 35 percent in 1989 (according to unpublished membership surveys carried out by the General Service Office in New York). In the United Kingdom, the share of women increased from 22 percent in 1972 to 35 percent in 1986 (A. R. Smith, 1993).

Gender relations in AA will be discussed in more detail in chapter 13.

Age

Clinical studies consistently report that the proportion of those having attending AA meetings is higher among older than among younger patients (Emrick et al., 1993). Because of the retrospective nature of the studies, the value of these findings is limited. On the average, older patients have had longer drinking careers, and the duration of drinking tends to correlate positively with any drinking-related experiences. Insofar as AA is particularly attractive as the last resort for

Table 9.3 Membership Composition of AA in Study Countries, by Percentage

	Austria	Finland	Iceland	Mexico	Poland	Sweden	German-speaking Switzerland	U.S. and Canada
Women	44	24	29	10	19	30	40	35
Men and women under 30 years old	9	7	30	32	16	9	8	22
Substantial involvement of working class	–	+	+	+	–	–	+	+

Source: The U.S. figures come from AA's own unpublished membership survey conducted by the General Service Office in New York. The remaining figures are based on data from ICSAA group surveys (Appendix B).

103

persons with extreme drinking patterns, it is likely that, even in a prospective analysis, older candidates would have a greater likelihood to affiliate with AA.

There is enough variation in the age of the membership to indicate, however, that under certain circumstances AA can attract substantial numbers of young members. The proportion of members under thirty years of age is under 10 percent in Austria, Finland, Sweden, and the German-speaking part of Switzerland, but it is around 30 percent in Iceland and Mexico, with Poland and the United States falling in between (Table 9.3). These figures indicate that there is no simple relationship between the age of the membership and the age structure of the general population, the maturity of the movement, or the nature of the surrounding culture.

Contrary to a widespread belief among the membership, Robinson (1979, p. 27) found no downward trend between 1963 and 1976 in age on AA admittance in Britain. In North America, however, the percentage of members who were thirty years old or younger increased from 7 percent in 1968 to 22 percent in 1989 (unpublished membership surveys carried out by the General Service Office in New York).

Social Class

In the literature, AA is described as a predominantly middle-class movement (Bean, 1975; Madsen, 1980, p. 166; Trice & Roman, 1970b), but the evidence is inconclusive. Trice and Roman (1970b) stress the importance of the dramatics of downward and upward mobility as presented in AA stories: "[B]y the emphasis on downward mobility due to drinking, the social mobility 'distance' traveled by the A.A. members is maximized in the stories. This clearly sets the stage for impressive 'comeback accomplishments' " (Trice & Roman, 1970b, p. 543) Despite their emphasis on social mobility, Trice and Roman found that the middle-class experience was not related to affiliation with AA. A recent meta-analysis (Emrick et al., 1993) also found no consistent correlation between AA affiliation and socioeconomic status. Here again, retrospective studies of clinical populations are of limited value. Unfortunately, few studies report comparisons between samples of AA members and members of other mutual-aid groups for drinking problems or independent clinical samples.

Kiviranta (1969) presents information from the early 1960s on the occupational structure of the membership of AA in Finland compared to the clientele of outpatient alcohol clinics and municipal or state-owned asylums for alcoholics. Of the three groups, asylum inmates quite clearly were recruited from the lowest social strata. In comparison to clinic patients, there were more lower white-collar and unskilled workers but fewer skilled workers among AA members. There were no differences in the percentage of upper white-collar workers.

In London in 1964, the two highest social strata of the general U.K. population were overrepresented in the membership of AA, and the two lowest underrepresented. Compared to hospital populations of patients treated for alcohol diseases, however, AA was found to draw its membership predominantly from social class III, with underrepresentation of both the two lowest and the two highest strata (Edwards et al., 1966).

In France, data from the 1970s and 1980s indicate that white-collar occupations and professionals are noticeably overrepresented among the membership of AA compared to the membership of another mutual-aid movement for problem drinkers, Vie Libre (Cerclé, 1985). It is worth noting, however, that Vie Libre is an explicitly left-wing organization with close connections to militant unions. In Sweden, a membership survey of alcohol-related mutual-aid movements (Kühlhorn, Helmersson, & Kurube, 1991) showed that Links members more often belong to lower social strata, while AA members tend to belong to higher social strata.

In Japan, married couples form the basic unit of Danshukai groups; professionals tend to refer married and better-off patients to Danshukai, and single and poor alcoholics to AA. Danshukai thus recruits mainly married male alcoholics, whereas AA newcomers are more often unmarried young people, women or divorced men (Oka, 1994).

In North America, Women for Sobriety seems to attract women in very high social positions. Since their occupational status is on average higher than that of AA members as a whole (Kaskutas, 1992a), the contrast would probably be even more marked if we could compare WFS members with AA women. Rational Recovery groups also recruit more members with higher educations than does AA (Galanter, Egelko, & Edwards, 1993).

In the study countries, the class composition of the membership of AA shows considerable variation (Table 9.3). In Austria and to a lesser degree in Sweden, AA members are mostly recruited from the higher echelons of society, whereas Finland, Iceland, and Switzerland report substantial working-class involvement. In Mexico as well, urban workers and rural poor are strongly represented in AA.

Historical contingencies may have a longlasting influence on the class composition of the membership. In Finland, the first autonomous AA groups grew out of the so-called Home Clubs for alcoholics working under the auspices of the social democratic temperance movement (Mäkelä, in press). The first Home Club was led by a social worker who recruited its members mainly from her working-class clientele. As a consequence, the first AA members in Finland frequently had a working-class background, in contrast to the situation in the United States.

The class background of AA members may be related to their channel of recruitment. People coming from institutional 12-step treatment centers are most likely to belong to the upper social strata, partly because of better insurance coverage. In Iceland and Sweden, the early old-timers were often blue-collar workers, whereas the middle class is overrepresented among the newer members coming from 12-step treatment centers (Ólafsdóttir, in press; Helmersson Bergmark, in press).

Drinking and Drug Experiences

Table 9.4 presents data on selected drinking problems experienced by AA members in our study countries. Any cross-cultural differences shown in the table may reflect as much general cultural differences as differences in the severity of members' drinking careers. To take one example, having been stopped for drunk driving is more common in the German-speaking part of Switzerland than having been arrested because of drunkenness, whereas the opposite is true in all other countries. This very likely reflects important differences in both drunken comportment and in systems of social control, but provides little ground to compare the severity of AA members' drinking careers in each country. Taken as a whole, however, Table 9.4 gives a picture of how extreme the members' drinking experiences have been. The table shows a great deal of despair and deviance among prospective AA members. Quite a few have attempted suicide, and prison experiences are not rare. At the same time, the table indicates that many members have by no means been social outcasts before entering AA. In all countries except Poland, only a minority report that they ever have lost a job because of their drinking.

A German study (Murken, 1994, pp. 76–77) shows that AA members with more extreme drinking experiences are more actively involved in the movement than less deviant drinkers. The severity of the members' drinking careers may have an impact on the dynamics of AA as a social movement.

It is generally thought that the number of newcomers with less extreme drinking careers has been on the rise in the United States, but corresponding cross-cultural speculations are not available. The experi-

Table 9.4 Types of Drinking Problems of Members in Iceland, Poland, Sweden, and German-speaking Switzerland, by Percentage

	Iceland	Poland	Sweden	German-speaking Switzerland
Hearing voices	60	53	N.A.*	22
Seeing things	54	56	N.A.*	25
Attempting suicide	45	54	33	47
Job loss	38	62	26	41
Being arrested	74	66	43	21
Drunk driving	68	23	30	43
Prison	39	21	20	18

Source: ICSAA membership surveys (Appendix B)

Question wordings:

When did you most recently experience the following physical problems related to drinking?

	Never	More than 12 months ago	In past 12 months
a. Not being able to go to work or do your work	1	2	3
b. Have had a health problem caused by your drinking	1	2	3
c. Have had a blackout after drinking	1	2	3
d. Have heard voices	1	2	3
e. Have seen things	1	2	3

When did you most recently experience the following problems?

	Never	More than 12 months ago	In past 12 months
a. Tried to commit suicide	1	2	3
b. Felt deep shame			
c. Felt extremely depressed			
d. Lost a job			
e. Been arrested by the police because of drunkenness			
f. Been in fights			
g. Severe financial problems			
h. Broken marriage			
i. Had no regular place to live			
j. Stopped for drunk driving			
k. Been to prison because of crimes committed when drinking	1	2	3

*N.A. = Not available

ences of most of the early members had been extreme and dramatic, and they often had become social outcasts because of drinking. From early on, however, room was made for members with less extreme drinking careers who had nevertheless come to think that the only way they could manage their lives was to stop drinking. A distinction was made between people with high and low "bottoms." The "main purpose" of the first revision of *Alcoholics Anonymous* (*Big Book*, 1955) was "to bring the story section up-to-date, to portray more adequately a cross section of those who found help. In general, one important purpose [was] to show that low-bottom drunks are not the only ones who can be helped" (Kurtz, 1991, p. 132).

From early on, members of AA have been telling each other that the background of newcomers has been changing. There are a number of psychological factors that support a tendency to exaggerate any ongoing changes. For a newcomer, the most dramatic recoveries have the highest visibility. Later on, the drinking experiences of more recent newcomers may look less impressive.

Comparing British AA members' alcohol-related problems in 1964 and 1976, Robinson (1979, pp. 28–29) found little support for the belief that those who had joined in the interim were joining the fellowship with fewer problems. He concluded that AA in Britain at the time still was, for most people, a last hope organization. The advent of institutional 12-step treatment may, however, have changed the situation. Twelve-step treatment centers tend to recruit employed people in relatively strong social positions. On the other hand, it seems that only a fraction of those treated in 12-step institutions actually join the movement. According to the 12-month follow-up interview in a Finnish controlled study of a 12-step treatment center, only 15 percent of the patients had attended an AA meeting during the two preceding months (Keso, 1988). In an American follow-up of patients treated at a variety of institutions, 18 percent had attended AA in the month preceding the four-year follow-up (Polich, Armor, & Braiker, 1981, Table 6.14).

In North America, it is also possible that the diffusion of 12-step thinking into the general culture has increased the number of people entering the fellowship early on in their drinking career.

It is very likely that multiple drug use is more common among AA members in the United States and Canada than elsewhere; in 1989, 42 percent of the membership reported that they were addicted to other drugs besides alcohol (Comments . . . , no date). In Mexico, the corresponding figure was only 14 percent, and 98 percent of these had been using marijuana only (*Encuesta* . . . , 1990).

Newcomers and Old-Timers

The rate of growth and maturity of the movement in each country (cf. chapter 7) is reflected in the length of sobriety attained by members of AA (Table 9.5). According to the group survey, the percentage of members with less than one year of sobriety varied from 24 percent in the German-speaking part of Switzerland to 69 percent in Poland. At the other end of the scale, more than one-tenth of the membership had at least ten years of sobriety in Finland, the German-speaking part of Switzerland, and the United States, whereas there were fewer experienced members in Austria, Iceland, Mexico, Poland, and Sweden. These differences have important implications, since early pioneers join a different movement, compared to later newcomers who are surrounded by experienced old-timers.

AA is based on equality, and experience is the only source of influence and power accepted by AA ideology. The fact that more experienced members have more influence is not only tolerated but welcomed: "They become the real and permanent leadership of A.A. . . . They do not drive by mandate; they lead by example" (12 + 12, 1986, p. 135).

Many longtime members restrict their activities to meeting attendance and may enjoy considerable prestige without ever participating in general service activities. The minority of members embarking on what could be called AA careers are, however, of great importance for AA as a social organization. As a matter of convenience, we can distinguish four major career paths followed by long term AA members: local service work, higher-level service work, becoming an AA speaker, and becoming an alcoholism professional. The careers are not mutually exclusive, but members tend to focus on one of the four roles.

"Many women were annoyed by the fact that there were no female speakers at the fortieth anniversary of AA in Finland. Two had been asked but had refused. Having heard this I volunteered, but they said I had not had enough sobriety time."
Finnish field interview (F, 48, 12)

"People who have a relapse after a long sobriety often have continuous problems. Although we are expected to learn to be humble, it seems difficult to come back as a newcomer after having enjoyed the prestige of an old-timer."
Finnish field interview (M, 45, 10)

Table 9.5 Percentage of AA Members in Study Countries with Short and Long Time Spans of Sobriety

	Austria	Finland	Iceland	Mexico	Poland	Sweden	German-speaking Switzerland	U.S. and Canada
With less than one year of sobriety	34	16	33	32	69	52	24	35
With more than 10 years of sobriety	6	26	4	8	1	1	11	12

Source: U.S. figures come from AA's own unpublished membership survey (General Service Office, New York). The remaining figures are based on data from ICSAA group surveys (Appendix B).

Some members become unusually active in the home group and local community. Typically, they work actively with newcomers, chair open meetings, and serve on AA intergroup committees. They also serve as a link between AA and local institutions and agencies working in the field of alcoholism, work with local alcohol treatment centers, and take part in committees and boards sponsoring alcohol action and education programs.

Careers in the High-Level Service Structure

An alternative to the local service career is to become active in the high-level service structure, particularly in Mexico and the United States, which have several layers of organization. In Mexico, this path seems particularly to attract working-class members of AA. In Mexico, AA can be seen as one among the many recent grassroots organizations that provide new channels of influence for underprivileged groups (Rosovsky, in press).

"My fifth year of sobriety marked a turning point. I felt no satisfaction from attending meetings. So I assumed responsibility for service tasks on the regional and national level, and that opened up a new world of important experiences. Five years often is a turning point: meeting attendance thins out and the risk of drinking again grows."

Finnish field interview (M, 39, 13)

The Speaker Circuit

In the United States, there is a recognized cadre of AA speakers who travel to major meetings with their expenses covered by the sponsoring organization. Some are internationally known through the distribution of tapes. The American cadre of conference speakers is a product of large open conferences that do not exist in all countries. In Finland and in Switzerland, for example, there is an informal pattern of traveling AA speakers who may be visitors from one group or meeting invited to speak at another meeting. The visiting speakers are often accompanied by friends, and the speakers are not so clearly differentiated as conference or platform speakers. In the French-speaking part of Switzerland, AA speakers are also recorded on videotapes to be shown as part of the program in treatment centers.

Alcohol Professionals

Working in alcohol treatment programs is another full-time career alternative, particularly in the United States where 12-step treatment is a dominant part of the professional system. For some, an alternative career may be necessary as a result of their having lost credibility in their previous occupation. Some alcohol counselors continue to attend local groups, but many become less active in working with alcoholics outside the institutions that employ them.

Membership Turnover

Little is known about how long members stay in AA, although membership turnover is a core feature of the dynamics of any mutual-help group. Mutual-help movements vary widely with respect to membership stability, and turnover rates also differ according to the phase of development of each movement.

One early study (Bill C., 1965) presents a probability curve for continued sobriety as a function of the duration of sobriety. Although the curve has been reproduced in the literature (Leach & Norris, 1977), closer inspection shows that it is pure guesswork with no real data base. AA's triennial surveys of membership in the United States and Canada present data on length of sobriety, and an attempt has been made to estimate membership attrition using cross-sectional data collected in 1977, 1980, 1983, 1986 and 1989 (Comments . . . , no date). The figures obtained are based on uncertain assumptions and relatively crude approximations, and the calculations are not reported in detail. The main conclusions of this survey are the following:

- About half of those coming to AA for the first time drop out in less than three months.
- About 40 percent of the members with less than one year of sobriety will remain sober and active in the fellowship for another year.
- About 80 percent of the members with between one and five years of sobriety will remain sober and active in the fellowship for another year.
- About 90 percent of the members with more than five years of sobriety will remain sober and active in the fellowship for another year.

More trustworthy calculations of rates of attrition require information on the same individuals at several points in time, but such data are usually not available. The anniversary announcements in the newsletter of the Finnish AA, therefore, provide a unique opportunity for analyzing the turnover of the membership of AA (Mäkelä, 1994). Of the total membership, having at least one year of sobriety, close to 90 percent continue as sober members for another year. Of those having reached their first year of sobriety, about two-thirds maintain sobriety into the next year. The survival rate of members with between two and five years of sobriety is about 85 percent. Among members with more than five years of sobriety, the survival rate is more than 90 percent. There are no gender differences in survival rates, at least not after the first year of sobriety.

Assuming an even inflow and no attrition, the number of members with 7 to 12 months of sobriety should equal the number of members with 0 to 6 months of sobriety, but the figures obtained in membership surveys are consistently much lower, indicating considerable early dropout. Unfortunately, the figures are usually not reported separately for men and women. One early exception is a study of the membership of AA in London in 1964 (Edwards et al., 1966) where attrition rates by sex can be calculated from the data presented on the duration of membership. The rate of attrition between the first and the second half year of membership is higher among men (.73) than among women (.56), but the small number of cases makes any conclusions tentative.

The survival rates of the membership of AA in Finland are quite high and of the same order of magnitude as those calculated on the basis of membership surveys in the United States and Canada (Comments . . . , no date). The Finnish data shed no light on the attrition occurring before the first full year of sobriety. Those who reach one year of continuous abstinence are a highly selected group compared to the clinical populations for which success rates usually are presented. If we look at the turnover from a mutual-help movement perspective, however, we can conclude that the sober membership of AA is exceptionally stable. It may be instructive to calculate the time by which half of the membership of a base year have left the fellowship. The 10 percent dropout rate among more experienced members means that after five years 53 percent of them are still in the fellowship.

Although the risk of dropping out is quite low among members with at least a few years of sobriety, it is large enough to be considered a threat and provide support to the conviction that meeting attendance should continue for a lifetime. The threat is strengthened by the fact that relapses of AA old-timers provide dramatic material for gossip.

Continued membership does not always mean frequent meeting attendance. Many among the older members go to meetings infrequently. On the other side, dropping out of AA does not necessarily mean a relapse in drinking. Natural death takes its toll among the older cohorts, and former members may continue to be sober, either on their own or by joining some functional alternative to AA. In the more religious parts of the United States, AA membership may be replaced by church activities, especially in churches that advocate abstinence. In Finland and Iceland as well, an initial period in AA may be followed by religious conversion and membership in an evangelical congregation. In the United States, ethnic or racial minorities sometimes find that AA does not provide a supportive social network for their long-term sobriety. Thus, in the southeastern states, black members may return to black churches after achieving sobriety in AA. Another alternative, especially in the United States, is transference from AA to other 12-step programs. Ties to other 12-step programs may be temporary, while the main identification remains with AA, or the person may switch his/her identification to the alternative program.

Conclusion

Affiliation with AA is often a prolonged and complex process. Early attrition is considerable, but dropout rates among more experienced members are quite low. Hence, the membership of AA consists of a relatively stable core and a large number of transient members.

Differences between countries in membership composition do not necessarily reflect cross-cultural differences in the demographic characteristics of problem drinkers. In the main, they seem to reflect internal developments in each of the national movements. Identification with older members is an important aspect of the affiliation process. If the first members of AA in a country or a community represent the working class, local groups will initially attract people having the same background. If the founders are college graduates, middle-class people will be most likely to join the movement. More recently, professional and institutional 12-step programs have begun to have an important impact on the recruitment process and the composition of the membership.

Part Four
AA as a Belief System and a
Program for Action

10
The AA Program as a Set of Beliefs and as a Program for Action

This chapter presents a general analysis of the nature of the AA program and a description of AA's view on alcoholism, spirituality, and human beings as psychological and moral entities. In chapter 12, we discuss in more detail the diversity of individual interpretations and program practices.

Origins of the AA Program

The AA movement started in the 1930s in the United States. The founders described themselves as "average Americans" (*Big Book*, 1955, p. 17), but most were Protestant, white, and middle-class. Their beliefs about religion, psychology, gender roles, and politics were a product of their environment. Pittman's (1988a) chronicle provides vivid illustrations of how early members absorbed ideas from religious, philosophical, medical, and psychological writings about the nature of alcoholism and man's relationship to the social environment and the cosmic order. A more systematic and rigorous account is presented by Kurtz (1991). Particularly important were influences from the evangelical Protestant tradition (Kurtz, 1991; McCarthy, 1984; Peterson, 1992). Another key influence was from philosophical pragmatism, because of its impact on American everyday thinking, especially as it was developed by William James (Kurtz, 1991; Rehm, 1993). Temperance ideology provided a negative point of reference (Room, 1989). With the aim of distancing themselves from temperance rhetorics, early AA members made a point of stressing that alcohol as such is not bad, that there are simply individuals who cannot drink moderately.

First among the key tenets of AA is the notion that the member has to *admit his/her powerlessness* before recovery is possible. This is expressed in the First Step: "We admitted we were powerless over alcohol, that our lives had become unmanageable." According to AA, before one can admit one's powerlessness one must "hit bottom": that is, one must find oneself in a totally hopeless situation.

The second crucial element is *belief*. Only by believing in a power greater than oneself (Step Two) and by having faith that this higher power will guide one's future actions (Steps Three, Six, and Seven) can one establish true recovery.

Taken together, admitting one's powerlessness and the commitment to belief may be seen in terms of a *conversion*. Conversion refers to a spiritual experience in which an old system of beliefs and thoughts is turned over and replaced by a new system (James, 1903b). This process is often called "spiritual awakening" by AA members (*Big Book*, 1955, p. 569). Conversion may happen suddenly or gradually.

Finally, the notion of *action* is crucial. For AA it makes no sense to elaborate on possible reasons for alcoholism. What is necessary is that the alcoholic must act. He or she must act by not touching the first glass, by following the Steps, and by spreading the AA message to alcoholics who still drink. This postulate of action is directly taken from philosophical pragmatism (Rehm, 1993). The central tenet of pragmatism is that ideas should be valued by their practical consequences and by their bearing on human interests.

The Twelve Steps

The Twelve Steps present the core formulation of the AA program (Appendix D). The wording of the Steps has not changed since they were first published, but there have been changes in their interpretation. There is not one but two equally authoritative texts describing the Steps. The original commentary was published in the *Big Book* in 1939 (1955, pp. 59–103), and the second in *Twelve Steps and Twelve Traditions* in 1953 (1986, pp. 21–125). Both texts mention specific behaviors and attitudes in connection to each Step, but there is a systematic shift in the later description away from traditional Christian language. In addition to these official interpretations, individual groups in North America from early on produced pamphlets on the AA program, and some have been translated into other languages. More recently, the publication industry connected to professional 12-step treatment has put out detailed instructions on how to work the Steps.

In themselves, the Twelve Steps are literally a program. They do not formulate a code of conduct to be interpreted but a series of tasks and problems to be solved. The Steps are often divided into three groups. The first three Steps—which call for admitting alcoholism, and putting oneself in the hands of God or a higher power—are called the decision Steps. Steps Four to Nine, which aim at changing one's relation to one's life, are called the action Steps. In these, the member makes a moral inventory and talks it over privately with someone, seeks assistance from a higher power in removing defects of character, and makes amends for harm done to others. The action Steps say nothing about drinking. In AA perspective, "liquor was but a symptom" (*Big Book*, 1955, p. 64). Steps Ten to Twelve are called the continuing or maintenance Steps. Step Ten requires self-examination and self-correction. Step Eleven consists of prayer and meditation. Step Twelve is about carrying the message to other alcoholics. In AA's conception, the primary reason for helping other alcoholics is to maintain one's own sobriety.

The Transmission of Beliefs and Methods of Work: The Place of Oral and Written Traditions in AA

AA is based on a special mix of written and oral tradition. It differs from many other mutual-help movements in having highly revered basic texts that provide a common frame to individual groups and members. In their comparison of AA and the Washingtonian movement of the 1840s in the United States, Blumberg and Pittman (1991, p. 207) point out that the *Big Book* facilitated at least a modest degree of uniformity between AA groups, whereas the lack of a central piece of literature made the Washingtonian societies more vulnerable to the conflicts and competition that led to their rapid decline.

At the same time, oral tradition plays a more significant role than in most modern organizations (Gellman, 1964, p. 60). The role of the oral tradition is closely connected to AA's emphasis on individual experience. The basic texts, especially the Twelve Steps and the Twelve Traditions, can be described as products of individual and group experience.

The Twelve Steps were written by Bill W. in a burst of inspiration, but they were circulated in draft and revised in light of the experience of other early members. The *Big Book* (1955) presents them as a summary *description* of what the early members *did* ("here are the steps we took") and as a "suggested Program of Recovery" (p. 59). It is also significant that most of the pages of the *Big Book* are devoted to individual stories of recovery. From its early beginnings, AA was based on learning by example.

In the same way, the Twelve Traditions grew out of a "vast welter of explosive experience" (*12 + 12*, 1986, p. 18). In corresponding with groups, Bill W. did not want to formulate prescriptions but to pass on the most successful methods groups had used to deal with organizational problems. Just as the emerging individual experiences of the early recovering alcoholics moved to written form in the *Big Book,* so the emerging experience of AA groups was codified in the Twelve Traditions.

The *Big Book* was written in the language of the time. However, in less than fifteen years and by the publication date of the second edition, the great success of the *Big Book* had rendered the original text too sacred for even the author to change (Kurtz, 1991, p. 132). Today, the opening chapters of the *Big Book* and the *Twelve Steps and Twelve Traditions* are seen as unchangeable by the majority of members, although many are critical of some of the language, which they find sexist and rigidly Christian. Rather than changing the basic texts, AA has chosen to add new stories to the North American *Big Book,* and national translations use local stories. It has also produced an increasing volume of pamphlets, which are periodically updated. These are oriented to different groups such as women, minorities, and professionals. They also address various problems or topics, such as AA's relation to other drugs, multi-drug users, and special aspects of the program. In general, these pamphlets deal with subjects that have come up and are seen as needing clarification. Finally, there are periodicals such as *A.A. Grapevine* for North America and its counterparts in other countries.

Despite the importance of the basic texts, the program and the methods of work are mainly transmitted orally. The *Big Book* outlines a personal program to follow and the *Twelve Traditions* provide organizational principles, but they offer no guidance on how to behave at meetings or what is expected of a good AA member. All of this is communicated either by example, during meetings, or orally, around the edge of meetings.

The format of the meeting, any prescriptions about what is to be said, or how it is to be said are decided by the group. This distinguishes AA, for instance, from the fraternal organizations of the late nineteenth century, including the temperance fraternities, which built their meetings around elaborate rituals set forth in centrally printed handbooks. More recent 12-step organizations often provide detailed written instructions on how to run a meeting.

In addition to the activities centered around AA meeting participation, there is another set of oral traditions that surround specific AA interpersonal activities. A crucially important part of AA is the sponsor-sponsee relationship. A sponsor is a person who advises another member in working the AA program (see chapter 12). Again, the idea of sponsorship is not part of the official program. While there is a pamphlet on sponsorship (*Questions and Answers,* 1983), and while references to the relationship can be found in such semiofficial literature as *A.A. Grapevine,* the form and content of the relationship are communicated mainly in the oral tradition.

The words of a successful sponsor will continue to be exchanged among his or her sponsees. There are orally acknowledged lineages of sponsors within AA. In the United States, it is possible to meet people whose sponsor was sponsored by one of the pioneers of AA. References to such lineages are often used to authenticate a view of the traditional way of doing things.

The role of oral transmission is related to the fact that AA does not formulate rules of conduct, but rather methods of behaving and ways of speaking. The methods of work and the ways of speaking are learned not as general rules that can be written down but by learning by example and by using more experienced members as models. In terms of MacIntyre's (1984) contrast between Aristotelian and modern ethics, in AA one learns virtues and experiential wisdom, not the rules of good conduct. Rules of conduct can be formulated, just as written legislation classifies actions as permitted or prohibited. Virtues such as fortitude, wisdom or serenity cannot be formulated in a set of rules classifying actions as brave, wise, or serene.

The role of learning by example means there is a lot of cultural and even local variation in what is seen as *the* belief system of AA. There are extremely doctrinaire and authoritarian variants but also very loose, open, and liberal variants.

"When I first approached the Fellowship, it was suggested that I get a sponsor. Now sometimes it appears the only choices are a guru or a Step Nazi. Thank God I was told that the timetable in working the Steps was between my Higher Power and me."

Marge R., 1993, p. 19

Slogans and Mottos as Guidelines for Behavior

A notable feature of AA's kit of tools is the wide proliferation of its slogans and mottos (Table 10.1); Pittman's list (1988b) includes more than 250. Along with a variety of other functions, these are used as guides to daily life (Taylor, 1977, p. 62). Some are limited to the oral culture ("keep the plug in the jug"), while others are considered suit-

Table 10.1   AA Slogans and Mottos

Not drinking
One drink is too many and a thousand not enough
(It's the) first drink (that) gets you drunk
Keep (/put) the plug in the jug

Belief and action
Act as if . . .
Fake it till you make it
Utilize, don't analyze (/don't intellectualize, utilize)
If it works (/if it ain't broke), don't fix it
Take what you can use and leave the rest
Keep coming back (—it works [if you work it])

Identification and listening
Get (/take) the cotton out of your ears and put it in your mouth
Sit down, shut up and listen
Stick with the winners
Identify, don't compare

Surrender to Higher Power
*Let (it) go and let God
Turn it over
(I) came, (I) came to, (I) came to believe
Expect miracles (/a miracle)

Daily praxis
*First things first
*Easy does it (but do it)
*Think, think, think
One day at a time
(Live today) just for today
Keep it simple (, stupid) (KISS)

Psychic state
Don't get too hungry . . . or too angry . . . or too lonely . . . or too tired—H.A.L.T.
(Get off) the pity pot
Poor me, poor me, pour me a drink
You're only as sick as your secrets

Tolerance and humility
*Live and let live
*(There) but for the grace of God (go I)
Self will run riot

Organizational principles
What you hear and see here (/what is said here) stays here
Principles before personalities

Source: The 32 slogans listed are those mentioned by at least two of the following sources: H. C. Johnson, 1987; Pittman, 1988b; M. Phillips, 1991; Taylor, 1977. Additional words in alternative formulations are included in parentheses; alternative wordings are in parentheses preceded by a solidus (/thus).

*These six slogans "are often seen hanging in meeting rooms" (Stewart C., 1986).

able for posting on walls. According to Stewart C. (1986), the six slogans marked with asterisks in Table 10.1 "are often seen hanging in meeting rooms," and *Staying Clean* (Anonymous, 1990b, p. 7) notes that five of these (omitting "let go and let God") are often hung "in meeting rooms around the world" in an order "arranged so the first word of each slogan offers sound advice to the addict when read from left to right: *Live Easy But Think First.*" Along with a specialized vocabulary, which Bill W. was already describing in 1953 as "AA slang" (*12 + 12,* 1986, p. 135), the slogans provide a framework of shared understanding among movement members. They also serve as boundary markers on membership in a subculture. Thus the use of the slogans in conversation may provide a means of recognition among movement members when outside the meeting. In many parts of the United States, the "Easy Does It" bumper sticker has become an identifier of membership in the more general 12-step movement.

"I've talked to you like an ordinary person, not doing AA talk like I would to another AA. You get into the way of switching on to the other. It just becomes automatic."

Robinson, 1979, p. 74

The substantive issues, which the commonest slogans address, are surrender to a higher power, tolerance, and humility. Also emphasized is an everyday praxis of generalized self-control, expressed in terms of focusing on the immediate moment, "one day at a time," and on applying the program and exemplars offered in AA, even if you have to "fake it till you make it."

The slogans range from very general and abstract sayings, which must be infused with meaning by interpretation, to very concrete and practical guides to action. Some express clear-cut norms: "Do not gossip about what you hear at closed meetings." Some express similar generalized psychological or other wisdom as proverbs: "If I'm angry or tired, there is an increased risk that I will take a drink." The most interesting ones are those that are instructions (not rules) for action. On the surface, they seem to be almost devoid of content. The point is, however, that they are deictic, that their semantic content is completely determined by their situation of utterance, by the concrete situation where they are addressed to oneself or to others. As pointers for conduct they can be likened to manuals on how to operate stereo equipment, utterly incomprehensible if there is no button B to push nor switch X to put in an upright position. It is because of the deictic nature of the instructions that the oral tradition of AA can infuse empty looking slogans with great wisdom.

Although most slogans are not, strictly speaking, norm prescriptions, they are recommended as tools to be used in the battle with the bottle. According to a study of AA in New York in the late 1950s, when a member had a slip others said that he did not pay attention to one or another of the slogans and, therefore, was more vulnerable (Gellman, 1964, pp. 109–110).

One might expect that many political and religious movements could use deictic instructions for action, but their proliferation in AA seems to be unique. This may be connected to the role of an oral tradition in AA and to the interrelations of belief and action. Using a concept from ethnomethodology (Garfinkel, 1967, pp. 1–34; Zimmerman & Polner, 1970), we may say that the proliferation of mottos is an indication of the situatedness of AA. AA is not about something out there but about here and now, about the existential condition of being an alcoholic.

Loss of Control and the Nature of Alcoholism

The prerequisite for continued membership in AA is to recognize the loss of control over one's life because of alcohol and to identify oneself as an alcoholic. While members differ in their views of alcoholism, we can identify some core beliefs of the movement (Eisenbach-Stangl, 1991b, 1991c).

Alcoholism is a categorical condition: "[T]here is no such thing as being a little bit alcoholic. Either you are, or you are not" (*44 Questions,* 1990, p. 8).

Alcoholism is unitary in the sense that it affects all aspects of a person as a human being. Alcoholism is at the same time physical, mental, and spiritual. The condition of being an alcoholic pervades one's whole life. Without addressing one's alcoholism, one cannot solve any of one's other life problems.

One is not morally responsible for one's alcoholism, but one has responsibility for doing something about it. "One should not feel shame at being sick, one should only feel shame at not doing anything about it" (*Big Book,* 1955, p. 33).

Alcoholism is a progressive condition. If there is no intervention, alcoholism leads to all kinds of endless suffering and, finally, to death.

The course of alcoholism cannot be halted by individual will power without outside support. "It was a statistical fact that alcoholics almost never recovered on their own resources" (*12 + 12*, 1986, p. 22).

In order to start one's recovery, one has to recognize one's alcoholism personally. Outside diagnosis and professional help cannot substitute for personal identification. This is why AA does not need codified criteria for alcoholism. In principle, outside diagnosis requires objective criteria. In contrast, the recognition of one's powerlessness over alcohol is not contingent on codified methods of diagnosis.

The condition of being an alcoholic is so basic that it outweighs all other individual and social differences. This belief is of strategic significance to AA, since it is the foundation of the basic equality of members. AA is based on interaction between equals who mutually recognize that they are tortured by the same demon (Eisenbach-Stangl, 1993). It is about mutual help rather than about self-help. "You see, our talk was a completely mutual thing. I knew that I needed this alcoholic as much as he needed me. This was it" (*Alcoholics Anonymous Comes of Age*, 1986, p. 70). One important difference from every type of group therapy is that there are no professionals involved in the process.

The progress of alcoholism can be halted, but alcoholism in itself is incurable. Lifelong abstinence is required, since an alcoholic can never resume moderate drinking: "Once an alcoholic, always an alcoholic" (*Big Book*, 1955, p. 33). Therefore, AA does not speak internally of recovered alcoholics but only of recovering alcoholics. Indeed, if a former member is reported to have successfully resumed moderate drinking, it is concluded that he was not a true alcoholic in the first place. This belief provides further support to the premise of equality among members. Although longtime members are highly respected because of their experience with sober life, the fragility of being an alcoholic puts them in the same situation as any other member. This fragility is ritually reconfirmed at every meeting, where participants identify themselves by the formula "My name is . . . and I'm an alcoholic." AA is about sobriety "one day at a time" (Pittman, 1988b, p. 221).

Old-timers in many countries emphasize the common vulnerability of all members by saying that the longest sobriety belongs to whoever woke up first this morning.

Alcoholism is a specific condition in the sense that the AA program is about alcoholism and alcoholism only. The program is not a remedy for human powerlessness in general, although it can be modified to address other life problems such as drug addiction or eating disorders.

It should be pointed out that these core tenets do not as such amount to a medical description of alcoholism as a disease (cf. Miller & Kurtz, 1994). They also make room for considerable variation in individual interpretations, as is shown in Finnish life-story interviews (Appendix B). One common response was to define alcoholism as an emotional condition, but generally the views of individual members differed a lot.

In the beginning, AA had an ambivalent stand on medical models of alcoholism as a disease. On the one hand, the founding fathers of AA generally avoided the quasi-technical term "disease" and used instead some synonym such as "malady" (Kurtz, 1991). Their emphasis was on the unity of human life and on the three-fold nature of alcoholism—as being at once physical, mental, and spiritual. On the other hand, AA literature abounds with fragmentary descriptions of alcoholism as a disease. Alcoholism is variously seen as a "physical allergy" but also as a "mental obsession" (*Big Book,* 1955, p. xxvi; *12 + 12,* 1986, p. 22). It is worth pointing out that similar discrepancies exist in medical and psychiatric texts about alcoholism. Furthermore, medical models of alcoholism often contain moral elements (Falk, 1975), and these change according to time and culture (Eisenbach-Stangl, 1991a; Miller, 1986; Room, 1978).

On being an alcoholic to oneself and to another: "And then I started to get alarmed myself that I could not quit drinking. Once I said to my husband that I'm an alcoholic. 'You're no alcoholic, [he said], you're perfectly able to stop; I am drinking, too, but I am better able to keep it within limits, or at least I am not showing anybody that I have those terrible hangovers like you do.' So this again turned into a terrible fight; he accused me of being a total alcoholic and 'alkie,' that I do not take care of things and so on."

Finnish life-story interview (F, 43, 1)

The psychological functions of looking at alcoholism as a disease are manifold. The shift provides relief from feelings of guilt, it helps to admit one's powerlessness, and it provides support for the requirement of lifelong abstinence.

In today's AA, some members adhere to particular scientific theories about the nature of alcoholism, whereas others focus on their existential powerlessness with respect to alcohol. Whatever the emphasis, the AA program is not interested in the causes of alcoholism. The application of the program differs from medical theories in the sense that it does not rely on expert techniques based on explanations of the genesis of the condition to be treated. Practicing the AA program is a collective undertaking of equals.

Spirituality and the Higher Power

Having admitted his powerlessness over alcohol, the AA member is expected to come "to believe that a power greater than [himself] can restore [him] to sanity" (Step Two) and to "turn [his] will and [his] life over to the care of God as [he] understands Him" (Step Three). Faith in God or a higher power is very much at the core of the belief world of AA.

In principle, the AA way of looking at the world is not tied to Christianity or to monotheism. AA advocates no theological or ontological beliefs. The lack of eschatological themes in AA literature and AA speech is striking. Rather, AA speaks of this life and has nothing to say about afterlife. AA is only interested in the relationship of an individual to her/himself, to other people and to some higher power.

At the same time, the historical roots of AA are firmly embedded in Christian and Protestant traditions. When the Twelve Steps were written down, some revisions were made in order to accommodate the worldview of those early members who were atheists or agnostics, and great care was taken to avoid any formulations that might offend Catholic thought. Kurtz (1991) describes how the language of the Twelve Steps reflects the conflict between those early members who wanted the AA program to be Christian in doctrine and others who objected to any references to God. According to Kurtz (1991, p. 71), "neither Wilson nor A.A. did ever solve this problem." Indeed, to Kurtz the unresolved tension between these two perspectives is a central feature of AA.

AA is emphatic about not being a religious society since it requires no definite religious belief as a condition of membership (*44 Questions*, 1990, p. 19). At the same time, the program is "based on acceptance of certain spiritual values," although "the individual member is free to interpret those values as he or she thinks best, or not to think about them at all" (*44 Questions*, 1990, p. 19). Members of AA emphasize the importance of spiritual principles both for the recovery of each individual and for the success of the organization as a whole.

"[Visiting a meeting in Poland,] I did not understand the language but I knew why they were there, and they knew why I was there. The room was filled with spirituality, and that can say more than a thousand words."

Kenta, 1992, p. 9

AA emphasizes individual solutions to the task of finding meaning in the world (Eisenbach-Stangl, 1993), and members often refer to *my* Higher Power. For some members, spirituality has a definite theological content, for others it may simply mean a certain type of relationship humans have with their life, an open-hearted and respectful attitude to life. Many members experience a contrast between their spirituality and organized religion. One important aspect is that AA as a spiritual community is cut off from any church or religion as a worldly power structure (Eisenbach-Stangl, 1992d).

Human Beings as Psychological and Moral Entities

The AA program as such does not hinge on any particular psychological theory. The basic texts of AA use an everyday moral and psychological vocabulary and show few traces of academic psychology, either positivistic or psychodynamic. Traditional AA is also wary of causal explanations of behavior. These are important features, because they undercut the attempts by professional 12-step programs to translate AA's system of belief and action into professional psychology.

Bill W. thought of human psychology in terms of "instincts" and "moods" (Kurtz, 1991, p. 225). The instincts, for "sex, security and society," could not be avoided during the recovery period from alcoholism, but rather could be "tempered and redirected." The problem for the alcoholic was not the instincts, but rather the moods or "passions," which grip the drinker in regard to the instincts. "We have drunk to drown feelings of fear, frustration and depression. We have drunk to escape the guilt of passions, and then have drunk again to make more passions possible. We have drunk for vainglory—that we might the more enjoy foolish dreams of pomp and power" (*12 + 12*, 1986, p. 44). There are two master moods or passions in Bill W.'s thinking: depression and grandiosity or pride, and two associated personality types, "the depressive and the power-driver." In discussing the moral inventory in *Twelve Steps and Twelve Traditions*, depression is dealt with in a single paragraph; guilt, self-loathing, and desperation are associated with it, and suicidal desperation is labeled as "pride in reverse" (*12 + 12*, 1986, p. 45).

Considerably more space is given to the discussion of pride, "big-shot-ism," or grandiosity, as it is variously called. Listing the traditional Seven Deadly Sins, Bill W. noted that "it is not by accident that pride heads the procession" (*12 + 12*, 1986, p. 48). Proceeding from pride are a variety of other passions, notably resentment and anger, but including also jealousy, envy, and self-pity (*12 + 12*, 1986, p. 90). Indulgence in these "disturbances" is what is meant by "emotional 'dry benders' " (*12 + 12*, 1986, p. 90).

The task of recovery, in Bill W.'s thought, is to curb these "disturbances," to limit the play of the passions. Although for historical reasons the word itself was carefully avoided, "the concept embracing the root virtue that Alcoholics Anonymous proclaims and seeks to inculcate is *temperance*" (Kurtz, 1991, p. 228). The terms used in Bill W.'s writings are "peace of mind," "serenity," and "self-restraint." Some of the other virtues listed in the writings are the opposites of pride and its derivatives: humility, kindness, tolerance, and unselfishness. Also prominent as integral parts of AA's program are surrender and hope, two qualities that might be apposed to pride and despair. But the view of human psychology in terms of governing passions, which need to be curbed, means that there is no exact symmetry in Bill W.'s thought between virtues and vices. The cardinal virtue, in fact, is the curbing of the vices.

These emphases in AA's canonical works are still very much on the minds of contemporary AA members in the United States. In a study comparing responses on the Rokeach value survey of the general population and of those with three or more years of sobriety in attendance at AA meetings in Missouri, Mississippi, and Arkansas, the widest differences were reported for the term "ambitious," which was devalued by the sober AA members. These same individuals ranked "inner harmony" most highly (Brown & Peterson, 1990).

The chart of positive and negative qualities in AA thought systems (Table 10.2) lays out a list of qualities prominent in the *Big Book* and the *Twelve Steps and Twelve Traditions*. In more recent AA sources, there is a tendency for the lists to become more symmetrical: for instance, "dishonesty" and "intolerance" make their appearance in Hazelden's *Little Red Book* as counterpoints to Bill W.'s honesty and tolerance. This symmetry becomes explicit in the *12 Rewards*, which are often read at the end of AA meetings in the United States (M. Phillips, 1991). Notable also in these is a shift toward viewing aspects of pride (self-respect, self-confidence) as potentially virtuous. The *Little Red Book* and the *12 Re-*

Table 10.2   Positive and Negative Qualities in
AA thought systems

Positive qualities	Negative qualities
Faith	Uselessness/purposelessness
Peace of mind	
Serenity	
Hope	Despair
Joy	
	Self-pity
	Anxiety
	Fear
Humility	Pride
Surrender	"Big-shot-ism"
Self-restraint	
Honesty	
Unselfishness	Selfishness
Tolerance	
Love	Hate
Courtesy	
Kindness	
Justice	
	Resentments
	Anger
	Jealousy
	Envy

Note: Included in the table are (1) the positive
and negative qualities from the paragraph
known as the "12 promises" in the *Big Book* (1955,
pp. 83–84); (2) entries with at least four references (including subentries of phrases including
the indexed word) in Stewart C.'s *Reference Guide
to the Big Book of Alcoholics Anonymous,* 1986; and
(3) the lists of qualities in the *Twelve Steps and
Twelve Traditions* (1986), plus terms from the surrounding text on pp. 70, 90, 92–94, and 107.

wards are not official AA literature, but they represent emerging systems of thought in the movement.

Bill W.'s writings reveal a deep mistrust of psychological explanations and justifications. In AA's practice, to offer a rationale for a behavior is suspect, and to regard the rationale as justifying the behavior is
erroneous. The suspicion of all rationalization, "our ancient enemy"
(*12 + 12,* 1986, p. 44), is based on a perception of rationalization as a
main tool of the alcoholic in maintaining his or her drinking. While
practicing alcoholics have no idea "how irrational they are" (*12 + 12,*

1986, pp. 32–33), they can always offer reasons for drinking (*12 + 12*, 1986, p. 44).

While rationalization is suspect and discouraged, it is when the rationalizations become justifications that they turn erroneous. Bill W.'s framing of this was primarily in terms of the pride or self-pity that he saw as motivating such justifications: "Pride steps in to justify our excesses" (*12 + 12*, 1986, p. 49). As alcoholics, AA members were never "skillful in separating justified from unjustified anger. As we saw it, our wrath was always justified. . . . These emotional 'dry benders' often led straight to the bottle" (*12 + 12*, 1986, p. 90).

Another distinction can also be drawn between rationales and justifications. Offering reasons for past behavior may or may not involve justifying it. But with respect to current or future behavior, to offer a reason is also necessarily to offer a justification. The act remains wrongful if the reason offered is not also a justification. To ban justifications is to demand that the act justifies itself in its own terms, not in terms of an external frame of reference, which is offered as justification.

The ban on justification for behavior goes along with a wider suspicion of excessive analyzing. This tendency to steer away from searching for reasons for behavior sets AA somewhat at odds with major traditions of psychodynamic therapy. Regarding justificatory rationales as erroneous thinking is also a source of tensions with feminist thinking, since a major part of consciousness-raising is the validation of new justifications for self-regarding behavior.

Belief and Action in AA

The AA program is as much a set of behavioral tools as a set of beliefs. The basic texts present a program for action rather than a codified belief system. Already in the written tradition, stories play an important role by presenting testimonies of personal experience, and the Twelve Steps can be interpreted simply as a description of what the early members *did*.

But in order to act, one needs faith, as shown in the famous example by William James (1903a) of the mountain climber:

> Suppose, for instance, that you are climbing a mountain, and have worked yourself into a position from which the only escape is a terrible leap. Have faith that you can successfully make it, and your feet are nerved to the accomplishment. . . . Refuse to believe, and you shall indeed be right, for you shall irretrievably

perish. But believe, and again you shall be right, for you shall save yourself. (p. 59)

According to AA, the alcoholic is in the same predicament as the mountain climber. In both cases, knowing how and why one ended up in the precarious situation is hardly relevant for the course of action, and only one course of action is known that may lead to escape from the predicament. Explanations are to no avail, the only thing that matters is the decision to jump or not to jump.

Of course, a radical course of action cannot be justified by asserting that belief or faith are generally more advantageous than doubt or reflection on causes. The justification of the AA position is, rather, that other alcoholics already have applied the program successfully: "Keep coming back, it works" (Pittman, 1988b, p. 221). This also explains why members so often reiterate how they had tried everything else but failed before finally accomplishing sobriety in AA.

Despite AA's emphasis on behavior, the behaviors are often meant to lead to certain beliefs. AA wisdom advises the newcomer to leave aside any ideological doubts. A person who prefers arguing about the program instead of trying it fails to meet the criteria for recovery as formulated in the *Big Book:* "If you have decided that you want what we have and are willing to go to any length to get it—then you are ready to take certain steps" (*Big Book,* 1955, p. 58). Depending on the tenets of each group and sponsor, this gives great indoctrinating potential to the AA program.

Various strains of AA differ in the relative emphasis they put on the content of beliefs. In some quarters, the openness of the belief system is just the means for guiding members to *a* particular religion, that is, to the religion of their childhood family. In much the same way, institutional 12-step treatments may propagate particular theories of alcoholism and human psychology.

11

The AA Meeting as a Speech Event

According to a typical definition presented in the scientific literature, "meeting" is "A.A. jargon for relatively formal, quasi-ritualized therapeutic sessions run by and for any alcoholics in the community who wish to attend them" (Leach et al., 1969, p. 509). In AA's own words, the purpose of a (closed) meeting "is to give members an opportunity to discuss particular phases of their alcoholic problem that can be understood best only by other alcoholics. . . . These meetings are usually conducted with a maximum of informality, and all members are encouraged to participate in the discussions" (*44 Questions*, 1990, p. 22).

In AA directories, a variety of regular weekly meetings are listed. The most important distinction is between closed meetings, which are reserved for alcoholics only, and open meetings where friends, family members, and interested outsiders are allowed. Another major distinction is between speaker meetings and discussion meetings. Discussion meetings may or may not begin with a short lead, but most of the meeting time is taken up by general discussion. At speaker meetings, one or more speakers tell their stories without discussion from the floor. There also are speaker meetings with speeches from the floor after the introductory stories. Some meetings are devoted to the study of particular texts—there are Step meetings, Tradition meetings, and *Big Book* study meetings. Other meetings are designed for specific categories of AA members—for example, newcomers, women, or gay and lesbian members.

In addition to regular meetings, AA organizes a great variety of gatherings, such as:

- business meetings of the group and at different levels of the service structure,

- information meetings in prisons and treatment institutions, and for professionals and the general public,
- weekend retreats, roundups, workshops and conventions, and celebrations and social events such as dinners and dances.

Although many particularities of the AA meeting format can be observed at almost any AA gatherings, the focus of this chapter is on regular weekly discussion meetings as a special type of speech event (Arminen, 1994). This restriction still leaves us with a bewildering assortment of meetings. Any description of "a typical meeting" runs the danger of being one-sided, and it is a difficult task to determine the core region in the field of family resemblances that connects AA meetings in different cultures. Denzin (1987) characterizes AA as a "white, Anglo-Saxon social movement" and describes "the moral, interactional and emotional code of AA" as remaining "embedded in the white, Anglo-Saxon culture." Denzin adds that "the emotional tone of the AA meetings, although tilted in the direction of emotional display, is a tone that is modulated by the white, male experience." Therefore, blacks and Hispanics who speak from "a different linguistic background" tend to have more frequent slips (pp. 164–165). In fact, the structure and tenor of AA meetings varies a lot even in the Anglo-Saxon world. H. C. Johnson's (1987) study is mainly based on groups in California, but she also points out that AA meetings in Zimbabwe are quite different from meetings in the United States. Systematic cross-cultural comparisons are rare, but the evidence available indicates that AA meetings vary widely in response to local culture (Jilek-Aall, 1978; Sutro, 1989). The success of AA in Latin America also proves that it can adapt to various cultural traditions of interaction.

Every meeting is a unique social event and never directly based on what happened at an earlier meeting, nor does it carry any promises for future meetings. What goes on in the meeting is the point of the meeting: the gathering does not have a collective purpose beyond the meeting's process. In the meeting, AA members share with each other (express their experiences and feelings) and identify with each other (listen empathetically). A high value is placed on spontaneity and immediacy—on reporting personal experience, and on relating it to the here and now. Still, an AA meeting is a social event scheduled at the same time each week in the same location with the same format. The continuity between meetings is taken care of by the repetition of the meeting's agenda, which usually remains the same.

The chairman opens the meeting: "Good evening, my name is Gylfi and I am an alcoholic. May I welcome you to this 468th meeting of the Monday Eight O'Clock Group."

Icelandic field observation

The Setting and the Order of Events

In a big city, meetings are held everyday of the week and it may be possible to attend an AA meeting at almost any time of the day. Meetings in the middle of the day are attractive to housewives, those who work on shift, the unemployed, and people who have just been in treatment and have not started work again. Meetings at lunchtime are popular among busy people. People who can control their own working time, like businessmen, small entrepreneurs, and some academicians also have the freedom to select their meeting irrespective of the time of the day. However, most people go to meetings after work.

Meetings are scheduled all through the year. No exceptions are made for Christmas or other holidays, although meetings on Christmas Day may be moved by a couple of hours.

In societies where punctuality is regarded as a virtue, meetings usually start on time. Less industrialized societies may have different attitudes to time and this will be apparent at AA meetings, too. Most meetings in Mexico begin with some delay with only a few members present, and more arrive in the next 20 or 30 minutes.

In California, up to a half of AA meetings are in facilities owned by fellowships and clubhouses and used solely for 12-step meetings, but in the other study sites meeting facilities reserved for AA meetings are an exception. The social hall of a church or a meeting room in a municipal facility is typical for AA meetings in many countries, but almost any type of facilities can be used. In Mexico City, for example, meeting places include the garage of what used to be a suburban middle-class home, a large room in a downtown nineteenth-century colonial palace that nowadays is decrepit and divided into several modest offices and workshops, a room in a church that during the daytime is used for children's catechism classes, and an auditorium owned by a union.

Quite commonly, AA texts are hanging on the walls, such as the Twelve Steps, the Twelve Traditions, the Serenity Prayer, and selected mottos and slogans, sometimes in calligraphy. Framed pictures of Bill W. and Dr. Bob are also to be seen in meeting rooms, particularly in the

United States and Mexico. Candles are frequently used in Polish meetings, and flowers and candles may decorate the meeting room in Mexico. Places used solely for AA meetings have more clues indicating the authority of AA over the space than places that AA groups share with other activities.

Copies of literature and a display of leaflets are regularly placed on a table even in the most modest meeting room.

The number of participants and the seating order have a fundamental influence on the meeting. Bigger groups use audience-style, while smaller groups tend to sit in a circle or a U-shaped line. Newcomers tend to sit in the back row, and people who want to refrain from speaking may indicate this by taking a seat furthest away from the chair or by sitting on the right side of the chair, if the etiquette of the meeting is to start on the left side. Such traditions of non-verbal communication are characteristic of AA meetings and obviously have to be learned by experience.

As groups seldom change their agenda, the schedule of each meeting remains the same from one meeting to the next. The universal or near-universal features of the AA meeting consist of opening rituals, announcements, discussion, money collection, serving of refreshments and closing rituals, but not necessarily in that order. The main part of the meeting is devoted to members talking in turn. Longer meetings often have a break.

In almost every AA meeting, refreshments are served, either before the meeting starts, during the meeting, or after. In most Icelandic meetings, a cup of coffee or water and a tea bag will be all that is offered. In some places, a lot of effort is put into making the meeting a social event by serving an array of drinks and food.

In Marin County in California, it is not unusual to see refreshments that consist of two or three different types of gourmet cheeses and crackers laid out, alongside a selection of chips and dips, freshly cut apples, carrots and celery sticks, grapes and strawberries, several types of cookies, a large selection of herbal and non-herbal teas, and freshly brewed caffeinated and decaffeinated coffee decanters.

Kaskutas, 1993

At the same time in every weekly meeting, usually before the break or just before the meeting ends, the collection of money takes place.

Newcomers and people with limited resources are not expected to contribute. Usually there is no collection at meetings in prisons and other institutions.

Opening Rituals: Separating the Meeting from Non-Meeting Time

The demarcation of an AA meeting from non-meeting time is emphasized by procedural rituals. The opening rituals separate the meeting from mundane interaction and anticipate its specific interaction order with its own turn-taking system and ways of speaking. The significance of the opening rituals is accentuated by the fact that deviations caused by mistake or ignorance will be corrected. This contrasts with the general lack of direct negative feedback at AA meetings.

The person opening the meeting will greet the attendants. Special attention is paid to guests, if there are any, and newcomers are given an opportunity to identify themselves. Opening rituals consist mainly of texts read from the AA heritage. Additionally, there may be a moment of silence, and physical rituals such as holding hands. Frequently used texts include "How It Works" from chapter 5 of the *Big Book* (containing the Twelve Steps), the AA Preamble, and the Serenity Prayer. The Preamble is read as an opening text at most meetings in Austria, Iceland, Mexico, and Poland. Chapter 5 of the *Big Book* is commonly read at Californian, Finnish, and Polish AA meetings. Some reading from the *Twelve Steps and the Twelve Traditions* is done at almost all meetings. In Iceland, it is customary to read all Twelve Steps and selected Traditions, usually the Fifth, Seventh, and Twelfth Tradition about the primary purpose of the group, financial self-sufficiency, and anonymity. Texts also vary depending on the topic of the meeting. In Step and Tradition study meetings the Step or Tradition of the day is read (with interpretations), and in newcomers' meetings Step One is read. The texts are always read from a paper even though many members know them by heart. This practice ensures that new and inexperienced members do not stick out by disclosing their imperfect knowledge.

Despite their diversity, all opening texts state the common condition of the persons present—the shared problem of alcoholism. Throughout the meeting, individual speakers reiterate the main content of the collective opening ritual by invoking their powerlessness in respect to alcohol. The first time a participant reads a text, makes an announcement or speaks, she or he uses the formulaic introduction, "I am [name], and I am an alcoholic."

The opening rituals handle delicate matters explicitly. They remind the persons present of the negative experience of being an alcoholic, about loss of control, and loss of face. Taken as speech acts, many of the utterances can be categorized as accusations, deprecations, and threats. However, the face threats are not responded to according to the conventional preference organization of ordinary conversations, where deprecations should be followed by denials (Levinson, 1983, pp. 332–339; Pomerantz, 1984). Instead, the whole frame of a meeting is carried away from the realm of ordinary conversation to another interaction order. Absolute humiliation and admission of personal powerlessness turn out to be a "firm bedrock upon which happy and purposeful lives may be built" (12 + 12, 1986, p. 21).

Both before the meeting started and after the break everyone sat leaning tensely towards the table; on both occasions they leaned back and relaxed as soon as the meeting got under way.

Finnish field observation

The amount of ritual elaboration varies from meeting to meeting, but rituals are not the point of the meeting, as is the case in, for example, religious gatherings. Their main task is to set the frame of the meeting and to separate it from non-meeting time. This is related to an unusual characteristic of AA: that it is a movement essentially without songs—in contrast, for instance, to the old temperance movement. Singing together may have smacked too much of the hymns of formal religion, and, for that matter, of the drinking songs of the saloon. The solidarity of a hymn or song is when the whole group focuses outside itself with a common goal—whether praising God or producing a beautiful sound—while AA's togetherness is of a different nature.

Outside the meeting, members step back to the conversational realm of everyday life with its ordinary moral impositions. The informal interaction before and after the meeting is complementary to the meeting, and helps strengthen the social network of the group. In addition, disagreements and animosities may be ventilated without threatening the meeting format.

Turn-Taking Rules

The most obvious difference between everyday conversations and an AA meeting is that in AA meetings turns of talk are preallocated (Sacks, Schegloff, & Jefferson, 1974). The chair has the right to talk first and to make short remarks after each speaker, and in this way can have a great impact on the flow of the meeting. The first speech after the opening turn by the chair is usually somewhat longer than the rest. In ordinary discussion meetings, the introductory speech may last between ten and twenty minutes. In speaker meetings with discussion, the first speaker is predesignated and may speck for more than half an hour. At some meetings, there may be several predesignated introductory speakers.

Turn-taking rules of the main discussion vary between meetings. At small meetings participants often speak in seating order. This format is seldom used in larger meetings of more than thirty participants. In alternative turn-taking systems, it may be up to the chair to select the next speaker, the current speaker may select the next, or participants may indicate their willingness to speak by raising their hands, signing up on a list, or lining up in a row. Another variant is used at "red ball meetings," where the chair throws a ball to the group and the person catching it becomes the next speaker.

Differences in turn-taking rules are significant since they obviously have an impact on the topical coherence of the discussion. All meetings are, however, organized around extended turns rather than around turn-reply pairs. Turns are not followed by immediate replies as in an ordinary conversation. Instead, the discussion in AA meetings is non-conversational and its turn-taking system is institutional.

Normally there are no limits on the length of a turn of talk, but meeting time tends to become divided evenly among participants. The average length depends on the number of participants, since ordinarily the duration of an AA meeting is limited to one or two hours. If somebody talks very long, other participants may become inattentive and restless but no overt sanctions are applied, and talking extensively is all right if the speaker is seriously distressed. If somebody has used too much time, more experienced members coming after him or her often pass their turn to save time for participants who may need it more urgently. Sometimes a stopwatch is used, but most meetings tolerate speeches of varying length.

"Meeting time is our food and has to be divided evenly like provisions on a life raft. But we should also follow the example of the shipwrecked who surrender their share for the benefit of the weakest."

Finnish field interview (M, 34, 3)

Talking more than once until everyone has had a chance to speak is considered impolite. Usually each participant speaks only once, though after the first round a call for seconds is common. The second round is rarely used.

Passing one's turn is perfectly acceptable. Members may attend the same meeting for long periods without ever speaking a word (Westerman, 1978). In this respect, AA meetings differ from all versions of group therapy.

"Attending meetings and just listening has proven sufficient for me during my five years in the AA program."

Icelandic field interview (M, 62, 5)

At small meetings, it is quite common that a majority or all of the members attending the meeting participate in the discussion. According to ICSAA meeting surveys (see Appendix C), at two-thirds of AA meetings in Austria and Finland, everybody attending the meeting had taken part in the discussion. The speaker-discussion format is ordinarily used in large meetings, and generally only a minority of members use a turn.

Rules of Discourse in AA Meetings

AA meetings are robust in the sense that blatant transgressions of the rules of discourse are often simply ignored, and thus do not disturb the main line of the meeting. The outside researcher, therefore, cannot resort to the usual sociological technique of ascertaining the content of norms by describing what aberrations are met by negative sanctions. The variability of meetings also contributes to making it difficult to pin down the core of the interaction order of AA (Zieliński, 1993). The following summary is mainly based on small meetings in Finland where everybody speaks in turn. On the basis of observations of meetings and interviews with members, the main rules of speech can be spelled out as follows (Mäkelä, 1992b):

1. Do not interrupt the person speaking.
2. Speak about your own experiences.
3. Speak as honestly as you can.
4. Do not speak about other people's private affairs.
5. Do not profess religious doctrines or lecture about scientific theories.

6. You may speak about your personal problems in applying the AA program but do not attempt to refute the program.
7. Do not openly confront or challenge previous turns of talk.
8. Do not give direct advice to other members of AA.
9. Do not present causal explanations of the behavior of other AA members.
10. Do not present psychological interpretations of the behavior of other AA members.

The first two rules are the most crucial. The first rule supports the non-conversational turn-taking system. The second rule restricts turn types to self-narratives. In AA parlance, members share their experiences; that is, they tell self-narratives. Regardless of whether the topic of the meeting is a Step, a Tradition, or a personal story, speakers are expected to cover it through their own experiences. The mode of turns is restricted to a specific type (self-narratives), but the content is free. This leads to a great variety of themes. In actual practice, the notion of personal experience is sometimes interpreted very broadly. It may be possible to get around the ban on political topics by discussing one's political feelings.

"Political speeches are avoided, but I sometimes discuss politics in my home group when I am really disgusted. However, I talk of political matters as a personal problem, how Holkeri [Prime Minister] or Koivisto [President] make me mad when I see them on television."

Finnish field interview (M, 38, 6)

The amount of overt connections to previous turns of talk varies from meeting to meeting and from culture to culture. Agreement is more explicitly expressed than disagreement. Opinions also differ with respect to how important it is to stick to the topic. In a very general sense, however, turns of talk can be said to confirm previous speeches or contain opposite experiences. "Member's monologues are 'put on the table,' with or without reference to anything said by the previous speakers. One person may describe a recent traumatic event in his life. The next speaker may discuss something trivial by comparison. This does not mean that the traumatized member is ignored in favor of minor concerns. Members are not talking past each other. The net result of an evening's monologues is to level the highs and lows of all members" (Sadler, 1979, pp. 391–392).

"The most important thing is that one can talk about what is weighing on one's mind at that particular moment. There are no unimportant matters: what makes you laugh makes me cry. After the opening address on one of the Steps a member may talk about something quite different that is worrying him, but the next speaker will revert back to the Step. Some groups insist on keeping to the topic but we think otherwise."

Finnish field interview (M, 55, 21)

The rules of discourse have to be learned by practice, but they receive support in AA literature. For example, direct advice to meeting participants is contrary to at least two items on the list of "what A.A. does not do" (*If You Are a Professional . . . ,* 1986): "Make medical or psychological diagnoses or prognoses," and "Provide domestic or vocational counseling." Thus AA members are reluctant even to answer a newcomer's question as to whether he or she is an alcoholic, since this would be a medical or psychological opinion about another person. Rather, members will tend to answer in terms of their own experiences with alcohol.

If somebody breaks the rules of discourse, later speakers can present some of their own experiences that indirectly point out the unorthodox nature of the earlier turn of talk. If somebody seems to speak insincerely, somebody else may tell about the problems he ran into when he wasn't honest to himself, but no overt sanctions are normally applied during the meeting against breaking any of the rules presented above. After the meeting, more direct feedback can be given.

"Comments and advice must be given privately, otherwise the spell of the meeting may be broken."

Finnish field interview (F, 48, 12)

Facework and Politeness at AA Meetings

The main characteristics of AA meetings can be discussed in terms of facework. "Face" is the public self-image that every member of a culture wants to claim for himself or herself. It consists of two related aspects, negative and positive face. "The human personality is a sacred thing; one dare not violate it nor infringe its bounds, while at the same time the greatest good is in communion with others" (Durkheim, 1953, p. 37). "Negative face" refers to freedom of action and freedom of imposition, "the want of every 'competent adult member' that his actions be unimpeded by others" (Brown & Levinson, 1987, p. 61). "Positive face" refers to one's desire to be recognized by others, "the want of every member that his wants be desirable to at least some others" (Brown & Levinson, 1987, p. 61).

The opening rituals and the repetition of their main content by each speaker create a strong bond of togetherness and equality: all participants are in the same situation, only one drink away from a slip. The common existential condition creates a warm atmosphere of positive politeness and solidarity. On a more technical level, however, the rules of talk in AA meetings are very much geared toward negative politeness—toward honoring participants' need for autonomy rather than their need for approval.

The ban on cross-talk is one important rule supporting the negative face of the speaker. In AA meetings the right to speak given to the person holding the floor is respected even when somebody has trouble in completing his or her turn. Allowing someone to choose to remain silent also amounts to honoring his or her negative face. Furthermore, the lack of direct negative feedback on previous speeches protects the negative face of all participants.

It is now the chairperson's turn to talk. She begins "My name is Leila and I am an alcoholic." A prolonged silence follows. After several minutes she restarts in a low voice ". . . I guess I should"—a long silence—". . . I guess I shouldn't"—silence again. The stammering continues. During her talk, which lasts longer than five minutes, Leila manages to say that she has been a tough and that one should not be a tough. Then she gives the floor to the next person. (The group took the silence and the stammering surprisingly well.)

Finnish field observation

By protecting all participants against infringements of their negative face, AA rules of talk create space for derogatory and humiliating self-narratives that in other contexts would signify a total loss of face. In AA, members have "to give up their fear of losing face in order to keep face" (cf. Scollon & Scollon, 1981, p. 170).

In ordinary conversation, giving feedback is not just a right but an obligation as well; it is part of the face management required by conversational involvement. AA meetings lack the negative feedback challenging the negative face of the speaker, but many newcomers also feel uncomfortable about not receiving enough positive feedback. There are clear elements of positive politeness in AA meetings, such as the ritual response "Hi, (name)" given to the standard self-introduction. As the meeting proceeds, the chairperson thanks each speaker, and in Iceland, Mexico, and California the audience expresses thanks for the speech with a ritual applause. Old friends may be embraced by the chairperson and a nervous newcomer may get a friendly slap on the shoulder. Someone seriously distressed often receives direct support. Denzin (1987) gives an account of the reaction to a relapsed man flooding out: "Each member who spoke after this individual thanked him for coming back. A box of tissues was passed to him as he cried. Members offered him rides to other meetings. His show of emotion was not taken, then, as a sign of the loss of face" (p. 116). Denzin's example, however, also shows a cool underplaying of emotionality that is typical of AA meetings. The demolition of face was played down—only a box of tissues was passed, and the meeting continued its ordinary course.

"If a member becomes emotional and reveals more than he intended, the subsequent speakers express support and appreciation ("it was good to get it off your chest, I'm sure it wasn't easy") to show that the group has not let him down. After such a speech the tension sometimes discharges itself in the form of physical cramps. When this happens we make sure that the speaker gets professional help."

Finnish field interview (M, 51, 9)

It is possible that some women experience the lack of direct and immediate support at AA meetings as particularly distressing. Studies of gender differences in everyday conversation have produced extremely complex results that often challenge common sense stereotypes. The evidence suggests, however, that females are more concerned than males in explicitly supporting another's need for approval and fellowship (Shimanoff, 1994). Female heavy drinkers in Finland who have attended AA meetings but have not remained in the movement repeatedly lament that they could as well have been talking to a wall as to an AA meeting (unpublished data collected by Marja Holmila, Social Research Institute of Alcohol Studies). In the United States, similar concerns contributed to the establishment of Women for Sobriety, which stresses more direct emotionality (Kaskutas, 1989b). Longtime female members of AA, however, are not disturbed by the relative lack of direct affirmation or comfort.

"The secret of AA is that you get the feeling that 'those bastards are not even interested in you.' Nobody in AA asks where you come from and where you are going."
Finnish field interview (M, 44, 8)

"AA is like a longtime analysis with the group as the analyst. It is important that members do not comment on each other but that each member is allowed to draw her own conclusions."
Finnish field interview (F, 48, 12)

Handling Trouble inside AA Meetings

The interaction order of AA meetings is a precarious achievement that is constantly threatened by outside rules of talk. In this section, we discuss various types of trouble that may disturb the regular flow of the discussion.

Most groups require that meeting participants should be sober, but the policy is flexible. A lot of latitude is also given to mentally disturbed persons. At most meetings there is a high tolerance of noise and other disturbances. Whispering and chatting between people sitting together may go on uncontrolled. Indeed, often people seem to behave in improper and disorganized ways in AA meetings. In nonsmoking meetings, smokers may rush back and forth for a cigarette during the meeting. Sometimes even general unrest may prevail. The important thing is that concurrent activities are usually treated as side activities, and the main line of the meeting is held unchallenged. Only occasionally different lines of the meeting get intertwined if, for example, somebody reacts to sideline activities. In those cases the frame of the meeting can be threatened. In California, smoking sometimes is such an issue. "Leaving for a cigarette became a source of tension at times, as sometimes the woman who was speaking when the smokers decided to go outside would take this exodus personally" (H. C. Johnson 1987, p. 116).

One of the women present has taken her two young children to the meeting. The kids sit quiet during the opening ceremony, but as the meeting proceeds they start to move around and in the end they are running all over the place. Nobody seems to mind.

Mexican field observation

Johnson offers many examples of the recurrent conflict between the egalitarian concerns of time-sharing and a variety of "ego-trips." People may vote with their feet; if somebody is speaking too long or uninterestingly, other people may simply disappear or start to chat. "Inattention, barbed comments, exaggerated comings and goings to and from the rest rooms and coffee bar, private conversations, and the like would result after about ten minutes of sermon" (p. 410).

A man compares his life to the pollution of the countryside where he was born. Everybody listens with great attention for about fifteen minutes. When he repeats the description of his visit to his old home for the third time, people start to become restless. A female member whispers to the man sitting next to her: "What about the Steps? This is supposed to be a Step meeting." The speaker now starts explaining how he has been working on the Sixth Step. The noise from people crossing their feet and moving the chairs is increasing. The chair seems unhappy but does not intervene. Finally, the speaker thanks the group for their friendship, and the audience becomes quiet again. After he has spoken, the chair says: "Thank you, Pavel, and may I remind all of us that we suggested we should talk about the Sixth Step. Because we are running out of time, may I ask the next speakers to be short."

Polish field observation

AA's emphasis on the individuality of spiritual beliefs may create problems for members who have had a religious awakening. Since their faith demands that they spread the Gospel, they come in conflict with the rules for AA speech. The conflict is often solved by the newly awakened leaving AA for a time or for good. The newly awakened can feel completely at home in AA only after the urge to spread the Gospel is no longer compelling. In a similar fashion, Weiss (1990, p. 1352) reports that the subjectivist flavor of "God as we understood Him" makes AA unattractive to Orthodox Jews in Israel.

In situations where most AA members are committed to the same faith, it may become difficult to distinguish AA from religious meetings. Quite commonly, however, special efforts are made to mark the distinction between AA meetings and religious gatherings.

Although most of its members are practicing Catholics, a group in Mexico City holding its meetings in the local Catholic church makes sure that the statue of the Virgin Mary is turned to the wall before each meeting.

Mexican field observation

In cases where somebody breaks the rules of talk, the turn-taking order in itself decreases the risk of escalation of conflict (cf. Garcia, 1991). In the following example, a person had behaved in an inappropriate way by directly criticizing some other participants of the meeting and by claiming that drug talk was not a proper topic. "Rob was never challenged, outright, in the meeting. . . . Subsequent speakers simply [discussed] their own experiences [with drugs] gently after Rob spoke. Since Rob had had his turn, he could not counter" (H. C. Johnson, 1987, p. 464). In this case, the turn-taking order of an AA meeting helped to prevent an argumentive explosion by constraining both the challenger and those who were challenged.

Emotional outbursts happen, especially among newcomers or after a crisis a member has experienced. Sometimes a member may seem to lose face totally. However, emotional leakages are not penalized, but are taken as signs of affective ties that bind the membership together and therefore encouraged and supported. "Crying, the revelation of deviance while under the influence of alcohol, discussions of bouts of insanity, mentions of crippling fears or depressions, and talk of failures in marriages and social relationships are all sanctioned and accepted within the talk of AA meetings" (Denzin, 1987, pp. 115–116). Even a torrid affective flood does not disturb the overall format of the gathering.

A *Big Book* study meeting of Zapotec Indians in a southern Mexican village introduces another type of trouble. Limited literacy prevents the ordinary course of the meeting because certain "obscure Spanish words or constructions" have to be repeatedly discussed. The course of the meeting is all the time disrupted as the meaning of the strange words or sentences has to be negotiated (Sutro, 1989, p. 18).

One of the newcomers becomes restless. His friend tries to calm him down but does not succeed, and they are almost fighting. A man intervenes by saying: "Relax my friend, let's listen." The young man becomes quiet but after a few minutes he starts again. He starts laughing and talking loudly. A man takes his arms as he says, "Let's go out for a smoke." The two of them walk out of the room. The speaker has stopped talking while this is happening and everybody's attention is now drawn to the episode. None of the following speakers mentions the disturbance, and the relaxed atmosphere created by the first speaker gradually returns.

Mexican field observation

The frame of a meeting hardly ever breaks. After a disruptive event, the meeting returns smoothly to its ordinary format, since little attention is paid to sideline activities.

The use of overt sanctions to support the rules of discourse is exceptional, and systematic aberrations are not uncommon. Many Hispanic meetings in Los Angeles practice what is known as *terapia dura* and are quite confrontational, and participants criticize each other in extremely foul language and abusive ridicule (F. Hoffman, 1994). Under special circumstances, cross-talk can be allowed over a prolonged period: "One alcoholic couple reveals the brittle nature of their relationship by interrupting and commenting on each other's monologue. This couple displayed such 'deviance' for a year yet no one voiced objection to their departure from the standard format" (Sadler, 1979, p. 392).

Very small meetings with little turnover tend to be more relaxed about the etiquette of talk. Participants may talk back and forth or even comment on what someone else has said. The format of the discussion thus moves toward the informal conversation that characterizes AA interaction after the formal meeting. Sometimes this leads to a domination by old-timers of small inbred meetings. Where this occurs, the typical AA resolution is not to engage in conflict, but to withdraw and start another meeting.

The rules of discourse remain implicit and have to be learned over an extended period. However, some groups in California have added to their opening rituals a line about "no cross talk or private conversations" (H. C. Johnson, 1987, p. 323). This formal expression of rules is in itself a sign of a weakening of the rules. Manifest rules are always more vulnerable than implicit ones.

Dimensions of Cultural Variation

In this chapter we have argued that, despite wide variation and frequent transgressions, the prototypical AA meeting is a unique speech event defined by a specific combination of rules of talk. Within the prototype, however, there is room for cultural variation. It is this diversity that allows AA to adapt to widely varying cultural contexts (Arminen, 1994).

Perhaps the most important intercultural variable is the relative emphasis on positive and negative politeness, since this dimension is a direct reflection of basic cultural patterns of face-to-face interaction and of the presentation of self. We noted above that men and women seem to apply and expect others to apply different politeness strategies. Whole cultures can be grouped along a corresponding dimension (Brown & Levinson, 1987, pp. 242–255; Kasper, 1990; Scollon & Scollon, 1981, pp. 169–188), and Barnlund (1975) gives interesting hints about "Eastern" and "Western" styles of the presentation of self (for a discussion of the complexities involved, see Morisaki & Gudykunst, 1994). Positive-politeness cultures value positive feedback and support to others. In negative-politeness cultures, the emphasis is on respecting each other's autonomy and freedom of action. But classification is relative: in the literature, Americans are presented as a typical example of positive politeness, whereas autonomy and keeping distance is characteristic of the British (in the eyes of the Americans) and the Japanese (in the eyes of the British).

Many of the rituals that are often regarded as essential to AA are not universal (Table 11.1). For instance, the standard greeting "Hi, x!" after every opening of a turn by "My name is x" is not used in Finland, Iceland, and Poland. In a similar fashion, ritual applause is rare in Austria, Finland, Poland, and Sweden. The ritual of holding hands is seldom used in Finland, Iceland, and Mexico. Body contact during or after meetings and eye contacts as supportive back-channel feedback are uncommon at meetings in Finland and Iceland. Finland and Iceland represent the extreme of this kind of negative politeness, viewing these kinds of rituals as intruding, embarrassing, and ridiculous. At meetings in northern California, however, all these same rituals and forms of back-channel feedback expressing positive politeness are ubiquitous.

Table 11.1 Positive Politeness in AA Meetings in Study Countries

	Finland	Iceland	Poland	Mexico	Austria	Sweden	French-speaking Switzerland	German-speaking Switzerland	California
Eye contact common at meetings	−	−	+	+	+	+	+	+	+
Body contact common before and after meetings	−	−	+	+	+	+	+	+	+
Ritualized response "Hi, x" common	−	−	−	+	+	+	+	+	+
Ritual of holding hands common	−	−	+	−	+	+	+	+	+
Ritual applause common	−	+	−	+	−	−	+	+	+

"The way previous speakers are complimented has started to irritate me. Both in the open and the closed meeting of our group the first speaker is habitually given credits in later speeches, elsewhere this happens very seldom. One should not pay tribute even to the opening speech, the speaker speaks in order to stay sober and there is nothing praiseworthy in that."

Finnish field interview (F, 48, 12)

The amount of ritual elaboration varies from meeting to meeting. Because of considerable intracultural variation, it is problematic to present strong intercultural generalizations. It is our impression, however, that meetings in Mexico, Poland, and California use more ritual elaborations than do the relatively plain meetings in Austria, Finland, Iceland, Sweden, and Switzerland. The degree of ritual elaboration cuts across any preconceived cultural classifications of our study countries.

Another important intercultural variable is the openness and social visibility of AA meetings. In Austria, Finland, Iceland, and Sweden, meetings tend to be small, intimate, and secluded, whereas large meetings are somewhat more common in Mexico and Poland. The main division runs, however, between California and the rest of our study sites. In northern California, almost one-half of AA meetings are open meetings, and large speaker's meetings are quite common. In the rest of the countries, speaker's meetings are exceptional, and relatively small discussion meetings predominate. The difference between California and the rest of the study sites can be seen as an indication that the distance of AA to mainstream culture is shortest in the United States.

The equality of all members is an important tenet in AA, but meeting arrangements may influence how fully this ideal is realized. Audience-type seating is more common in Iceland, Mexico, Poland, and California, whereas in Austria, Finland, Sweden, and Switzerland circular seating arrangements predominate. Circular seating arrangements emphasize the equality of participants. In Finland and Sweden, speaking in seating order also is the most common turn-taking system. In Switzerland, the chair usually picks the next speaker, whereas in the rest of the countries speaking on request is the most prevalent format. In the United States, some traditional groups require that newcomers not speak unless their sponsors are present. Alternatively, newcomers may be instructed not to speak until they have attended a certain number of meetings. These customs are not widespread, but they bring out the difference in status between newcomers and more experienced members.

Conclusion

Despite all variability, an AA meeting is a very particular social formation. It does not require the same predispositions and skills as bureaucratic Western organizations, but it is also dissimilar from traditional forms of spontaneous social organization. It is informal, yet it is more structured than most informal gatherings. Both turn-taking and types of speech acts or turn-types are institutionally restricted. First, AA's system of turn-taking is based on extended turns that exclude discussion in the ordinary sense of the term. Second, turn-types inside the meeting are delimited to self-narratives in a way that restrains direct comments to previous turns of talk. The rules of talk at AA meetings, therefore, differ from most forms of professional group therapy. It is also worth pointing out that the confrontational and interpretative style of 12-step meetings at many professional treatment institutions systematically deviates from traditional AA meetings (see chapter 14).

12
Practicing the AA Program

The goal of this chapter is to draw a picture of the cultural and individual variability in working the AA program. In the first section, we discuss the degree of involvement of members in working the Twelve Steps. We then describe differences in members' beliefs about spirituality. The remaining sections deal with specific program activities: the talking out of alcoholism and telling one's story, sponsorship, and 12th-step work.

Working the Steps

Members show different degrees of involvement in the Twelve Steps as a formal program. Some find it helpful just to attend meetings, without committing themselves to the program in other respects. There are members with years of sobriety who maintain that it suffices to admit one's powerlessness over alcohol (Step One) and to work together with other alcoholics (Step Twelve). In AA parlance, this is known as two-stepping. Official AA literature warns that two-stepping is not enough to guarantee genuine sobriety (*12 + 12*, 1986, p. 112).

In the daily praxis of AA, all Steps do not receive equal attention. At meetings, the decision Steps are discussed much more frequently than the action Steps, and the maintenance Steps receive the least attention (Table 12.1). In addition, the actual discussion is often loosely related to the Step that is supposed to be the topic of the meeting. The distribution of articles published in the Finnish AA journal show a similar imbalance (Table 12.1). In *Twelve Steps and Twelve Traditions*, however, more pages are spent, on average, on the maintenance Steps than on the earlier Steps (*12 + 12*, 1986). In comparison, meetings and journal articles are more oriented to members working on the earlier parts of the program.

Table 12.1   Steps Addressed in AA Meetings in Austria and Finland and in Articles in the Finnish AA Journal

	In meetings in Austria[a]	In meetings in Finland[a]	In articles in the Finnish AA journal[b]
Steps 1–3	49%	48%	49%
Steps 4–9	43%	38%	34%
Steps 10–12	8%	14%	16%
Total	100%	100%	99%
Number of meetings or articles			
addressing specific Steps	35	58	263
Step not specified	2	4	—
Other topics	22	6	—
Total	59	68	263

[a]The data for meetings in Austria and Finland are from ICSAA meeting surveys (Appendix B). If a meeting addressed some other topic in addition to a Step, it was classified as a Step meeting. If a meeting addressed more than one Step, a proportionate fraction was added to the frequency of each Step.

[b]The figures refer to articles having a specific Step as their main topic and published in the Finnish AA journal *Ratkaisu* in the years 1952–1988 (Aaltonen 1990, p. 36).

"There are people in AA who think the Steps should be worked on one each year; but I think that most of the Steps should be worked on simultaneously."
Mexican field interview (M, 45, 16)

Even among those who define themselves as committed to the program, there are widely varying interpretations of what that implies. Opinions differ as to whether the Steps should be worked in order, whether they should be worked through once or repeatedly, how fast they should be worked, and how important the various Steps are. Part of the variability is related to the openness of the basic texts of AA. In addition, the Twelve Steps are learned and worked in conjunction with other AA members. The oral tradition of AA provides a continually changing context for working the Steps. AA members also refer both to working "the" program and working "my" program, it being accepted that "my" program may be different from "yours." A survey of persons working 12-step programs in the United States showed a wide range of responses when people were asked what activities they had carried out in connection to each Step (Brown & Peterson, 1991).

> "I was quite enthusiastic after reading the program and the Twelve Steps. It was beautiful, it was easy. I was sure that I would be able to do everything in a few weeks. My AA friends advised me to be careful and to take it slower. I understood my mistake only after having had a quick relapse."
>
> Polish life-story interview (N, 43, 5)

One dimension concerns the overall importance of formally working the Steps. Many longtime AA members insist that all Twelve Steps must be worked on for continued sobriety. Other members maintain that they did not work all the Steps but concentrated on working a daily program. The main issue here is that some members look at the Steps as a systematic schedule and itinerary, while other members put more emphasis on the program as a collection of tools and techniques. The distinction is not very clear, since the Steps themselves are often seen as tools for accomplishing specific purposes.

Opinions also differ regarding the pace at which the Steps should be taken. In the United States, traditional members are critical of the fact that many people come to AA from alcohol-treatment programs after having rushed through the first five Steps. On the other hand, newcomers are commonly advised not to unnecessarily postpone working on the program Step by Step.

> "It took me eight years before I did Steps Four and Five thoroughly. Many people had told me that I should not postpone things, that AA is a program of action. Now I feel good about having taken my time. Earlier I did not understand Step Five well enough. If I would have tried to take it, it would just have amounted to psychological exhibitionism."
>
> Finnish field interview (M, 51, 12)

> "Some people say that Step Four has not been taken thoroughly if it changes afterward. This is not true, since history changes all the time when you look at it from the present."
>
> Finnish field interview (M, 37, 2)

> "I have not done Step Five in one sitting as some people require. I do it in bits and pieces with several different people."
>
> Finnish field interview (M, 34, 5)

Members eagerly discuss how each Step can best be taken. Unorthodox interpretations receive criticism, and stories are told about people who have harmed themselves or other persons by working some Step imprudently.

> "I have heard speakers relate how they put their name first on their Eighth Step list and how they 'forgave themselves' and that they now 'feel good about themselves.' I can't find any such thing in AA literature."
>
> Harry F., 1993

> "As separate performances, Steps Eight and Nine are alien to Finnish culture. We do not thresh human relationships, and we do not ask for or give absolution in so many words. I cannot bulldoze my parents into an emotional discussion. Change is not expressed in words but in behavior."
>
> Finnish field interview (F, 40, 5)

> "One guy wanted to make amends to a one-night stand he felt he had humiliated many years ago. With a lot of trouble he found her address and visited the home of this happily married couple 'to make his amends.' "
>
> Finnish field interview (M, 48, 8)

The diversity of interpretations provides room for a lot of variation not only among individual members but also among groups. Members learn to know the differences in emphasis between groups, and sometimes the name of the group may provide an indication of its school of thought. In one Finnish town, the "Traditional AA Group" tends to bring together the more fundamentalist members.

> In Mexico, members recognize "schools" of groups. "Bill W." groups often sponsor speakers' meetings with life stories and a lot of humor and laughter. "Dr. Bob" groups emphasize spirituality and organize Big Book study meetings.

When an AA community grows older, an increasing number of people gain a thorough acquaintance with the official literature. This usually means that a systematic approach to the Twelve Steps receives more emphasis, although most members may continue to be eclectic. In the beginning of AA in the Italian-speaking part of Switzerland, only the first three Steps and Step Twelve received attention until exchange with AA members in other parts of the country led to a more orthodox coverage of the full range of Steps. In the German-speaking part of Switzerland, new groups were formed around 1990 explicitly to address the full range of the Steps. These groups were called "Step Groups" to distinguish them from groups perceived not to be working the full program.

"It wasn't until a group of us began a Step meeting, and agreed to use only Conference-approved literature, that I began to see our Twelve Steps as a truly spiritual program."
Harry F., 1993

Variability of Spiritual Beliefs

There are marked regional and cross-national differences in interpretations of spirituality. As an outward sign of this variability, AA meetings close with the Christian Lord's Prayer in many parts of the United States and in some Icelandic groups, whereas this custom is uncommon or non-existent in other study countries (ICSAA meeting surveys; Appendix C), as well as in France (Anonymous, 1989c). Madsen (1980) suggests that within the United States a traditional religious orientation is more typical in the Midwest and the South, while a non-religious approach is more prevalent in California and the urban Northeast. Another indication of the prevailing diversity is that interpretations of spirituality among gay and lesbian AA members vary along several independent dimensions (Bloomfield, 1990).

Data from membership surveys in five of the study countries (Appendix C) illustrate the variation of beliefs about spirituality both within countries and cross-culturally. Only a tiny minority openly acknowledge that the "power greater than ourselves" means nothing to them personally (Table 12.2). Some selection may be involved in the sense that more unorthodox members have been less likely to participate in the survey. Quite obviously, however, most members experience a higher power as personally relevant. The proportion of members interpreting the higher power as referring to the Christian God varies widely from 13 percent in Sweden to 56 percent in Poland; in most countries, Christians form a minority. In all countries, around 60 percent interpret the higher power as referring either to the Christian God or to God but not the Christian God. Alternative interpretations are not seen as mutually exclusive. A substantial number of individual respondents think that the "power greater than ourselves" refers both to God and to the AA fellowship. The same phenomenon is visible at the level of countries. In Poland and Sweden, the same proportion selects the AA fellowship as a higher power, although there is a large difference in the degree of belief in the Christian God.

Some feminists in 12-step groups describe the higher power as "the Goddess within," others as "my higher self."

Haaken, 1993

"God and I have made a deal: I don't have to believe in him but he takes care of things for me, except for making coffee."

Icelandic field interview (M, 43, 2)

"I never could believe in a God as the Higher Power but I know that I am an alcoholic and that I need my fellow AA members."

Mexican field interview (M, 58, 30)

"Sometimes it feels as if I have found a Higher Power, but in the next moment everything is swept away and I am in deep despair. . . . I have met AA members that really have achieved serenity. I envy them, and I am prepared to sacrifice everything to reach the same goal."

Uffe, 1992, p. 30

The number of AA members professing Christianity is related to the strength of Christian belief in the surrounding society. Catholicism is strong in Poland and Mexico, and Sweden is the most secularized of our study societies. Iceland is somewhat of an exception in the sense that a high percentage of AA members believe in the Christian God although they live in a very secular society. The impact of the surrounding society on the frequency of worship attendance is even stronger and more systematic (Table 12.3). About half of AA members in Mexico and Poland but only about one in ten in Iceland and Sweden go to church at least once a month, and the majority of members in Sweden attend worship less than once a year.

Data from the membership surveys can be complemented by mate-

Table 12.2   Meaning among AA Members of "Power Greater than Ourselves" as Mentioned in the Twelve Steps, by Percentage

	Iceland	Mexico	Poland	Sweden	German-speaking Switzerland
It means nothing to me personally	2	2	1	<1	4
It refers to the Christian God	52	40	56	13	30
It refers to God, but not the Christian God	13	16	9	38	30
It refers to the cosmic order	28	11	9	19	27
It refers to the AA fellowship or power of the group	47	34	58	59	37

Source: ICSAA membership surveys (Appendix B)
Question wording:
  What is your understanding of the concept "Power greater than ourselves" as mentioned in the Twelve Steps? (*check all that apply*)
  ( ) It means nothing to me personally
  ( ) It refers to one's inner strengths
  ( ) It refers to some other power than "I"
  ( ) It refers to the Christian God
  ( ) It refers to God, but not the Christian God
  ( ) It refers to the cosmic order
  ( ) It refers to the balance of nature
  ( ) It refers to the AA fellowship or power of the group
  ( ) Other, describe
Note: Percentages do not total 100 because multiple choices were allowed.

rial from interviews with Finnish members who told their life story on tape (Appendix B; Arminen, 1991a). One of the questions asked about the respondent's views of the higher power. The total of 37 responses may be classified in four groups:

God of organized religion (3 responses)
Theistic God but not of an organized religion (15 responses)
Non-theistic spiritual power (13 responses)
Natural power (AA group, internal human force, etc.) (6 responses)

All respondents endorsed some higher power but interpretations were quite varied. Many members had a rather diffuse concept of spiri-

Table 12.3   Percentage of AA Members Attending Worship Services

	Iceland	Mexico	Poland	Sweden	German-speaking Switzerland
At least once a month	13	47	52	7	17
Less than once a year	46	15	9	62	39

Source: ICSAA membership surveys (Appendix B)
Question wording:
   How often do you attend worship services?
      1 Every week or nearly every week
      2 About two to three times a month
      3 About once a month
      4 4–10 times a year
      5 About 1–3 times a year
      6 Less than once a year
      7 Never

tuality, and quite a few explicitly denied the possibility of being specific about the higher power. On the average, longtime members professed more elaborated ideas of spirituality.

"It is God for me, the God of the Lutheran Church."

"I have been able to get rid of my mother's opinion of God, or what they taught in school, a kind of severe God. I use the name God of my Higher Power, but He is a loving, merciful God."

"The Serenity Prayer is all I need, so I learn to accept those things that I can't change and to change those things that I can. The word *God* is difficult for me."

"I consider the AA community and the program to be a Higher Power in the sense that they are clearly smarter things than what I myself could have ever been able to create."

"I look at myself as a humanist. My Higher Power is inside me, something existing inside human beings."

Excerpts from interviews with Finnish life-story tellers

Characteristically, AA members in Finland make a sharp distinction between church doctrines and the spirituality of AA. Only a small minority were committed to a specific religion. The majority preferred to use the term "Higher Power" and avoided the expression "God," and many of those who used it explicitly dissociated themselves from the teachings of the church. Many respondents felt that the religion taught to them at school or at home had stressed the severe, punishing nature of God, whereas their own higher power was loving and merciful. Naturalistic interpretations of the higher power that do not seem to have any supernatural component were also common.

In their early sobriety, many members experience a period of euphoric optimism. In AA terminology this is referred to as sitting on a pink cloud. Most people climb down from their cloud in an orderly manner but a person can also be pulled down from the cloud by a serious personal crisis. The abrupt fall from the pink cloud may cause acute despair, for which an instant solution may be found in religious conversion. According to Finnish members of AA, some of the people who experience such despair join a revivalist congregation and leave AA but stay sober, some return to drinking, and some come back to AA. The point here is that those coming back to AA tend to look at their religious period as a surrogate for genuine spirituality: "Instead of working on myself I wanted to believe that the blood of Jesus washes away all troubles" (Finnish field interview).

Talking about the Private in AA

The AA process of "talking out of alcoholism" (Robinson, 1979) has two aspects, "transforming the unspeakably private into public discourse" and "talking a biography." In this section, the focus is on the first aspect. Telling one's story is discussed in the next section.

If one wants to speak about one's private problems, one has two basic choices. One may seek professional help or one may open up to a peer. The second choice is related to how one defines one's existential problem. One may decide either to reveal one's secrets or to search for one's unknown authentic self. By combining these choices we obtain the fourfold classification depicted in Table 12.4, where each cell contains one example of ways of transforming the unspeakably private into public discourse.

Originally, AA was more about disclosing the secret than about searching for the authentic self: "We are only as sick as our secrets" (Pittman, 1988b, p. 221). The emphasis, therefore, is on honesty rather than on spontaneity or authenticity. It is then another matter if, by disclosing one's secrets, one also learns more about oneself.

Reciprocity is a key feature of AA. Psychotherapy and confession usually are not reciprocal. A borderline case worth mentioning is the

Table 12.4   Ways of Transforming the Unspeakably Private into Public Discourse

	Private brought into speech	
	With a professional	With peers
Disclosing the secret	Confession	AA
Searching for the repressed	Psychoanalysis	Feminist and men's consciousness-raising groups, etc.

technique adopted by Frank Buchman and later widely used in Oxford groups: "I have found a way to draw confessions. It is to confess first myself" (Peterson, 1992, p. 58).

In AA, the principle of reciprocity is taken beyond the meeting and to the revealing of one's innnermost secrets privately to one's sponsor. The Fifth Step advises members to admit the exact nature of their wrongs to God, to themselves, and to another human being. The wording of the Step does not specify with whom it should be taken. Many members of AA recommend, however, that it should be taken with another member and that it should involve reciprocity. In the most painful moments of the process of taking the Fifth Step, the sponsor should assist the sponsee by revealing his own most embarrassing secrets first.

In AA, the boundaries between private and public are clearly gradated, although this is done by concrete examples rather than by abstract norms, as is everything in AA. At least three levels are identified: what one speaks about with one's sponsor, what one can speak about at a closed meeting, and what is acceptable at an open meeting. These gradations are talked about from two perspectives: what should not be spoken of in order to avoid embarrassing others and what should not be spoken of in order to safeguard one's own interests. The oral tradition of AA is full of stories of what happens when these boundaries are not observed.

"Some guys use the meetings to do Step Five on the tribune, but this is no good."

Mexican field interview (F, 41, 14)

The disclosure of sexual experiences is a special cause of contention within the movement. The most tormenting secrets of many members are of a sexual nature, but this is also a field where the step from sincere confessions to explicit boasting is unusually short.

> "When someone is annoyed by the way fellow members share, repeating the same intimate experiences over and over, somebody else often reminds him of the story of the farmer who always told about how he fucked his cow. Some members complained and they relapsed but *he* didn't!"
> Mexican field interview (M, 43, 6)

At AA meetings, the private may be disclosed in tiny pieces over an extended period or in sudden outbursts where the speaker may afterward not know exactly what he or she has been telling. When old boundaries collapse it may be difficult to erect new ones, which in an adequate way take into account the culturally expected variation in intimacy by situation.

Sometimes members make confessions that impose a burden on the listeners to know. Confidential information revealed to other members has no legal protection. In extreme cases, members may have to testify in court about what they have heard in AA meetings.

> "A man with a number of years of sobriety was chosen to have the first turn. Clearly enjoying the situation he unveiled the whole range of his sexual experiences, perhaps for the benefit of the many women present. The speaker had every reason to be pleased with himself, because he made a great impression. Without exception, the subsequent speakers were embarrassed."
> Finnish field interview (M, 36, 8)

Members of AA learn to speak openly to each other and without embarrassment about matters that in our cultures usually are kept hidden from strangers. As one visitor commented, "These young people say things to a roomful of 100 people that I wouldn't say to my parish priest!" (Blau, 1991). Sometimes they find it difficult to remember that the new borders of what is public are not shared by the general culture and may talk about their private lives to strangers or non-AA friends in ways others find annoying or embarrassing. "It always amazes me that people will go on TV and talk about what I would think of as intimate things. There is *no* sense of privacy." (Larimer, 1992) This may be one of the reasons why members of AA sometimes restrict their social life to other members.

In Larchmont, New York, a carpenter in his mid-twenties had been telling his fellow AA members that he thought he had killed a couple in their bedroom during a drunken blackout. The case had remained unsolved for more than four years until the police learned of the carpenter's confession and were able to match fingerprints found in the bedroom with those taken from him. At the trial, six AA members testified that the defendant had confessed to the crimes in private conversations. None of the AA members who testified came forward until they were subpoenaed. As news of the trial spread, members of mutual-help groups flooded the National Self-Help Clearinghouse in New York with calls of protest.

Berger, 1994; J. Hoffman, 1994

Telling One's Story

Telling one's story is a central activity in AA (Arminen, 1991b; Cain, 1991; Denzin, 1987; Humphreys, 1992; Robinson, 1979) and in other 12-step movements (Rappaport, 1993). When people join AA, their life most often is shattered and entangled by secrets and lies. Who am I? Why have I committed all these destructive and immoral acts? How did it happen that I wrecked my life and harmed the people closest to me? By candidly telling about their lives, AA members gradually build up a new identity as sober alcoholics and compose a meaningful autobiography, a coherent interpretation of the course of their lives. The AA story is a cognitive tool and a device for self-understanding (Cain, 1991). As members tell their personal stories, they reinterpret their past as evidence of their alcoholic identity.

Putting together one's autobiography is a key aspect of individual recovery, but storytelling also has important functions for AA as a mutual-aid movement. By listening to the stories, members learn to know each other more quickly and intimately than is common in social life. Recovery stories are often the means through which newcomers identify with and join AA. The stories provide a basis for potential members to identify themselves as alcoholics, enabling them to compare their lives to the lives told in the stories. Identification works in the opposite direction as well. The pain and despair of the newcomer provides a vivid reminder to the more experienced members of what could happen if they were to start drinking again. Later on, descriptions of how longtime members have coped with the crises of sober life offer concrete examples of ways of solving life's problems.

"In the beginning, telling one's story is putting oneself together. Later on, it's dissecting oneself into pieces that help others to identify."
                                        Finnish field interview (F, 48, 12)

"A man I met told me that if I didn't think I belonged, I should hang around and I'd hear my story. Then a few weeks later, this girl got up and as she spoke, it started to dawn on me. I was so engrossed . . . every word she said I could relate to where I had come from. Here was this woman with seven or eight years in the program telling my story."
                    American field interview, A. R. Smith, 1993, p. 696

Data from ICSAA membership surveys (Appendix C) indicate that telling one's story indeed is almost universal in AA. Excepting Sweden, only between 0 and 5 percent of the respondents with at least one year of sobriety said they had never told their story at an AA meeting; in Sweden, the percentage was 14. It is not easy to explain why Sweden stands somewhat apart, but perhaps some of the Swedes in the study understood the question as referring only to a more formal presentation at a speaker's meeting. In any case, however, it should be pointed out that, while telling one's story is a very common AA activity, not everyone does it. In a study of the English AA, 13 percent of the members with more than ten years of sobriety had never told their story (Robinson, 1979, p. 66). For some members, at least, telling their story is not an essential part of staying in AA.

The building of a biography is usually a gradual and sequential process spread over a long series of AA meetings. The details of the personal history will not necessarily be drawn together into a single narrative account. Looked upon as narratives, stories may vary from the incoherent outburst of a newcomer to the highly polished performance of an old-timer on the speaker circuit.

"In the United States, meetings are bigger and open meetings are more common. This supports a circuit of performing stars. They perform, they don't tell their story. In Finland, meetings are smaller and more down to the earth."
                                        Finnish field interview (M, 74, 39)

Most members report that their stories have changed over time (Robinson, 1979, pp. 70–72), and this is supported by comparisons of the same person's story at different stages (Cain, 1991). According to members' reports, their stories have become more honest and have begun to contain less drinking and more recovery as a way of life (Robinson, 1979, pp. 70–72).

"In the beginning, I exaggerated both my drinking and my social successes. I have later on noticed similar things in other people, but in AA that's accepted, nobody wants to edit other people's talk. In due time, the boast and exaggeration gets left out."

Finnish field interview (M, 60, 17)

Sponsorship

The word *sponsor* is not found in the original text of the *Big Book* (1955), but it appears later in *Twelve Steps and Twelve Traditions* (1986, p. 61) and in an AA pamphlet on sponsorship (*Questions and Answers on Sponsorship*, 1983). The designation comes from the early days of AA, when members sponsored newcomers into a hospital for detoxification, vouching that the bill would be paid. The sponsor would visit the person during treatment and upon release take him or her to a meeting.

Sponsors serve as role models for younger members. They are used as a sounding board, to bounce off ideas with, and to turn to for encouragement, discipline, praise, and guidance in working the program. Ultimately, the sponsor often is the person to whom a member turns in telling the most intimate details of his or her story in completing Steps Four and Five. The personal style of individual sponsors varies widely. In some cases sponsorship becomes intense, and the sponsor may spend hours and nights with his sponsee struggling with the problems of early sobriety or later crises.

There are large differences between countries in how commonly AA members have sponsors (Table 12.5). In Poland, the sudden increase in membership makes it difficult to find experienced sponsors. In Sweden, the central role of 12-step treatment institutions is likely to have weakened the institution of sponsorship. There are, however, differences in sponsorship even between countries with a well established traditional AA. Having a sponsor is more common in California and Mexico than in Iceland and Switzerland. A widespread ideal norm, par-

Table 12.5   Percentage of AA Members Experiencing Sponsorship

	Iceland	Mexico	Poland	Sweden	German-speaking Switzerland	California
	All members					
Has a sponsor now	57	78	25	35	31	72
Has ever had a sponsor	62	84	27	47	49	87
	All members with at least one year of sobriety					
Has a sponsor now	61	83	26	43	35	74
Has ever had a sponsor	69	90	39	57	63	92

Source: ICSAA membership surveys (Appendix B)
Question wordings:
  Have you ever had a sponsor?
    1   No
    2   Yes
  Do you now have an AA sponsor or sponsors?
    1   No
    2   Yes

ticularly in the United States, requires that every member, including oldtimers, should have a formal sponsor. As shown in Table 12.5, however, in many countries the majority of members do not have a sponsor. Even in California, a substantial minority report that they presently have no sponsor.

Sometimes people select a sponsor for their Fifth Step only. Some members who have done a Fifth Step in a 12-step treatment center do not feel the need for a sponsor later on. Others are reluctant to enter into formal sponsorship, although they may gradually build close personal relationships with one or a few experienced members. This may be related to cultural traditions. In the Finnish life-story material (Appendix B; Arminen, 1992), nearly a half of the interviewees did not like to use the term "sponsor." They preferred to speak about "a close AA friend" or a "support person." Some of the male respondents saw themselves as unsuitable to become sponsored because of their independence or "egoism" and "pride." Some explicitly felt that formal sponsorship was an indication of how AA in the United States tends to be overly rigid and systematic.

Although in some countries the majority and in all countries a considerable minority of the membership do not have a sponsor, sponsorship is highly important for AA networks. While a sponsor may be compared with a parent or a psychoanalyst, the relationship is different in that, ideally, a sponsor should be as self-revealing as they expect their sponsees to be about themselves. Sponsorship is a bond based on detailed sharing of the most embarrassing and regretted parts of the lives of both persons. This ideal of reciprocity distinguishes AA sponsorship from most mentor relationships.

12th-Step Work

AA members regard recruiting new members as an integral part of the mutual-help process of AA. "To keep it, you have to give it away" (Pittman, 1988b, p. 223). In AA parlance, membership recruitment is known as "carrying our message to the next suffering alcoholic" (*12 + 12*, 1986, p. 109) or doing 12th-step work. The content of the concept is somewhat fluid. Bringing a newcomer to a meeting or just talking about AA to individual drinking alcoholics is certainly regarded as 12th-step work. Talking at information meetings or at meetings held in prisons or treatment institutions also qualifies. The main text discussing Step Twelve includes meeting attendance under 12th-step work (*12 + 12*, 1986, p. 110), but most members would probably classify only more outward-oriented activities as 12th-step work.

Table 12.6 presents data on 12th-step activities. Because of the diffuse meaning of 12th-step work, the figures cannot be meaningfully compared with whatever data are available on proselytizing activities of members in other organizations. Nevertheless, they show that in most countries a majority of AA members have been engaged in what they interpret as carrying the message. The more concrete question on bringing a newcomer to an AA meeting also shows a high level of engagement. Depending on the country, between 30 and 60 percent of the membership reports that they have brought a newcomer to an AA meeting in the past twelve months.

Commitment and Diversity

As shown in this chapter, many AA members are deeply committed to the program and experience fundamental shifts in their worldview. Corresponding to what we would expect to find in any organization, however, there is a great diversity of program practices, and varying degrees of commitment. Members show varying involvement in the Twelve Steps as a formal program, and interpretations of spirituality differ widely. There are longtime members who have never told their story, and in many countries the majority of members do not have a

Table 12.6 Percentage of AA Members Performing 12th-Step Work

	Iceland	Mexico	Poland	Sweden	German-speaking Switzerland	California
	All members					
12th-stepped a newcomer in past 12 months	50	71	64	48	56	76
Brought a newcomer to an AA meeting in past 12 months	40	58	40	32	39	44
	All members with at least one year of sobriety					
12th-stepped a newcomer in past 12 months	62	66	79	65	76	88
Brought a newcomer to an AA meeting in past 12 months	44	59	60	43	48	45

Source: ICSAA membership surveys (Appendix B)
Question wording:
How recently did you engage in the following AA activities?
— 12th-stepped a newcomer
1 In past 4 weeks
2 In past 12 months
3 Earlier
4 Never
— Brought a newcomer to an AA meeting
1 In past 4 weeks
2 In past 12 months
3 Earlier
4 Never

sponsor. Hence, we should guard ourselves against stereotypic descriptions of AA as a strict treatment regime or as a monolithic community in which members are immersed. It is in many cases more accurate to say that members use and apply AA rather than convert to AA.

13
Men, Women, and AA

Gender, AA, and Al-Anon

From its early days, AA emphasized the unifying existential condition of being an alcoholic. The fact remains, however, that the two founders were men, that most of the AA literature is written by men, and that men in all countries have constituted and still constitute the majority of members. The founding fathers of AA also adhered to rather traditional family values and to conservative gender roles. Dr. Bob, for example, was not happy about letting women into AA (N. Robertson, 1988, p. 37).

AA had its first continuing female member, Marty Mann, as early as 1937, two years after AA's inception. However, more often than not women stayed "in the woman's place." Non-alcoholic wives of recovering men remained at the side of their husbands. In the beginning the wives even attended AA meetings, but when AA developed into a movement for alcoholics only, they were left aside and later formed Al-Anon Family Groups.

In the eyes of the early members, women had more of a social stigma (e.g., as a whore) and a less independent social identity (e.g., as a wife rather than an individual) than men when joining the fellowship. In both colloquial and structural terms, the female AA member was "the other woman." In the 1940s in the United States (Vourakis, 1989) and in the 1950s in Finland (Rosenqvist, 1992b), wives attempted to start women-only groups. This can be interpreted as support for alcoholic women, but also as a means of protecting wives' relationships with their husbands.

Despite the initial ambivalence, AA now shows an active interest in recruiting women into the fellowship. Among our study countries, Finland, Mexico, and the United States have had national working parties on women's issues, and from 1967 to 1972 the Finnish General

Service Board upheld quotas for female members (Rosenqvist, 1991). The interests of women were also repeatedly mentioned in the minutes of the Board (Suomen AA-palvelun ja toimikuntien suosituksia 1961–1986, 1986).

AA, Al-Anon, and later Alateen developed around modern nuclear family roles, AA being primarily for the father, Al-Anon for the mother, and Alateen for the child. Gender polarization was thus a reality: women were in Al-Anon and men in AA. Even today, relationships between AA women and Al-Anon women are sometimes strained (Rosovsky, Guadalupe, Gutierrez, & Casanova, 1992, p. 603).

"There are female AA members who refuse to participate in open meetings because Al-Anon women may come there."
Finnish field interview (F, 42, 3)

"Al-Anon women envy us for the way we develop as human beings in AA."
Finnish field interview (F, 49, 7)

As a parallel to the greater influx of women into AA, Al-Anon appears to be changing both in terms of its membership and its program (J. E. Martin, 1992; Rosenqvist, 1992b). Rather than helping women adjust to their husband's alcoholism and recovery, the traditional Al-Anon aim, it now emphasizes the 12-step program in the interest of its own members. The shift is most evident in the United States, where 13 percent of the present membership is male (Wolf/Altschul/Callahan, Inc., 1990). In Switzerland as well, there are men in Al-Anon, but in the remaining study countries, male Al-Anon members are rare, and Al-Anon continues to function as the "women's section" of AA.

"I had done the Fourth and Fifth Step with my male sponsor. Then his wife became jealous, which was natural. After all, in these activities the sponsor serves as a platform for takeoff, there is spiritual, holy transfer, but from the outside it may look different. I did not notice anything, but others did, and older more experienced members said that this could not go on. So I got another sponsor."
Finnish field interview (F, 42, 3)

In Mexico, many aspects of Al-Anon and AA can be seen as reflections of the prevailing family system (Rosovsky, Guadalupe, Gutierrez, & Casanova, 1992). For example, Al-Anon meetings are held in the daytime, which assumes that Al-Anon wives do not work outside the home or that they cannot go out alone after dark. In contrast, most AA meetings are held after working hours. Family ties also seem to be fairly close between Polish AA and Al-Anon. Half of the AA groups collaborate directly with an Al-Anon group. While Al-Anon as the women's section was swiftly established in the Polish movement, it remains rather weak in Sweden, a society with less traditional family patterns. The interrelations of AA and Al-Anon continue to indicate a context of family structures.

Female Drinking, Recruitment to Treatment, and Recruitment to AA

As noted in chapter 9, there are big differences in the percentage of women in AA among our study countries. The percentages range from 10 percent in Mexico to 44 percent in Austria and up to 50 percent in Switzerland. In this section, the rate of female participation will be discussed from two perspectives. First, we will discuss factors that may explain cross-cultural variation. Second, we will compare the proportion of women in AA to their proportion among heavy drinkers in the general population and in clinical populations.

One might expect that the increasing equality between sexes would tend to increase the number of women in AA. Our study countries can be arranged in three groups according to the relative position of women in the five social areas of education, employment, social equality, health, and marriage and children (Population Crisis Committee, 1988). The standing of women relative to men is highest in the Nordic countries and in the United States, and lowest in Mexico, with the Central European countries (Austria, Poland, Switzerland) falling in between. The proportion of women in AA is lowest in Mexico, but otherwise the correspondence is far from perfect. Despite the strong social position of women in the Scandinavian countries, there are fewer women in AA than in Austria and Switzerland.

The proportion of female members in AA should be put in relation to the number of female heavy drinkers in each country. Much attention has been paid to the presumed or actual increase in alcohol consumption by women after the Second World War. Still, in all countries women drink less often, drink smaller quantities, and are less often drunk than men. The differences in men's and women's drinking appear to persist irrespective of the prevailing levels and patterns of drinking. In Finland, for instance, women consumed one-fifth of all alcohol drunk in 1984 (Ahlström, 1987). In Austria in the latter half of 1970, Austrian women drank about one-third of the amount men drank. Judging from trends in alcohol-related consequences, the situation did not change much in the 1980s (Eisenbach-Stangl, 1986). In Switzerland as well, women drink considerably less, and less often than men (Fahrenkrug & Müller, 1989). The unequal distribution of alcohol consumption between the sexes implies that female heavy drinkers certainly constitute a minority among those eligible for AA.

Women's drinking is more stigmatized than men's, and attitudes more strongly oppose alcohol use and intoxication among women than among men (Eisenbach-Stangl, 1986; Schmidt, Klee, & Ames, 1990). It has also been shown that women are less often than men referred to alcohol treatment through social control channels such as physicians, employers, or judicial authorities (Duckert, 1989), and that the informal network may prevent a woman with alcohol problems from seeking help (Thom, 1986). On the basis of these and similar findings, it has often been assumed that women are underrepresented among populations seeking treatment (Weisner & Schmidt, 1992). Contrary to this expectation, the share of women in treatment populations is higher than their share of heavy drinkers or alcoholics in the general population in most countries for which data are available (Table 13.1). For the United States, the conclusion depends on which criteria for problem drinking we apply. The percentage of women of persons in treatment is lower than the percentage of women of those in the general population meeting the criteria for alcohol dependence *or* alcohol abuse, but much higher than the percentage of women of those meeting the criteria for both alcohol dependence *and* alcohol abuse.

A number of factors may contribute to the fact that so many women seek help for their alcohol problems. Several studies indicate that women in general seek help for health and other problems more readily than men (Duckert, 1989; Schmidt, Klee, & Ames, 1990; Thom, 1986). There also are indications that health problems in women appear sooner after the onset of heavy drinking, and that women are more sensitive to different signs of ill-health (Dawson, 1994; Klee, Schmidt, & Ames, 1991). In general, there seem to be differences between males and females in how they find their way to treatment. Problems in the workplace are often the main signal pushing men to treatment, while for women family-related issues are often the most salient ones. The gendered system of social responsibilities is visible in data on alcohol problems experienced by Swedish AA members before they

Table 13.1 Percentage of Women of Heavy or Problem Drinkers in the General Population, of Clients in Professional Alcohol Treatment, and of AA Members in Study Countries

	Finland	Iceland	Mexico	Poland	Sweden	German-speaking Switzerland	United States
Heavy or problem drinkers in the general population[a]	10	11	5	8	17	20	26 13
Clients in professional alcohol treatment[b]	20	25	N.A.[c]	9	18	28	21
AA members[d]	24	29	10	19	30	40	35

[a]Sources are as follows. Finland: Simpura, 1987 (heavy alcohol consumers, 1984); Iceland: Helgason, 1984, calculated from Table V (positive on a summary index of alcohol abuse, combined data from 1974 and 1979); Mexico: de la Fuente, 1992, Table 1 (frequent heavy drinkers, 1988); Poland: unpublished survey data collected by Janusz Sierosławski (heavy alcohol consumers, 1993); Sweden: Österling et al., 1993 (Mm-MAST positive in a birth-year cohort in Malmö, 1983); German-speaking Switzerland: SFA, 1993, Figure 4 (heavy alcohol consumers [men: at least 48 grams alcohol daily; women: at least 36 grams daily], 1992); United States: Grant 1992, Table 2 (upper figure: respondents meeting DSM IV criteria for alcohol dependence or alcohol abuse, 1988; lower figure: respondents meeting DSM IV criteria for alcohol dependence and alcohol abuse, 1988).

[b]Sources areas follows. Finland: Lehto, 1991, Table 1 (alcohol clients in outpatient health facilities, 1987); Iceland: Helgason, 1984, calculated from Table V (first admissions to inpatient alcohol and drug treatment, 1976–1980); Poland: Woronowicz & Zieliński, 1992 (clients in alcoholism treatment, 1980s); Sweden: Löfstedt, 1991 (clients in inpatient alcohol or drug treatment, 1990); German-speaking Switzerland: SAKRAM, 1991 (clients in alcoholism treatment, 1990); United States: unpublished data from the National Drug and Alcohol Treatment Unit Survey, U.S. Department of Health & Human Services, Rockville, Maryland (clients in alcohol treatment facilities, 1992).

[c]N.A. = Not available

[d]Sources are as follows. Finland: ICSAA group survey (1989); Iceland: ICSAA group survey (1989); Mexico: ICSAA group survey (1989); Poland: ICSAA group survey (1989); Sweden: ICSAA group survey (1989); German-speaking Switzerland: ICSAA group survey (1991); United States: Anonymous, 1990 (AA's own membership survey 1989); see Appendix B.

come to AA. Financial problems and job losses ranked higher among men than women. Women more frequently mentioned separation as an alcohol-related problem (Kühlhorn, Helmersson, & Kurube, 1991). In stories written by Finnish AA members, treatment agencies are often mentioned by women as being a part of their past experiences, whereas men emphasize the role of control agencies such as prisons and the police on their way to AA (Aaltonen & Mäkelä, 1994).

The original literature of AA has a rather patriarchal flavor, and many AA groups still seem to be based on very traditional sex roles. It is a strong indication of the flexibility of the AA program that, in all countries for which data are available, AA meetings attract an over-representation of women as compared to professional treatment systems (Table 13.1).

A number of factors have been proposed as explanations for the fact that there are more women in AA than in professional treatment (Beckman, 1993). AA is free and may attract women with limited economic resources. It may be easier for women to undergo the cognitive shift in attitudes and values necessary for the AA member since their values and beliefs may at the outset be closer to the AA philosophy. Women are generally more willing than men to disclose emotions and intimate topics and in this way are better prepared for the rules of AA discourse. It is worth noting that 12-step movements arising in the wake of AA have been strongest in areas of female concerns: fatness and eating disorders, love and relationship upheavals, and family problems.

Men and Women in AA Service

In society at large, women are subordinated to men, and the division of labor is gendered: nowhere do women enjoy equal status with men, and some tasks belong to women and others to men. On the other hand, AA emphasizes that all members are equal in their alcoholism and that no alcoholic is worth more than another. Within AA, it is also argued that all service tasks are as important both for the group and for individual recovery. Serving coffee or chairing a meeting are said to be equally valuable. Despite any ideological declarations, however, it would not be surprising if the division of service tasks would be influenced by external views on what a woman should do and what a man should do.

ICSAA group surveys (Appendix C) contain data on the sex of each officer (Ólafsdóttir, 1992). The small number of cases renders the analysis inconclusive, but there are surprisingly few traces of a gendered division of service tasks. In some countries, individual tasks are indeed unevenly divided between the sexes, but in many cases the direction goes against traditional role expectations. In Austria, women are underrepresented as chairpersons and treasurers, but in Iceland women are more often than men entrusted with money. The cleaning-up chores seem to be done mostly by men in Sweden and Poland, but in Finland women are slightly overrepresented in the cleaning and coffee-making area. In most countries, women were not underrepresented as chairpersons, treasurers, and secretaries, although in most organizations these are predominantly male tasks. On the whole, women were also not systematically overrepresented in cleaning and coffee-making, which are traditionally considered to be female tasks. Although our overall impression is that gender relations in AA are fairly traditional, our survey suggests that, at least in the division of service tasks at the group level, AA is an equal-opportunity movement.

This is not the case with positions in the higher echelons of the AA structure (Rosenqvist, 1992a). These are firmly in the hands of men. Sweden and Switzerland are the only countries in which women are not markedly underrepresented as members of the national service board compared to their share of the total membership. In Iceland, women were not at all represented in the service board during five of twelve years between 1979 and 1991. In Finland, the first female chairman of the general service board was elected in 1969 and the third in 1989. On the whole, however, women have been clearly underrepresented in the general service board. In addition, women in the Finnish AA have been almost totally excluded from AA Publishing, which is the main center of economic decision-making in the Finnish fellowship. Women accounted for only 4 out of 180 membership years on the AA Publishing board during the period from 1960 to 1989. Moreover, in the programs of annual meetings or information meetings, which are meant for larger audiences, women are seldom speakers or chairpersons. Finnish AA women also do not contribute as much as could be expected from their numbers to discussions in the national AA magazine on Steps and Traditions or on matters concerning the structure of AA (Aaltonen & Mäkelä, 1994).

Gender Separation and Women-Only Groups

Although the proportion of women is growing, they still are a minority in AA. According to our group survey, Austria and Switzerland are the only countries where groups commonly have a relatively equal representation of men and women. Groups in Finland, Iceland, Poland, and Sweden quite often have no or only one or two female members. About half of the Mexican groups have only male members. As a consequence, women's issues are seldom discussed at general meetings, and female members may feel unable to compete with men for the floor. Women may also feel uncomfortable about being "hit on" by men for dates and sexual favors, and competition between women for the attention of men may be a distracting factor. One solution to these problems is to establish women's groups.

Special topics discussed at women's meetings include emotional relationships, menstruation, menopause, abortion, incest, sexual discontent, and the neglect of one's children. In addition to sexuality and motherhood, dependence emerges as a common theme in women's groups. For women, the issue of dependence connects with female roles in general. Many think that women's meetings are needed during the early phase of the AA experience, when the first steps toward independence are taken.

"There are things men do not understand in women's lives: problems with periods, menopause, and so on . . . get wrongly interpreted as signs of alcoholism."

Finnish field interview (F, 41, 12)

"I found it difficult to be honest about my sexual experiences in front of men, but the most embarrassing thing was to talk about how I had neglected my children. Polish culture has little understanding of women failing their duties as mothers. It can only be discussed in a group of women having similar experiences."

Polish field interview (F, 48, 6)

There are women-only meetings in all study countries, but only in the United States do they have any quantitative significance. The popularity of same-sex groups in the United States is not explained simply by the number of women in the American AA. AA groups in Austria and Switzerland have a high proportion of female members but no women's groups.

The need for women's meetings may depend on the prevailing format of mixed meetings. Women may feel safer and more anonymous at the closed meetings that predominate in the Scandinavian countries, Austria, and Poland. In meetings where speaking in seating order is the rule, as in Finland and Sweden, women also do not have to compete for speaking turns. In Europe, large speaker's meetings are uncommon. In the United States, many meetings are speaker's meetings, and discontent with consistently having male speakers has been a stimulus for women's meetings (Vourakis, 1989).

"They [women-only meetings] seemed to talk about feelings more openly. In the women's meetings all of a sudden I felt I was doing more growing. It was new to me to discover that I could have friendships with women. I was saying things I never said in the mixed meetings. . . . Now I can go into a meeting where there are men—I really don't feel the same way I used to, and I can talk about what I came to talk about without hoping they'll like me."

American field interview (F, more than
6 years), in Vourakis, 1989, p. 172

More importantly, countries vary in how they define women's issues. The most important dimension can be described as "equality versus difference." The struggle for equality focuses on a demand that women be treated in the same way as men. An emphasis on difference requires that characteristically female features should not be erased but recognized and valued. In the United States from the 1960s onward, there has been a shift in emphasis from equality to difference, but this shift is less evident in Scandinavia (Bock, 1991). In Sweden, for instance, gender equality has been interpreted as "sameness" rather than as striving for the recognition of difference (Hoem & Hoem, 1988). Feminism was fairly strong in the United States in the 1960s and 1970s. The mushrooming of women-only groups in the United States can be seen as one facet of the American strain of feminism. Depending on how we phrase it, we could say either that Scandinavian women have become sober on male terms or that they have not felt a need to separate themselves from men. In Scandinavia, there is some opposition to women's groups among women as well as among men.

Gender Identity in AA

In AA, alcoholism is not a condition one has. Alcoholism is something that one *is*, and being or becoming an alcoholic is part of one's identity. The existential commonality of being an alcoholic is emphasized, over one's identity as man or woman. At the same time, many AA members, both men and women, appear to take for granted that men and women are different and that they do not understand each other in many areas. Thus, AA can be seen as the prototype of a fellowship where the two genders are seen as "two different kinds of people attempting to discover each other through having common experiences" (Haavind, 1984, pp. 139–140).

"Now I think of myself as an alcoholic first and a woman second. I had to haul down the feminist flag. And curiously enough, by doing that, I have arrived at the place where I have always wanted to be anyway. In the twelve years that I have been sober, I've made some good friends in the Fellowship—and many of them are men."

Joyce H., 1975, p. 37

"I am a woman with almost six months sobriety and am having a terrible time dealing with the blatant sexism of the *Big Book*. It is just not written to me! . . . I don't really feel 'the Fellowship' as everyone else seems to, and in my isolation I find that even the *Big Book* somehow looks right past me, because I am a woman."

M.E., 1990, p. 39

Comparisons of male and female life stories illustrate gender differences in the AA process. There are important differences in the time structure of female and male stories both in the articles published in the AA Finnish journal (Aaltonen & Mäkelä, 1994) and in the taped stories collected for the life-story project (Appendix B; Arminen, 1991b; Swiatkiewicz, 1992a). Women and men pay as much attention to the time when they were drinking, but women discuss in more detail their time spent in AA, whereas men talk more about their childhood and the time before they started to drink. The temporal focus in female stories is closer to AA ideals. In AA, members are advised not to spend too much time trying to explain their former behavior. It is also felt that it is important to discuss one's experiences with working the AA program as a support to newer members on their way to a sober life.

Women pay more attention than men to their relationships with other people (Aaltonen & Mäkelä, 1994; Swiatkiewicz, 1992a). Children and spouse are seen as an integral part of one's personal life and drinking problems. Women also tend to discuss their work as a social network, whereas men generally just mention it as a place of work.

Women's emphasis on social relationships is also visible in that they make more frequent comments than do men about their sponsor, AA friends, and their home group.

As a general tendency, women more frequently use phrases and expressions related to AA and the AA program. Consequently, women keep their stories more strictly in the program line, though in this area gender differences are not dramatic. There also are differences in the use of spiritual terminology. Speaking about God can be seen as an expression of traditional religiousness, while the use of the term Higher Power emphasizes individualized AA spirituality. This term is used with equal frequency by both sexes, but women more commonly use the word God. Women in AA seem to be more traditionally religious (Aaltonen & Mäkelä, 1994).

According to a phrase often repeated in AA meetings, alcoholism is an emotional illness (cf. Denzin, 1987, pp. 72–73). Learning to speak about one's emotions is an important part of the AA program. Male stories express more emotions than would normally be expected of Finnish men, but the incidence of terms referring to emotions is still higher in female stories. In particular, women more frequently than men dare to express positive emotions. The difference is particularly striking for such a global term as "happiness," which seems to be too big to be written down by Finnish males. There also are interesting differences in the register of negative emotions. Men vacillate between pride and defiance, and feelings of inferiority and seeking acceptance. Women waver between selfishness and self-pity, and shame and guilt. The crucial dimension for men seems to be related to personal competence and achievement, whereas the negative emotions of women rotate around their social worth. In AA stories, the ego of the drinking man is threatened by feelings of inferiority and the ego of the drinking woman by shame and guilt (Aaltonen & Mäkelä, 1994).

In some AA activities, gender differences are given special saliency. Since sponsorship touches upon the most intimate, often sexual, aspects of a member's life, AA advises that only men sponsor men and women sponsor women. In practice, women sometimes have difficulties in finding an AA sponsor of the same sex. Therefore, women often have older men or Al-Anon women as sponsors. In contrast, Al-Anon men as sponsors of AA members are unheard of.

In the Finnish life-story material (Appendix B), men and women put the sponsorship relationship to different uses. Women kept more frequent contact with their sponsor and spent a lot of time talking about their daily joys and sorrows. To men, the relationship with the sponsor was more clearly separated from daily life and reserved for a thorough mulling over of one's innermost personal problems, often of a sexual nature.

"My period was approaching, and I had always started drinking then. My sponsor thought I should see a woman, they were really afraid I would fall off the wagon. They took me home to one of the members to meet his wife, and that really helped."

Finnish field interview (F, 51, 12)

"Personally I have always relied on men, as I did on my grandpa during childhood. For instance the other night, when I just felt bad, I phoned around. Finally I got hold of an elder statesman's young wife, chatted cheerfully with her, and then when I, at last, got to talk to him—I immediately started crying."

Finnish field interview (F, 51, 12)

Self-Restraint or Self-Confidence?

Bill W. used the terms "peace of mind," "serenity," and "self-restraint" as synonyms for "temperance," to stand for what sobriety was about (see chapter 10). These terms were very far from what Californian women's groups aimed at in the 1980s. A distinction was commonly made between alcohol work and personal growth work, and women's groups were seen as more supportive of serious personal growth work than mixed groups (Vourakis, 1989, p. 157). Personal growth work aims at self-discovery, self-development, and self-realization, rather than at humility and at the recognition of the limits of human existence, the original tenor of the AA program (Eisenbach-Stangl, 1991c). Women for Sobriety (WFS), a women-only mutual-help movement, also sees combatting shame and guilt as a key task in female recovery from alcoholism (Kaskutas, 1992b). Rebuilding confidence and self-esteem is what WFS sees as the most important aspect of recovery work (Kaskutas, in press). But rebuilding confidence and self-esteem may already be taking place within AA. This view is supported by the fact that many women go to both AA and WFS (Kaskutas, 1989b).

Women for Sobriety seems to attract women in very high social positions. The movement specifically addresses women's psychological and social needs, but it attracts women that can be assumed to be wealthier, stronger, and more independent than those attracted to the male-dominated movement. This seeming paradox is a reflection of the general rule that, in any disfavored social group, the strongest members of that group are the ones that start the struggle for emancipation.

Bill W. felt that recovering alcoholics must combat two master moods, depression and pride or grandiosity; however, the bulk of his writings dealt with the latter, the more male of the two moods. As noted in chapter 10, in more recent literature inspired by the AA program there has been a shift toward viewing aspects of pride (self-respect, self-confidence) as potentially virtuous. The emphasis in the AA canon on pride as the cardinal vice, on "admitting we were powerless," and on turning one's will and one's life over to a higher power as primary steps in recovery, run very much against the grain of modern feminist thinking, which aims at inculcating pride in and empowering women. Given general differences in the societal position and in characteristic mental problems of the genders, the advent of large numbers of women to AA is likely to have tilted the emphasis more on besetting moods such as depression and away from pride.

Gender and AA

In the same way as AA has adapted to various cultural traditions of interaction, it has been able to attract significant numbers of females. The alcoholic experience is different for men and women, and their way of communicating these experiences differs. With its individualistic emphasis, AA entails different learning tasks for men and women. Men in AA learn to share personal problems with others. Women more often come to AA with a relational orientation and have to learn to look at their problems as individual problems and at themselves as individuals. It is an important sign of the general flexibility of the AA program that more women attend AA meetings than go to professional alcohol treatment.

"In AA, you meet the new man."
                    Austrian field interview (F, 46, 3)

Part Five
AA and the Outside World

14
AA and the Professional Treatment System

In discussing the complex interplay between AA and the professional treatment system, it is important to distinguish between traditional alcohol treatment and professional treatment directly based on or inspired by the Twelve Steps.

From its earliest years, AA has used the services of, worked with, and been used by, social and health agencies, but the interconnections between AA and the welfare state vary from one country to another (Stenius, 1994). Under some circumstances, mutual-help fills in for professional treatment. In countries where professional treatment services are scarce or expensive, mutual-help may be the only available cheap alternative. In Mexico, AA can be seen as the poor or middle-class man's treatment, whereas the rich have many options. With contracting welfare resources, low cost may also be the key factor behind attempts of the state apparatus to promote mutual-help movements. The goal of cutting prison and welfare costs may be the most important explanation for the expansion of referrals to AA by courts and Employee Assistance Programs in the United States. In other situations, the AA movement may stimulate the growth of professional treatment systems. In the United States, individual members of AA joined forces with scholars and clinicians to form the "alcoholism movement" and to promote the disease concept of alcoholism in order to provide medical treatment for alcoholism (Room, 1983).

It should be pointed out that alcohol-specific treatment services have expanded in most developed societies irrespective of the strength of AA or the diffusion of the disease concept (Mäkelä et al., 1981, pp. 63–65). Alcohol-specific treatment grew slowly in the first decades after the Second World War, but in the 1970s a radical expansion took place in most western European countries and in the United States. With the expansion came growing specialization and professionalization, especially within medicine, where alcohol treatment became an increasingly legitimate specialty (Mossé, 1992). The expansion of special health services for alcohol problems coincided with a general wave of investment in public health and social security in most industrial countries, and direct impact from AA was in no way a necessary prerequisite (Rosenqvist & Kurube, 1992). AA is strong in Latin American countries that have few professional services available, but it is also strong in Anglo-Saxon and Scandinavian welfare societies. Internationally, it is difficult to detect any correlation between the growth of AA and the strength of the professional treatment system.

Isolation, Autonomy, or Hegemony

The present relationships of AA to professional treatment vary considerably from one country to another (Eisenbach-Stangl, 1992c). In some countries the distance between AA and professional treatment is large. There alcoholism treatment is dominated by professionals who take pride in their technical training and skills and are suspicious of lay activities. Austria comes close to this pure type of *isolation* of AA.

In other countries, the treatment system is based on a mixture of professional skills and everyday wisdom. There may be some rivalries between AA and treatment professionals, but AA has an easy access to most treatment institutions. Few treatment professionals are, however, recovering alcoholics, and the 12-step program of AA is not an integral part of professional treatment regimes. Finland offers a good example of this type of AA *autonomy*.

In still other countries, all kinds of interconnections between professional treatment and AA exist, and the Twelve Steps have been adopted as an important component of professional treatment programs. The United States is the clearest representative of this type of *hegemony* of AA.

Table 14.1 presents a summary of the relationships between AA and the professional apparatus in the study countries along two dimensions. The first dimension has to do with the relationships between AA and the traditional machinery for handling alcohol problems. The second dimension describes the impact of the 12-step program on the professional treatment system itself. The order of the countries is not the same in these two dimensions. In the first dimension, the order is determined by the life span and strength of AA in each country. In the second dimension, the order is modified by the independent impact of the spread of institutional 12-step treatment in Iceland, Sweden, and the French-speaking part of Switzerland. The first dimension represents the consolidation of traditional AA, while the second dimension traces stages in a process of translating AA ideology into a product for professional markets.

AA has good contacts with the treatment system in all countries where there are many groups per inhabitant, irrespective of the size of the treatment system. This may not come as a surprise, but it shows that AA is not generally an antagonistic alternative to treatment. At the same time, there are several alternative trajectories for AA in its relations to professional treatment. AA may continue to lead a rather secluded life, with little contact with the treatment system, and with a slow growth. It may develop as a respected alternative for subpopulations of heavy drinkers. Or it may be regarded as the ideological basis for an integrated part of the treatment system, with an ensuing rapid growth of the movement.

AA and the Public View of Alcohol Problems

AA does not engage in political activity or controversy, and does not seek to change the societies in which it functions. Its attention and energies are directed inward, at individual recovery and mutual help. Nevertheless, AA members, particularly in the United States, have played an important role in forming or reforming the societal response to alcohol problems.

In the main, these impacts have been mediated through organizational forms other than AA. As an organization, AA has remained faithful to its traditions of non-involvement in external matters. But individual AA members have frequently been involved in political action, public relations, and other promotional efforts. When these actions and efforts have related to alcohol issues, and when they have involved groups of AA members acting in concert, the restrictions maintained by the traditions have sometimes worn thin.

The prototype of social action stimulated by the existence of AA and relying on AA members but without involvement of AA as an organization was the formation of the U.S. National Committee for Education on Alcoholism in 1943. The Committee soon became the National Council on Alcoholism (NCA), and is now the National Council on Alcoholism and Drug Dependence. The final form of AA's anonymity traditions were worked out in part in the course of internal disputes in AA concerning the early publicity about the NCA, which had included identified AA members on NCA's letterhead (Kurtz, 1991).

As the NCA precedent established, members of AA are free to engage publicly in political or social activities, as long as they do not mention their AA membership in connection with those activities.

Table 14.1 Relationship of AA to Professional Treatment Systems in Study Countries, and Role of Institutional 12-Step Treatment, 1990

Relationship of AA to traditional machinery for handling alcohol problems	Austria	Sweden	Poland	Finland	German-speaking Switzerland	French-speaking Switzerland	Iceland	Mexico	United States
AA allowed to organize meetings at treatment institutions*	+	+	+	+	+	+	+	+	+
AA actively organizes meetings at treatment institutions*	+	+	+	+	+	+	+	+	+
AA allowed to organize meetings in prisons*	–	+	+	+	+	+	+	+	+
AA actively organizes meetings in prisons*	–	–	+	+	+	+	+	+	+
Professionals frequently refer patients to AA	–	–	–	–	+	+	+	+	+
Private professional referral important pathway to AA	–	–	–	–	–	–	–	+	+
Mandatory referral to AA exists	–	–	–	–	–	–	–	–	+

Role of institutional 12-step treatment	Austria	Poland	German-speaking Switzerland	Finland	Mexico	French-speaking Switzerland	Sweden	Iceland	United States
Institutional 12-step treatment exists	–	–	–	+	+	+	+	+	+
Institutional 12-step treatment important pathway to AA	–	–	–	–	–	+	+	+	+
12-step treatment important or dominant part of institutional treatment	–	–	–	–	–	–	–	+	+
AA members form a significant proportion of treatment professionals	–	–	–	–	–	–	–	+	+
Officially recognized formal courses available for AA counselors	–	–	–	–	–	–	–	–	+

*Items on AA organizing meetings at treatment institutions and in prisons refer to regular AA meetings. In Austria, AA is allowed to and does organize information meetings in prisons.

189

Probably the most common form of social action catalyzed by AA membership has been efforts to improve the social response to alcoholism. Such efforts are often regarded by those involved as a form of 12th-step work, and thus a part of the recovery process.

From its founding in 1943 through at least the 1970s, the NCA served as the main political arm in the United States for the alcoholism movement. It was a loose alliance of public relations activists and entrepreneurial scientists promoting the recognition of alcoholism as a disease and a public health responsibility who were seeking government funding for treatment and research (B. H. Johnson, 1973; Room, 1978). In Keller's formulation, the alliance involved a "capitulation" of the scientists to "the lay wisdom of Alcoholics Anonymous" as a success story—"a way of dealing with alcoholism that worked" (Keller, 1972). The alcoholism movement took from AA the terminological choice of "alcoholism," and the focus on loss of control over drinking as the "pathognomic symptom" of the disease (Jellinek, 1952; Mann, 1950). But where the main texts of AA had emphasized the spiritual dimensions of alcoholism as a "sickness," NCA's emphasis was on alcoholism as a medical disease. The focus on securing government funding for treatment centers also contrasted with the mutual-help approach of AA. Nevertheless, AA members served as the main cadre of foot soldiers for local NCA "alcoholism awareness" campaigns in the 1960s and 1970s, tirelessly distributing brochures on the "warning signs of alcoholism" and collecting contributions for the cause.

In individual capacities, AA members have also served the U.S. alcoholism movement in many other ways. AA members in state legislatures have often functioned as legislative leaders on issues relating to public alcoholism treatment, and such connections played a key role in the rise of state-level alcoholism agencies and eventually of a federal-level agency (Hughes, 1988; Pike, 1988; Smithers, 1988).

During the 1970s and 1980s, there were recurrent publicity campaigns in which U.S. celebrities announced they were recovering alcoholics. While membership in AA usually is not mentioned, such membership is probably taken for granted by many in the audience. The celebrity status of recovering alcoholics may be seen by many as conferring a positive moral worth; unlike the ordinary person, the alcoholic has wrestled with powerful personal demons and overcome them. American culture appears to differ from others on this; being a recovered alcoholic would not lend added stature, for instance, to a British politician.

Another venue in which recovered alcoholics have put their talents to work on behalf of the movement is through the mass media. The tradition of troubled drinkers or ex-alcoholics making representations of alcoholism to the public began with the Hollywood alcoholism movies of the late 1940s (Denzin, 1991; Room, 1989). By the 1960s, such representations were a staple of television, both in soap operas and in prime-time series. Quite often, the presentations have included reference to AA, either by name or in thin disguise. With the dominance of U.S. films and television programs on the world market, these efforts by U.S. media professions play a significant role in many other societies as well.

The John Laroquette show, a half-hour prime-time situation comedy on U.S. network TV, which started in fall 1993, is the first such show to have the main character's membership in AA as the organizing premise of the show.

In the United States, the alcoholism movement has been quite successful in imposing its view of alcohol problems and their management. Again, AA as an organization has not been involved in the enforcement of this view, although the view certainly owes a good deal to AA thinking. Questioning of the disease concept of alcoholism (Fingarette, 1988; Peele, 1989) draws heated objections from medical as well as alcoholism movement sources. A particular flash point has been the proposition that some alcoholics may be able to go back to controlled drinking (Roizen, 1987), an idea which contradicts AA's axiom that an alcoholic can never drink again, and which is excoriated as potentially life-threatening to any alcoholic who acts on this proposition. Efforts to maintain the hegemony of AA's view on this issue have extended to efforts to cut off research funds for projects that do not presume abstinence as necessary for recovery (Room, 1983). In Great Britain and the rest of Europe, debates over controlled drinking have never reached similar levels of prominence (Miller, 1993).

In study sites other than the United States, the impact of AA on the public view of alcohol problems has been less pervasive, at least until quite recently. In Finland, for example, AA is quite strong and widely known, and popular magazines may carry stories about the recovery from alcoholism of public figures. Nevertheless, the disease concept has had relatively little impact on the prevailing views of alcohol problems, which continue to represent these problems mainly as social and behavioral problems (Bruun, 1971; Taipale, 1979; Takala & Lehto, 1992). In Austria, the small AA community is secluded and isolated from the rest of the culture (Eisenbach-Stangl, in press). In Switzerland as well, the public visibility of AA has been very limited compared to the situation in the United States. As in the United States, show business in Mexico has taken up the issue of alcoholism, but AA identities and issues seem less likely to surface in Mexican politics. In Iceland and Sweden, the aggressive marketing efforts of private 12-step treatment institutions have increased the visibility of their version of the AA program and the disease concept.

From the very beginning, Polish AA aspired for public visibility. A large number of journalists were invited to the first General Service Conference. The conference was given broad press coverage, and many active members were interviewed. Most but not all maintained anonymity. Members of AA regularly present themselves on a popular TV program called "Vodka, Let Us Live," which earlier featured mainly members of the Abstainers' Clubs. The goal of the program is to educate the public about the mechanisms of alcoholism and to give advice to people with drinking problems. Members of AA are presented by first name only, but the faces of those featured are fully visible.

In the beginning of the transition period in Poland, members of AA did not take part in the public discussion on alcohol problems and policies. However, advocates of free alcohol markets used selected AA texts to argue that the availability of alcohol had nothing to do with the incidence of alcoholism, which was determined by genetic factors and individual life experiences. More recently, members of AA have publicly argued against further liberalization of alcohol controls. Consequently, members of AA have been opposed to draft legislation defining beer as a non-alcoholic beverage, and have presented dramatic examples of "beer alcoholism" to a Parliamentary Commission.

The Criminal Justice System and Mandatory AA Attendance

Each day the police and criminal justice system deals with far more alcohol-involved cases than does any other system of social or health handling of alcohol problems. In countries like Finland and the United States, where urban public drunkenness has traditionally been handled as a crime, dealing with alcohol-specific offenses forms a large part of the daily burden of policing. In recent decades, drunk driving has risen to prominence in the arrest statistics, at least in northern Europe and English-speaking countries. In addition, those staffing the courts and prison systems are well aware of the heavy drinking of many of those convicted for non-alcohol-specific offenses. From its earliest years, AA often found itself being invited into prisons and courts as a resource by prison wardens, judges, and others staffing the criminal justice system.

The form of these relationships with the criminal justice system has varied by place and time. The practice of making visits to jails and prisons and holding AA meetings in them started relatively early in AA's history. The first AA meeting in an institution in northern California was held at San Quentin State Prison in 1942 (Kaskutas, 1989a, p. 30). Organizing meetings in prisons is a regular activity in all our study sites except Austria and Sweden (Table 14.1).

Another early form of cooperation with the criminal justice system in the United States was an informal assistance and vouching function in municipal courts as magistrates or judges processed public drunkenness cases and other petty offenders (Gellman, 1964, pp. 64–66). In these early relations, those in an AA capacity maintained a strict separation of functions from those who were officers of the state or representing the criminal justice system. This pattern remains the rule in the other countries in this study. In recent years, however, the relation of AA to the criminal justice system has substantially changed in the United States. It is now common practice in many parts of the United States for the judge to require attendance at AA meetings as part of the sentence for drunk driving or for other criminal offenses. To verify attendance, the secretary of the AA meeting signs or initials the "court card" carried by the probationer. The practice appears to have started in the late 1960s in southern California, at the initiative of enthusiastic judges and with considerable doubt among old-timers in AA, but the practice is now so widespread in the United States that it is taken for granted. Discussions continue, though, about the difficulties this new form of association with the criminal justice system has caused for AA's functioning.

Of our study sites, it is only in the United States that the formal practice of "court-carding" has taken root. In a less formal style, however, the criminal court process in Mexico and Sweden also encourages affiliation with AA, and holds out the prospect that this liaison will secure more lenient handling in the courts. In future years, AA may come under pressure in a wider variety of countries to serve a formal social control function on behalf of the criminal justice system.

The issue of compulsion is not limited to the criminal justice system. Mandatory treatment is increasingly prescribed not only because of homelessness or public deviance but also because of insufficient work performance or family problems (Takala, Klingemann, & Hunt, 1992), which means that it is spreading to new groups of the population. In the United States, for instance, employers sometimes request AA meeting attendance of their employees.

Institutional 12-Step Treatment

From the earliest days of AA, members frequently took new "pigeons" into their homes, and by the 1950s such group living arrangements under the supervision of a recovered alcoholic had become formalized into "half-way houses." As state aid for alcoholism treatment gradually became available in the United States, half-way houses became an important component of the treatment system (Cahn, 1970). It was primarily in connection with half-way houses that the possibilities and problems of AA's interaction with formal treatment systems first became manifest.

As in the United States, AA members in other countries were keen to increase the availability of specialized institutional treatment for alcoholics. Soon after the first AA group was founded in Iceland, AA members formed an organization that set up two treatment institutions, one of which is still run by members of AA (Ólafsdóttir, 1991). The Norwegian AA started the so-called AA clinics only one year after the first AA group was founded in Norway, in collaboration with the State Health Directorate (Krogh, 1989).

The first attempts to translate the 12-step program into a professional treatment regime, which may be regarded as marking a new phase in the relationship between AA and professional treatment, date back to the late 1940s in the United States. Of the first three established treatment centers, Pioneer House (1948), Hazelden (1948) and Willmar State Hospital (1950), two were established by ex-alcoholics, and one was established within a professional treatment setting (D. J. Anderson, 1980; Cook, 1988). It was not until the 1970s, however, that a marked growth was seen in the application of 12-step treatment in the United States. Today, 12-step treatment is a dominant part of the professional treatment system in North America. Closely connected to the growth of 12-step treatment was the proliferation of AA-oriented books and pamphlets by outside publishers such as the Hazelden Foundation and the Johnson Institute. These commercial publications helped to increase the public visibility of AA as well as the 12-step treatment.

From the late 1970s the model spread to several other countries. Of our study sites, institutional 12-step treatment was introduced first in Iceland in 1978, and in the early 1980s in Finland, Mexico, Sweden, and the French-speaking part of Switzerland.

Some of the countries importing 12-step treatment had had limited experience of traditional AA (Stenius, 1991). From 1977, Iceland experienced a sudden expansion of institutional 12-step treatment. As a result, AA grew from 9 groups in 1976 to 179 groups in 1986, and an astonishing 10 percent of all men in their forties had by the end of 1985 been admitted to inpatient alcoholism treatment at least once in their life (Ólafsdóttir, 1988). In Sweden, AA for a long time had great difficulties surviving in the shadow of the local Links (Kurube, 1991a, 1991b). The situation was suddenly changed in the mid-1980s with the advent of institutional 12-step treatment, and the number of AA groups grew from about 20 in the beginning of the 1980s to 278 in 1990 (Helmersson Bergmark, in press). The first 12-step center in the French-speaking part of Switzerland was established in 1986 in the canton of Vaud, where the number of AA groups increased from 3 in 1984 to 12 in 1990 (Mariolini, 1992). In Israel, a private 12-step treatment center was established in Nahariya in 1989, at a time when only 9 AA groups were active in the country (Weiss, 1990).

Institutional 12-step treatment consists of an intensive program for a period of up to four or six weeks. Patients attend lectures on AA, read AA literature, and go to AA meetings at the institution or outside. AA members visit the institution and talk about their personal experiences. Key positions in the treatment personnel are often held by recovering alcoholics who are doctors, psychologists, nurses, and, particularly, so-called alcoholism counselors. The latter are recovering alcoholics with varying degrees of formal training. In the course of the institutional program, the patient goes through the first four to five Steps of AA. A common formulation is that institutional 12-step treatment is an introduction to AA, where the real recovery should take place.

There is considerable variation among 12-step centers. In her study of 12-step treatment in Denmark, Steffen (1993) describes one "old-fashioned" and one "modern" center. In the former, the atmosphere is informal and egalitarian and reminiscent of traditional AA groups, and most of the personnel have no formal training. The clients have serious social problems that have prepared them for the AA message. In the latter, the emphasis is on professional competence, hierarchical structure, and a strictly regulated treatment schedule. Most of the clients have a relatively good social standing, and the main task of the treatment is to "break their denial" and to "raise their bottom."

The growth of institutional 12-step treatment has been related to a social demand for the treatment of new groups, in particular heavy drinkers employed by industry. As a consequence, newcomers from 12-

step centers tend to have less extreme drinking careers than traditional members.

"With the proliferation of treatment facilities that took place in the 1970s we aren't seeing as many alcoholics holding half-empty cups of coffee at their first meeting because they are shaking too hard to hold full cups. Thank God, it's been at least ten years since I've seen a member go into an alcoholic convulsion at a meeting."

L.F., 1983, pp. 3–4

In Scandinavia, 12-step treatment has been able to benefit from changes in treatment financing. Increasing public and private insurance coverage for alcohol treatment has, together with the trend toward decentralization and privatization, opened up a new market for treatment. In Iceland and Sweden, for example, 12-step treatment has been mainly privately organized (profit or nonprofit), but has been financed by public means (Stenius, 1991).

Institutional 12-Step Treatment and AA as a Social Movement

With the growth of professional 12-step treatment, the belief system of a social movement is transformed into a treatment modality. This transformation has important implications for the research agenda. Sociologists and historians may be interested in the dynamics of growth and decay of social movements, but these are not evaluated in any technical sense. The situation is different when mutual-help groups are used as adjuncts to public treatment or their program is applied by professionals. It now becomes pertinent to evaluate the overall efficiency of the treatment modality (Bradley, 1988; Brandsma et al., 1977; Ditman et al., 1967; Emrick, 1994; Emrick et al., 1993; Galanter et al., 1990; Glaser & Ogborne, 1982; Keso, 1988; McCrady & Irvine, 1989; Walsh et al., 1991) and to design analytic studies of specific components of the program (Anderson & Gilbert, 1989; Miller, 1990). Such issues, however, are beyond the scope of the present volume. In the following section, we focus on the impact of professional 12-step treatment on AA as a mutual-aid movement.

The Impact of Institutional 12-Step Treatment on the Structure and Activities of AA

The most direct impact of the 12-step treatment on AA is the influx of new members. Newcomers from 12-step centers have decisively contributed to the growth of AA, and the marketing of the 12-step treatment has, in many cases, also included a "marketing" of AA. In the United States, Iceland, Sweden, and the French-speaking part of Switzerland, the 12-step treatment has become a major channel to AA.

The organizational issues related to the impact on AA of the 12-step treatment can be summarized into three topics:

(1) AA as part of mandatory treatment and its effects on the autonomy of the AA movement;
(2) the impact of the influx of poorly motivated newcomers on the social networks of AA; and
(3) the role of members of AA who at the same time are treatment professionals, and the decline in sponsorship and direct 12th-step work.

Traditional AA thought strongly emphasizes voluntary participation. According to Tradition Three, "the only requirement for A.A. membership is a desire to stop drinking." In explicit opposition to the doctrine of hitting bottom, D. J. Anderson (1980, p. 8) argues that "initial motivation for treatment is unrelated to outcome," and V. E. Johnson (1986) has written a work with the subtitle "How to help someone who doesn't want help." This change in basic premises has had important implications for 12-step institutional treatment.

In the vocabulary of 12-step treatment, the problem of the alcoholic is his denial of the fact that he cannot control his drinking. Treatment, especially if the patient is under external pressure to undergo it, may offer a situation where the denial can be broken down. In a very systematic way, institutional 12-step treatment has used the influence of the family and the workplace to urge the patient to go into treatment.

Traditionally, AA has emphasized its autonomy in the face of the state and the professional apparatus. In countries or regions where AA grows as a consequence of the 12-step treatment so that most groups consist almost exclusively of former patients, the autonomy of AA may become largely dependent on the attitude of the treatment centers. In Sweden, for instance, the head of a treatment center was apprehensive that AA groups in the vicinity could easily be transformed into after-care groups and become completely dependent on the center (Swedish field interview).

In the United States, the most obvious drawback for traditional AA groups is the swamping of meetings by more or less unwilling and often sullen participants. It is not only the "court-carders," but also busloads of clients from inpatient treatment centers, that have often threatened the viability or transformed the process of established meetings.

Groups vary in their policy with respect to mandatory meeting attendance but many AA secretaries sign court cards or report to Employee Assistance Program counselors (Walsh et al., 1991). Exactly when during the meeting the secretary will sign the court cards sometimes becomes an issue; signing cards at the beginning of the meeting is a way of immediately getting rid of those who do not want to stay.

"At one point in the experience of my group as many as sixty percent of those attending our open speakers meeting were from treatment centers. Our group panicked. What was going to happen to us? Would we go broke making coffee? Would the group lose its character and closeness? . . . The new people came in a body; they sat together in a corner and we in ours. We decided to write a letter to the local centers and tell them they were limited to sending ten people each."

C.C., 1981, p. 27

In Pennsylvania, many publicly funded inpatient rehabilitation centers and sobriety houses refer their patients, often coming from distant communities, to local AA groups. In sobriety houses, attendance at ninety meetings in ninety days is mandatory. Further, area justice system officials routinely urge their clients to attend AA meetings, and failure to attend can result in incarceration. The influx of reluctant and transient newcomers has put the traditional AA network under heavy strain, and sponsorship has become nominal and frustrating for both parties (Milofsky et al., 1988). Reports from other parts of the United States similarly indicate that the large number of newcomers from institutional treatment causes resentment among members who would like to devote the meetings to later stages of the recovery program (H. C. Johnson, 1987). The report on the surveys of the membership of AA in North America pays special attention to the high rate of early attrition, suggesting that the causes include individuals sent against their will and individuals who are not convinced of their alcoholism (Comments . . . , no date).

A U.S. pamphlet from 1967 entitled *Cooperation without Affiliation* (no longer produced) still stressed that AA is a voluntary program, and that experience proves alcoholics do not accept AA under duress. But the policy has changed. As AA received greater numbers of newcomers from treatment centers, courts, and the workplace, attention has shifted from the source of the referral to the persuasive power of AA itself. What has changed is not that AA members are unused to the idea of having to force other alcoholics into a state of reasonableness, but that this state is more commonly stimulated today by a formal agency of social control instead of by some internal mechanism of the drinker (M. Phillips, 1988).

The contradiction between court-required attendance and AA's principle of "attraction" still causes some unease. But AA old-timers in Marin County, whose sobriety went back to the early 1960s, seemed to accept the advent of the court-carders, feeling that those coming "with deep resentment" might nevertheless be "attracted" by "exposure" to "a good way of life;" AA was "big enough [to] handle" it, given "the possibility they're going to get some good out of it" (Kaskutas, 1989a, pp. 19–20).

Attendance under duress also offers opportunities to small-time entrepreneurs operating at the fringes to distort AA's practices. In southern California, the owner of a clubhouse used by AA meetings was said to be pocketing the collection from several meetings attended by court-carders (H. C. Johnson, 1987, pp. 602–651).

"I have seen head hunters from treatment centers come to AA meetings and pounce upon new members the moment they enter the room. If they have insurance, they are whisked away to a treatment center."

Jack F., 1993, p. 29

Institutional treatment based on the 12-step program also may have reduced 12th-step work. In some parts of the United States, new-comers are told to attend institutional treatment before they are ripe to join AA, and field reports from the international AA project show that people identifying themselves as newcomers by raising hands on an invitation from the chairperson may be left alone after the meeting. The decline in sponsorship has caused lively discussions within the movement. Some members also feel that the responsibility for fellow-members who are in trouble has been given over to professionals.

Twelve-step treatment programs usually require the completion of Step Five before discharge. Where Step Five is completed in an institutional setting, there is no compelling reason for a newcomer to take a sponsor or share their Step Five with another AA member. The basic symmetry in taking Step Five and the resulting strong social bond is also lacking at most treatment institutions. Anderson, a pioneer of institutional 12-step treatment, is quite explicit about the shift from peer mutuality to professional expertise: "Ordinarily, most members of AA make their fourth step and their fifth step with one or another lay member of AA. . . . [W]e elected to use trained clergymen for this significant therapeutic experience" (D. J. Anderson, 1980, p. 16).

"The question is: Who's carrying the message these days, AA or Sunnybrook Farms?"

B.L., 1989, p. 22

"After six months in AA I went to 12-step treatment. I still consider it the best thing I have ever done. The only reason I could think for having a relapse is that it would permit me to go to treatment again."

Swedish field interview (M, 47, 5)

D. J. Brown's (1989) study of professional 12-step counselors provides a further indication of how pervasively 12-step professional treatment permeates today's AA in North America. Judging from how the author presents his results, each of the thirty-five counselors with whom he spoke had had a professional 12-step therapist, and in all cases this alcohol professional and not a traditional AA sponsor seems to have been the most important person in the recovery process.

"When we AAs speak more about our counselors and our therapists than our AA sponsors . . . how does it appear to the newcomer?"

David A., 1989, p. 9

Within the movement, the role of professional counselors is in many ways ambiguous (Kurtz, 1991, 1992). Counselors talk about their jobs much in the same way traditional members would speak of doing 12th-step work, only they get paid for it. "My successes in recovery, including being a counselor, would be seen by patients and those who helped me get sober" (D. J. Brown, 1989, p. 25). Most of Brown's interviewees report that they had made more money in their previous line of work, but others had been under financial strain: "Where else could I go and put bulimic and alcoholic on my resume and get hired?" (p. 28). It also seems that some respondents decided to become counselors in order to have more time for their own recovery: "At work, before I got this job, I would take extended lunches so I could attend A.A. After I got into recovery, I told my old boss that overtime jeopardized my program" (p. 21). Being a counselor was also seen as supporting one's own sobriety: "Being a counselor would force me to remain abstinent or else get fired" (p. 23).

In his classic analysis of the structure of AA, Bales (1944) presents a discussion of the functions of 12th-step work for AA as a social movement. According to Bales, the cohesion among AA members is based on their past drinking experiences. Therefore, "the articulation of ideas and sentiments relevant to action, which is a necessary and natural product of group life, can take place only in the areas of orientation toward the past and the immediate present, rather than toward the future, if the solidarity of the group is not to be endangered" (Bales, 1944, p. 271). Twelfth-step work "brings into prominence and utilizes to the fullest extent the one general basis of solidarity in an organization otherwise residually defined—the past common experiences and the present common characteristics of the members as compulsive drinkers" (p. 272).

To Bales, 12th-step work is the main guarantee for the unity of the movement and against hierarchic organization. His analysis gives special weight to the observation that the growth of institutional 12-step treatment seems to have had a negative effect on the extent of direct 12th-step work within the movement.

"Previously, we used to visit alcoholics. Once I traveled from Reykjavik to Rome in order to accompany an alcoholic to the Freeport Hospital; that must have been one of the longest 12th-step calls ever. Today, everything is left to the treatment institutions. No one visits people in their homes. You may give a drinker a lift to the treatment facility but that is all."

Icelandic field interview (M, 50, 13)

Institutional 12-Step Treatment and the Interrelations of Belief and Action in the AA Program

Despite the central importance of the disease concept for AA, most traditional members have focused on their existential powerlessness with respect to alcohol. In contrast, many professional 12-step centers profess codified theories of alcoholism. Institutional 12-step programs often employ detailed and elaborate educational packages about alcoholism containing strict and codified theories of the disease and its development. In the beginning, AA promoted the disease concept particularly as a means of convincing recruits what would happen if they went on drinking. "This 'conscious technique' was the stark portrayal of the early symptoms of alcoholism as these were understood by Alcoholics Anonymous, joined with a dreadful stress on the inevitability of the 'progression' of these symptoms" (Kurtz, 1991, p. 115). When this is communicated from one alcoholic to another, it is something radically different from when it is presented with the authority of an institution to a patient.

From the perspective of AA as a social movement, the scientific adequacy of these theories is beside the point. More important is the fact that the theories tend to change the interrelations of belief and action in the AA program. There is more emphasis on scientific doctrines, and the tools of action come to be regarded as corollaries of a systematic theory.

"Carl learned at closed meetings that he lacked the necessary knowledge of alcohol and body chemistry that he would only get 'in treatment.' "

J.M., 1989, p. 42

"It's good if newcomers go to treatment first, otherwise they disturb meetings too much. Newcomers are a mess."

Swedish field interview (F, 46, 3)

It is also possible that professional 12-step treatment is bringing about a new systematization of the belief system concerning the higher power, a generalized spiritual codification rather than a traditional religious codification. Corrington (1989) used Whitfield's Spirituality Self-Assessment Scale to study the interrelations of spirituality and life contentment among AA members. It is hardly a surprise that the two scales are correlated, since they include numerous items with almost identical content. It is more surprising that there is no clear correlation between spirituality and length of AA membership. One possible explanation lies in the many items that refer to the new codification of spirituality taught at professional 12-step treatment institutions: "I live in the Here and Now;" "I have a sense of being able to differentiate my mind (or ego) from my spirit (or higher self)." It is conceivable that this type of spirituality is more alien to AA old-timers than to newcomers from rehabilitation centers.

Twelve-Step Treatment and the AA Meeting as a Speech Event

The rules of speech at 12-step institutions are significantly different compared to traditional AA meetings. First, at 12-step treatment institutions, there is strong and overt pressure for everybody should talk. Second, patients' accounts of their experiences and behavior are regularly confronted and challenged in the interest of breaking denial. Third, counselors tend to hand out causal explanations and psychological interpretations of the patients' past and present behavior (Cook, 1988; Denzin, 1987).

"They go to therapists. The therapists arm them with buzz words and send them to AA. . . . AA isn't just a place we go to talk about our daily problems. It's still life and death for a lot of us."

Dolph L., 1989, pp. 2–3

"I gathered from them that the linchpin of good living was some spongy concept referred to as 'getting in touch with your feelings'. . . . The free-for-all group therapy that developed at our little meeting was simply not AA. . . . Spending an hour or two with people who are trying to 'feel better' is quite a different thing than spending an hour or two with people that are trying to recover from a fatal disease."

Gary R., 1989, p. 5

"So I do have some qualms when I hear a speaker waxing Freudian about his secondary alcoholism or his passive/ aggressive alcoholic subconsciousness. But then I look around and see all the young people getting and staying sober."

Jim N., 1988, p. 4

"I care a lot that an eighteen-year-old, fresh out of rehab, can articulate his feelings about himself better than some wise old deacon who has blanketed his resentments with a sense of humor and sits, uncomprehending, in judgment of how the program is changing."

Anonymous, 1990a, p. 23

Early AA members absorbed ideas from religious, philosophical, medical, and psychological writings at various levels of popularity

(Kurtz, 1991; Pittman, 1988a). The program was seen as complementing rather than challenging professional knowledge, but AA also was seen as something else than lay psychotherapy. The program was about solving existential problems within everyday speech, and traditional AA discourages scientific psychological explanation and interpretation.

Early members of AA adopted a mixture of non-normative technical terminology and morally loaded everyday language. In dealing with the outside world and with potential "pigeons," the term "alcoholic" was a clear choice; its medical provenance underlined the major strategy of argument that the potential recruit had "a sickness, a fatal malady," which set him or her apart from the normal drinker. But in the internal dialogue, much of the language fell back again on temperance terminology—but used now with a double layer of irony, as AA members spoke of themselves to each other as "rummies" or "drunks," and talked of "going on" or "falling off the (water) wagon" (Room, 1989, p. 380).

Psychodynamic discourse has to some degree become part of everyday language, which makes it difficult to distinguish between everyday wisdom and scientific knowledge in AA. Nevertheless, the influence from 12-step treatment has caused marked disagreements about how much psychological explanation and interpretation should go into an AA meeting. The disagreements concern the importance of "getting in touch with your feelings" and the role of psychodynamic vocabulary in the recovery process.

"There is only one group left in Stockholm for me to go to. All the others have adopted the new fashion of introducing oneself with, 'Hi, I am X, I am an alcoholic,' and everyone present responds with 'Hi, X.' That's treatment people, I just cannot stand their practices."

Swedish field interview (M, 61, 16)

Groups dominated by members having come to AA through 12-step treatment add new variants to AA meetings. As the debate in *A.A. Grapevine* testifies, many traditional members feel uncomfortable with "treatment psychobabble," but the dissatisfaction is reciprocal. As long as the rules of talk at AA meetings and particularly AA's organizational principles are not seriously infringed upon, disagreements between traditional members and recruits from 12-step centers are likely to just add to the diversification of AA, provided that traditional meetings continue to be available.

"Members who have gone through treatment feel more easily at home in 'feeling groups, social groups, support groups, or loving-confrontation groups.' "

E.O., 1981, p. 6

Twelve-Step Treatment and the Future of AA as a Mutual-Aid Movement

A clear distinction should be kept between AA as a mutual-help movement and professional 12-step treatment (Humphreys, 1993). Twelve-step treatment aims at producing quick changes in the patient's drinking behavior. This means that there is a rationale for confronting and challenging the drinker's accounts of his or her experience and behavior in a way that is foreign to the rules in traditional AA meetings.

Twelve-step treatment has been able to modify the AA program to meet many of the new demands on alcohol treatment. Institutional 12-step treatment is short and has a clearly formulated goal of abstinence. The model undermines the belief that treatment should be voluntary and supports the legitimacy of compulsion. Also, it has declared alcoholism a disease among other diseases, demanding treatment initiatives from society. At the same time, it stresses individual responsibility for sobriety. The disease cannot be cured through changes in society. In its most elaborated forms, 12-step treatment combines the personal witness of the living example of recovery with professionalism and entrepreneurial spirit. In Scandinavia, the integration of AA into the treatment system has been seen as a solution to the financial crisis of the public sector. Advocates of 12-step treatment often extol the merits of private enterprise within the social sector and appeal to neoliberal tendencies.

In her study of 12-step centers in Denmark, Steffen (1993) describes institutional treatment as an initiation rite to AA and sees no fundamental conflict between the movement and institutional branches. On the contrary, she argues, the movement will be able to sustain its egalitarian and non-bureaucratic structure precisely because 12-step treatment provides an institutionally established channel of recruitment. It is of crucial importance, however, that the distinction between AA and professional 12-step treatment continues to be clearly demarcated. In some regions, the growth of 12-step treatment has blurred the borders between mutual-help and professional work and between coercion and commitment in a way that challenges AA's basic organizational principles.

Two types of arguments seem possible: the viewpoint that institutional 12-step treatment poses a challenge or a threat to AA as a grassroots movement; and the viewpoint that the 1980s mark the golden age of AA in that its ideology was recognized in a number of countries as responding to the basic demands of society.

"Many AA members have always feared that the treatment institutions gain too much influence over AA. Yet, they think it is good that alcoholism counselors hold service positions in AA since they teach better AA in treatment facilities if the personnel is actively engaged in AA."

Icelandic field interview (M, 59, 9)

15
AA and Other Mutual-Help Movements for Alcohol Problems

In addition to AA, there are a number of organizations providing mutual-help for alcohol problems in the industrialized world. In the first part of this chapter, we present an overview of parallel mutual-help organizations in Europe and Japan. The second part of the chapter discusses AA's offspring and alternatives on its home turf.

Mutual-Help Movements for Alcohol Problems in Europe and Japan

Before the Second World War, the main influence in the formation of mutual-help groups concerned with drinking problems had been the temperance movement, which was frequently intertwined with religious denominations. Temperance-based mutual-help associations were an important part of the scene in English-speaking countries prior to the First World War, but nothing of the kind was left on the American scene when AA was founded. Catholic- or Protestant-based movements remain in the picture, however, in such countries as France, Switzerland, and Germany, and continue to offer an alternative to AA (Appel, 1988; Cerclé, 1985; Prestwich, 1988). The following estimates by Alain Cerclé (oral communication, February 1993) on the membership of various mutual-help movements for problem drinkers in France provide a picture of the relative strength of alternative organizations in the late 1980s. To enhance comparability, the figures used here include only former problem drinkers, not family members and other support membership.

AA	7,000
Amies de la Santé (including Joie et santé)	10,000
Croix d'Or	20,000
Croix Bleu	6,000
Vie Libre	20,000

Among the movements initiated after the Second World War, most have been to some degree influenced by AA. Particularly in the earlier years, the influence might have been remote and nonspecific—simply the news that a mutual-help movement for recovering alcoholics existed and was reported to be successful—and in many cases the influence was in part as a negative example. Of the AA-influenced movements, Links in Sweden, the Polish patient clubs, and Danshukai in Japan were all founded before the first AA group in their country.

Despite its spiritual emphasis, AA represented a step away from the direct connection between mutual-help and religion in such organizations as the Croix d'Or and the Blue Cross. AA's ideology is explicitly nondenominational. It avoids formal connection with any church and insists that it is a spiritual and not a religious movement. Nevertheless, in several instances founders of mutual-help groups have welcomed the example of AA but have rejected the spiritual nature of its program. For instance, the higher power is conspicuously downplayed in the Seven Points of Swedish Links, otherwise derived from AA's Twelve Steps (Kurube, 1992a). The Seven Points contain one reference to a higher power, but it is commonly understood as the strength of the collective power of the Links Society. In Links, the message for recovery is not "surrender" as in the AA program but "solidarity," where solidarity is to be understood as a political concept—the solidarity of Swedish mass movements.

The alteration might be interpreted in terms of the greater secularism of Swedish society. Strictly secularity in European mutual-help organizations also often reflects other, wider influences: Marxist ideology, in some cases, and the influence of professionals, who are perhaps the most rationalist segment of most societies (Rehm & Room, 1992).

The origin of most mutual-help organizations was not completely spontaneous, in that the initiative was often taken by professionals or non-alcoholics. The founder of the Swedish Links was an inspector at the Temperance Board in Stockholm who mobilized seven recovered alcoholics from different temperance organizations and the Oxford Group Team to start the first Links group in 1945, but the movement quickly became autonomous (Kurube, 1992a).

The first Polish mutual-help groups were founded by medical professionals in the form of patient clubs in the late 1940s. They were called "AA clubs," and were based on modified AA principles, but without references to spirituality. The first Abstainers' Club was founded in 1960 by a few alcoholics. During the 1970s the patient clubs again became tied to health care centers. The Polish clubs were influenced by community psychiatry and experiences from Yugoslavian clubs for alcoholics. The clubs ran extensive prevention and rehabilitation projects by collaborating with local commissions for mental health protection (Morawski, 1988; Woronowicz, 1992).

In the Japanese case, Danshukai, we find a combination of AA influence, initiatives from the temperance movement, and the involvement of medical professionals. The ideological concepts of AA were introduced through the temperance movement to form a mixed product of the two organizations. On the initiative of medical professionals, many of the associations were founded as patient clubs located in clinical facilities for alcoholics (Kurube, 1992b).

Where professionals have been involved in the founding of mutual-help movements, one frequent issue has been the autonomy of the group. Here AA provided an uncompromising model, of self-governing autonomous groups of alcoholics, which challenged professional ideologies about the appropriate role for patients in general and about the dependency of alcoholics in particular. In the case of the Polish Abstainer Clubs, an impediment to the move towards autonomy were the doubts of the "club protectors" (clinicians who had helped to organize the clubs) about the ability of alcoholics to manage their own affairs, even though the protectors had been influenced by the thinking of humanistic psychiatry (Świątkiewicz, 1992b). As with the early Polish Abstainer Clubs, each of the several hundred Yugoslav Clubs of Treated Alcoholics founded by Hudolin, a leading psychiatrist, would have "a general practitioner, social worker, or paraprofessional" working with it (Bennett, 1984). As a consequence, there are important differences between a meeting of such a club and an AA meeting.

"First of all, [in a Yugoslav Club of Treated Alcoholics] no one is anonymous: a membership roster is kept, and a roll is taken at each meeting. . . . Secondly, the philosophy behind the clubs is not based on religious premises, and no reference is made to a higher supernatural power. Third, professional staff constitute an integral part of each club's activities. Officers, however, are selected from among the treated alcoholics group, and they preside over each meeting. Each member takes antabuse [disulfiram] . . . over the first year. As names are read from the roll, each alcoholic goes to the front of the room where a tray of glasses and pills have been placed and takes a pill."

Bennett, 1984

One frequent disagreement between AA and other mutual-help movements is about membership identity. Alternative movements often stand in opposition to AA's insistence on the lifelong nature of being an alcoholic. For example, the overlap in membership of AA groups and Abstainer's Clubs in Poland often caused conflicts about whether participants should present themselves as "abstainers" or "alcoholics" (Woronovicz, 1992).

Unlike AA, most other mutual-help movements are formally organized under a hierarchical superstructure. The basic unit is in principle the group, which is called a "society," "association," "section," or "club," but local, regional, and central boards function as executive and control agencies for the organization's activities. Professionalization of leadership and decision-making by majority is common in all movements.

Only AA, among the six French "movements of former drinkers" compared by Cerclé (1985, p. 21), is not organized as a legal association. Links was organized from the first as a legal and fully accountable association; within a year of its founding, Links had asked for and received a grant from the Stockholm municipal government (Kurube, 1992a). The history of repeated splits in the Links movement and of expulsions of members is tied to the issues of outside financing and accountability. An early split in the movement was over whether the association should establish a subsidized convalescent home, and what official oversight this would require. In a complicated history of splits, the most serious was whether the movement should become a bureaucratic, hierarchical, and professionalized organization, or whether it should follow the model of AA. Nowadays Links is organized into seven different organizations. Several Links societies have their own convalescent homes, holiday resorts, or hostels, and the National Federation of Societies of Links, for example, aspires to be accepted as a social "institution."

As in Sweden, it has been common for European mutual-help movements for alcohol problems to be subsidized by government bodies, and this inevitably affects the internal structure and functioning of the organization. Economic support from the government requires that at least some members give up their anonymity. A dependence on government funding also threatens the survival of the movement if the funding is withdrawn (Świątkiewicz, 1992b).

In legal associations, regulations are required regarding who has voting rights. In the Swedish Links, a member who violates the bylaws of the society, obstructs the execution of its resolutions, or has been an unworthy member, can be expelled by the board (Kurube, 1991b). After a relapse, a member can regain the right to vote after a total abstinence of one or two months (Kurube, 1991b). In La Croix d'Or, one year of sobriety after relapse is required (La Croix d'Or Française, 1989).

Primary membership and voting rights usually are reserved for alcohol abusers, but support membership is available to family members and others who want to promote the goals of the movement. The family is seen as a victim of alcoholism and, therefore, in need of help. At the same time, support from family members is regarded as an important resource for recovery. The emphasis on family participation is particularly strong in Vie Libre, Danshukai, and the Polish Abstainers' Clubs.

With respect to anonymity, a distinction should be made between external and internal anonymity. Individual anonymity with respect to the outside world is generally protected to a high degree. Opinions are more divided regarding anonymity within the organization. The Swedish Links, for instance, argue that anonymity and solidarity do not fit together.

Unlike AA, some movements take on a social action agenda alongside their mutual-help agenda. The French movement Vie Libre has had from the beginning the aim of struggling "against the social and political causes of alcoholism" (Cerclé, 1985, p. 32), along with its mutual-help aim. In fact, its 1976 congress adopted resolutions that, among other matters, proposed a ban on gambling games in cafes, a reduction in the price of non-alcoholic drinks, and an increase in the health budget (Cerclé, 1985, p. 49). The National Society of Links has for a long time attempted to influence alcohol policy and other alcohol-related matters. The Links movement has been a vocal opponent of compulsory treatment. The movement is also against privatization of alcohol treatment and critical of 12-step institutions run by private foundations. Its argument is that alcoholics suffer from an incurable disease, which a private organization should not be allowed to profit from (Kurube, 1992a).

North American Movements for Alcohol and Related Problems Started by Former AA Members

In the United States, the numerical and ideological strength of AA has meant that other movements in the alcohol field are defined in explicit apposition to it. The three main such movements in the United States are Rational Recovery Systems (founded 1986, reporting 350 groups), Secular Organizations for Sobriety (also known as Save Ourselves and SOS, founded 1986, reporting 1,000 groups), and Women for Sobriety (founded 1976, reporting 350 groups) (Galanter, Egelho, & Edwards,

1993; White & Madara, 1992). The authors of the primary texts of each of these movements "were pioneering souls who attended AA and left for various reasons, including dislike of the sexism, the powerlessness concept, rigidity, religiosity, the cult-like atmosphere, and the all power-ful God approach" (Kasl, 1992, p. 163).

SOS rejects the spiritual aspect of AA, but has kept the auto-cephalous structure, with each meeting "an autonomous, grassroots gathering of sober alcoholics and friends and families of alcoholics" (Kasl, 1992, p. 175). The suggested "six guidelines," which substitute for the Twelve Steps, drop any mention of the higher power, but also have no equivalent of the Twelfth Step, which is often seen as being associated with indoctrination. The founder of SOS says, "in sobriety I think we'd do well to avoid sponsorship, approaching each other as equals, walking side by side" (Kasl, 1992, p. 174).

Rational Recovery's rejection of the AA model is more wholesale: "[T]here are no 'higher powers,' no moral inventories, and no substi-tute dependencies or endless meetings to attend" (Kasl, 1992, p. 177). The movement's approach is built around a form of cognitive therapy called "Rational Emotive Therapy," which "aims to help people root out irrational thoughts and beliefs that impede them from reaching their goals" (Hall, 1990). Along with rejecting AA's higher power, Ra-tional Recovery's *Small Book* teaches that "it is pure drivel to think that alcoholics are powerless over their addictions" (Kasl, 1992, p. 177). The movement's emphasis on rationalism, secularism, and individual-istic personal empowerment makes it attractive to psychotherapists; it is reported that "chapters are being started by therapists seeking alter-natives to Alcoholics Anonymous for their patients" (Hall, 1990).

Women for Sobriety (WFS) was founded by Jean Kirkpatrick, a Ph.D. in sociology, as a feminist alternative to AA (Kaskutas, 1989b). Kirkpatrick had found that AA meetings "just did not meet [her] needs. . . . The men were set in their ways and ideas, they dominated the meetings, their stories were often lurid and contained an ego ele-ment of bragging, and their descriptions of women were often very chauvinistic" (Kasl, 1992, p. 166). Influenced by Emerson's essay "Self-Reliance," and American writers on the power of positive thinking (Kaskutas, 1992a, pp. 68–69), Kirkpatrick substituted "13 Affirma-tions" for AA's Twelve Steps, dropped the idea of a higher power, and stressed the member's powerfulness rather than powerlessness. WFS diverges substantially from AA both in meeting procedure and in orga-nizational structure. Meetings are divided into a discussion on a set topic, often one suggested in the newsletter from the movement's head-quarters, and a session of sharing the personal highlights or crises of the past week. The telling of drinking histories is discouraged, while cross talk is allowed. Meetings are run by a "certified moderator" who has two years sobriety, has shown an adequate knowledge of the program, and has signed an agreement to transmit dues of U.S.$ 2 per meeting per member to the movement's headquarters (Kaskutas, 1992a, pp. 90, 100–102).

Despite the ideological and organizational differences between WFS and AA, Kaskutas (1992a) found that about 30 percent of WFS members also regularly attend AA. While there are discernible differences in beliefs between WFS members who attend and do not attend AA (Kaskutas, 1992b), the discrepancies in approach did not seem to discomfort members who attended the meetings of both organizations. Kaskutas' analysis offers a useful caution about the dangers of overemphasizing written ideologies of mutual-help organizations in understanding what they actually mean in members' lives.

Perhaps the most influential U.S. movement founded by an AA member was Synanon, which exerted an extraordinary influence on thinking about treatment for heroin and other drug addiction in the 1960s and 1970s. As Glaser (1981) noted, Synanon pioneered the idea of the drug-free therapeutic community (TC), which remains a major modality of drug treatment in the United States and elsewhere. Chuck Dederich, the founder of Synanon, has given a detailed account of the emergence of Synanon from his involvement in AA (Casriel, 1963). Dederich devoted most of his spare time to the AA movement, picking up alcoholics, having dinner with them, and going to a meeting or clubhouse. After reading Emerson's "Self-Reliance," he resigned his job and, taking every 12th-step call he was given, with two or three other AA members, went into "the business of drying out alcoholics." By July 1957, he "worked for a Twelve Step House and had to live there," since he had no money for an apartment. But he was growing estranged from the AA meetings. "I was bothered by the religious overtones of the meetings and the lack of the utilization of thoughts of anthropology, psychology, philosophy, and sociology" (Casriel, 1963, pp. 19, 21).

By early 1958, the "bull sessions" among alcoholics that evolved into Synanon's basic therapeutic method had begun at Dederich's new apartment. "The first meetings were nondirective; they were à la AA. . . . After the third or fourth meeting it became apparent that the meeting took on a different quality when I maintained a stout and rigid control. I became the inquisitor and the leader of the group. I began to demonstrate the mechanisms and methods of ridicule and cross-examination. . . . I demonstrated this by a powerful manipulation of the people present; they used to attack me, but they never won. My approach was the one which gradually developed into the synanon method" (Casriel, 1963, p. 22).

The first drug addicts started to come to the meetings, which were often at Dederich's apartment. When some people moved in with him, the group moved into an empty store. By July 1958, Dederich was convinced he had something that would work on addicts. As someone who had always "wanted to make history," he realized, "my search was over, and my dedication began" (Casriel, 1963, p. 25). He incorporated the Synanon Foundation, putting on the board "those who would do as I told them to do. I needed dummies that I could control" (Casriel, 1963, p. 27). Many of the alcoholics began to drift away or complain, feeling that the organization was going further and further away from AA principles, and after a series of conflicts, Synanon and AA parted company completely (Casriel, 1963, pp. 26–27).

In the meantime, the Therapeutic Community movement took root, taking up many of Synanon's departures from AA: an organized and incorporated structure; an openness to state financing; a therapeutic modality of residence in a "total institution" (often viewed as a patriarchal family); and, above all, the replacement of the "no cross talk" rule with rules of discourse in meetings that emphasized the therapeutic value of a humiliating stripping down of whoever is in the "hot seat."

AA also has had important offshoots in Mexico, where the "24-hour groups" movement first split off from AA in 1975, and then later split into two movements: the Grupos 24 Horas Condesa, and the Grupos 24 Horas y Therapia Intensiva de Alcoholicos Anonimos (Rosovsky, in press). In its service manual, one of the 24-hour movements explains that the "radical change in [AA's] traditional conception" was due to the "necessities of our country," including "its socioeconomic characteristics," which required setting up "centers for assistance of the marginal alcoholic" (*Manual de Servicios,* 1990, p. 2). The 24-hour movements have come to differ from AA in many ways: not only in providing an "annex" (for sobering up) to each group that is open 24 hours a day, but also in its more confrontational meeting style, complete with a "hot seat" tradition reminiscent of therapeutic communities, and in its tradition of much more directive sponsors, with members rounding up drunks on the street and bringing them to the annexes to be sobered up. The 24-hour movements also have a system of farms where men are taken for recuperation by working as farm laborers.

It would be hard to imagine more divergent outcomes from a dissatisfaction with AA and a reading of Emerson than a Women for Sobriety meeting and a Synanon game. Yet they still share some common elements derived from AA: for instance, a commitment to abstinence as the sole goal for the alcoholic or addict, and the idea that help will come from others' life experiences—through sharing and identification—rather than from professional training.

AA and Alternative Mutual-Help Movements

Considerable variation exists in mutual-help approaches to alcohol problems. Some organizations offer clear ideological alternatives to the Twelve Steps, but the greatest range of variation involves organizational principles.

Three main types of mutual-help organizations for heavy drinkers can be identified (Mäkelä, 1992b): (1) groups of patients under professional leadership and supervision; (2) the Swedish Links organization, which represents an expansion of the principle of solidarity of classic mass movements into a category of individual deviance; and (3) AA and its offshoots, which build on affinity among individuals facing a common existential situation.

Mutual-help movements that do not apply the 12-step program have not diffused internationally like AA, but they continue to attract a large membership in their home countries. Most of the national models have existed for more than thirty years, and some have been in existence even longer than AA.

In the last ten years, the AA movement has grown in all the countries discussed in this chapter. In Poland and Sweden, for example, changes in the political system and the impact of institutional 12-step treatment contributed to its rapid growth. In some cases at least, each movement seems to have found its own recruitment group. The national models thus continue to provide alternatives to AA.

16

Diffusion of the 12-Step Program to Problems Other than Alcohol

AA began in the 1930s as a mutual-help movement aiming at inner reform and addressing the existential problems of a small minority. The end result is that important segments of the general public in North America are deeply affected by a range of 12-step programs.

As of 1991, it was reported that there were 260 12-step programs—movements—modeled on AA but applied to problems other than drinking (V.R.M., 1991, p. 1). The first of these, Al-Anon, was founded in 1951 for members of the families of alcoholics. It is organizationally separate from AA, but the two movements often cooperate on conventions and other activities. All other movements are completely separate from AA: AA's role is limited to giving permission to use the language of the Twelve Steps.

Table 16.1 shows the founding dates of major 12-step movements in the United States. Among all the 12-step movements, AA remains by far the largest, with Al-Anon taking second position. In a representative sample of U.S. adults in 1990 (Room & Greenfield, 1993), 13.3 percent had attended a 12-step meeting sometime in their lives, 9 percent had attended an AA meeting, and 4.6 percent had attended an Al-Anon meeting. The corresponding figures for attendance in the last year are as follows: any 12-step meeting, 5.3 percent; AA, 3.4 percent; Al-Anon, 1.7 percent. Meeting attendance and membership are not necessarily the same thing, since many people go to AA meetings out of curiosity or out of concern about someone else's drinking. In the same sample, 3.1 percent reported having been to AA sometime in their lives for help with an alcohol problem of their own, and 1.5 percent in the last year (for comparison, AA's own count of membership amounts to about 0.5 percent of the U.S. population).

Irrespective of the quantitative significance of 12-step groups, they have high cultural visibility. Even a superficial reading of American newspapers and magazines shows that AA wisdom has definitely

216

Table 16.1   Selected 12-Step Movements in the United States

Date founded	Name	Number of groups	International	Headquarters
1951	Al-Anon Family Groups	32,000	+	New York
1953	Narcotics Anonymous	22,000	+	California
1957	Alateen	4,100	+	New York
1957	Gamblers Anonymous	1,200	+	California
1960	Overeaters Anonymous	10,000	+	California
1971	Emotions Anonymous	1,200	−	Minnesota
1976	Adult Children of Alcoholics	1,800	+	California
1976	Debtors Anonymous	400	−	New York
1976	Augustine Fellowship Sex & Love Addicts Anonymous	1,000	+	Massachusetts
1982	Survivors of Incest Anonymous	800	+	Maryland
1982	Cocaine Anonymous	1,500	+	California
1985	Nicotine Anonymous	500	+	California
1986	Co-Dependents Anonymous	3,500	+	Arizona

Source: White & Madara, 1992
Note: Emotions Anonymous is listed as national, although groups in other countries exist. In situations where two or more movements coexist in the same problem area, only the largest has been included.

moved from the margins to the center of prevailing culture. Comic strips now assume a knowledge of 12-step language and thinking. For example, in the *Washington Post* (28 August 1992), one character offers a parody of the Serenity Prayer: "Know what I pray for? . . . The strength to change what I can, the inability to accept what I can't, and the incapacity to tell the difference" (Calvin and Hobbes). Another offers a joke about denial: "I think the way I'll handle this is to just assume that was a Freudian slip, and go into denial—that's the name of the bar across the street" (Fusco Brothers).

The first 12-step movement addressing problems other than alcohol, Narcotics Anonymous, was founded in 1953. From early on, drug addicts had posed a problem for AA groups. Since the membership requirement was a desire to stop *drinking,* persons addicted to other drugs were not eligible. Narcotics Anonymous was started by dually addicted members of AA, but it soon gained organizational momentum of its own.

The other early movements not related to drinking were Gamblers

Anonymous (1957), Overeaters Anonymous (1962), and Emotions Anonymous (1971). With the exception of Emotions Anonymous, the early non-alcohol 12-step groups dealt with highly specific compulsive behaviors. It is likely that members of AA played key roles in starting these movements. New 12-step groups seem to have been started by AA members who wanted to discuss in more detail some of their other problems besides drinking.

The great proliferation of 12-step movements started in the 1970s and continued in the 1980s. Only a selection of the more important movements is listed in Table 16.1. Many of the newer movements continue to address highly specific problems. The most important development, however, may be that the 12-step program is now applied to problems that are much more generic than drinking, gambling, or overeating.

In a way, this represents a logical extension of AA's philosophy. To Bill W., writing in a letter in 1961, "the whole world is on a terrific dry bender." Members of AA "are fortunate, of course, to have suffered a malady that has not only threatened us with extinction but which makes it impossible to pass the blame on other people. Being thus forced to 'hit bottom,' as we say, the way to spiritual awakening is opened. . . . In the world around us, however, the bottom is hit alright, but this is always somebody else's fault" (Kurtz, 1991, p. 381). As seen from this excerpt, the main difference between AA and the more diffuse maladies of the newer 12-step movements lies in the specificity and concreteness of the experience of hitting bottom.

Membership Maladies of 12-Step Movements

The structure and organizational principles of AA probably do not suffice to explain its continuing vitality as a grassroots movement: the existential situation of the membership is an important additional factor. The concrete threat of starting to drink binds the members together and motivates old-timers to a lifelong commitment that also provides a safeguard for the continuity of the movement.

The existential condition of being an alcoholic is not given: it has to be construed in AA discourse and in AA meetings. The construction of existential identity cannot be carried out arbitrarily, however. The nature of the membership malady has a bearing on the task of contructing existential sameness among members of each 12-step movement (Mäkelä, 1992b). Table 16.2 presents a tentative summary of the following features:

(1) the degree to which the malady overshadows the member's total life experience;
(2) the specificity or diffuseness of the membership malady;
(3) the specificity and objectivity of criteria for what constitutes a relapse;
(4) the severity of objective and subjective risks attached to a relapse; and
(5) changes in physiological mechanisms connected to the malady.

The classification of each of the fourteen membership maladies in Table 16.2 is based on summary judgments and can be contested. It is difficult, for example, to classify membership maladies in terms of how pervasively they overshadow overall life experience. What to an outsider looks like a minor problem can paralyze an individual. This variable has been included in Table 16.2 to distinguish between nicotine addiction and other membership maladies. Nicotine is highly addictive and tobacco use involves a set of concrete behaviors, but smoking usually is not an existential problem to the same extent as are the other membership maladies listed in Table 16.2.

The specificity or diffuseness of the malady refers to patterns of behaviors and may vary widely within the same movement. The malady of members of Sex and Love Addicts, to take one example, may vary from highly specific compulsive behaviors to a diffuse vulnerability to sexual and emotional exploitation. Despite unclear borderline cases, there is a difference between specific addictions or compulsive behaviors and diffuse feelings of *mal-aise* or *dis-ease*.

Depending on the behavioral specificity of the malady, the clarity of the criteria for what constitutes a relapse varies widely. For drinking and drug taking, relapse can be defined unequivocally. A compulsive gambler is also able to easily recognize a "jump." In other membership maladies, there is more individual variability. Overeating can be broken down in specific behaviors, jointly providing the definition of what constitutes a relapse. The same may be possible with respect to certain sexual behaviors. Members of other 12-step movements may in their discussions aim at similar behavioral specifications, but a relapse in codependency necessarily remains more diffuse than a drinking bout.

The severity of the risks attached to a relapse is, at least in part, a highly subjective matter. If both the membership malady and the criteria for relapse are behaviorally diffuse, however, the risk cannot be similarly concrete and imminent, as in drinking, drug taking, or compulsive gambling. There may be scientific disagreements about the fatality of the first drink and the possibility of relearning moderate drink-

Table 16.2   Membership Malady Characteristics of Selected 12-Step Movements

	Pervasive impact of malady on life	Behavioral specificity of malady	Clear criteria for relapse	High risks attached to relapse	Malady connected to clinically identifiable changes in physiological mechanisms
Alcoholics Anonymous	+	+	+	+	+
Narcotics Anonymous	+	+	+	+	+
Cocaine Anonymous	+	+	+	+	+
Nicotine Anonymous	−	+	+	−	+
Gamblers Anonymous	+	+	+	*	−
Overeaters Anonymous	+	+	*	−	+
Debtors Anonymous	+	*	*	*	−
Sex and Love Addicts Anonymous	+	*	*	*	−
Emotions Anonymous	+	−	−	−	−
Al-Anon	+	−	−	−	−
Alateen	+	−	−	−	−
Adult Children of Alcoholics	+	−	−	−	−
Co-Dependents Anonymous	+	−	−	−	−
Incest Survivors Anonymous	+	−	−	−	−

*Variable

ing, but AA experience and folklore provide dramatic examples of the catastrophic consequences of a relapse.

The possibility of a somatic foundation for different membership maladies raises many debatable issues. To counteract problems related to the diffuseness of membership maladies, and because of the growing importance of postulated disease entities for 12-step thinking (Peele, 1989), attempts have been made to claim that, for example, codependency has a somatic foundation. Genuine scientific disagreements concerning the physiological basis of some of the membership maladies remain even after sorting out the most preposterous claims. These disagreements should not, however, be allowed to erase the difference between addictions with a clinically identifiable set of somatic symptoms and vaguer conditions.

Rival 12-Step Movements with the Same Problem Area

Among the newer 12-step movements, a diversity of organizations dealing with a particular life problem is not uncommon. Thus there are presently four significant 12-step movements in North America that deal with sex and love addictions: Sex and Love Addicts Anonymous (SLAA, Augustine Fellowship; 1,000 groups, founded 1976, headquarters Boston); Sex Addicts Anonymous (SAA; 500 groups, founded 1977, headquarters Minneapolis); Sexaholics Anonymous (SA; 700 groups, founded 1979, headquarters Simi Valley, California); and Sexual Compulsive Anonymous (100+ groups, founded 1982, headquarters New York) (data from White & Madara, 1992). The three biggest movements started within a few years of each other and tend to have different regional bases; SAA, for instance, is particularly strong in the midwestern United States. There are also differences in program emphasis between the movements. Kasl (1992, p. 387) notes that "SAA welcomes anyone with a sincere desire to cease compulsive sexual behavior and supports people in defining their own sobriety. By contrast, SA defines sexual sobriety as sex only within a heterosexual marriage." An informant who attends both SAA and SLAA reports that he goes to SAA for his "core physical addiction" but to SLAA for his addiction to romance. In SAA, apparently men and women tend to meet in different groups (Kasl, 1992), while SLAA's *Big Book* emphasizes all four affectional preferences (male and female, homosexual and heterosexual) coming to the same meetings and learning from each other (*Sex and Love Addicts Anonymous*, 1986, pp. 131–133). These various differences may help explain why there are four different movements for a common problem-area; but it is worth noting that equal differences on most of these dimensions can be found within AA. The one exception might be the differences in the bottom line of sexual sobriety; AA would be unable to tolerate differences within it on its bottom line of total abstinence from drinking.

AA and the Growth of a Generalized 12-Step Consciousness

In the course of the 1980s, many of those who participated in Alcoholics Anonymous and other 12-step groups in North America came to think of themselves as belonging to a more general phenomenon, a 12-step consciousness transcending AA or the other particular groups they attended (Room, 1992). This shift in consciousness came in the wake of the growth of the Adult Children of Alcoholics (ACOA) movement, which got under way in the early 1980s. Where earlier 12-step movement members shared a struggle with a specific obsessive behavior of their own, ACOAs, drawn together by the idea that their life problems were attributable to the specific behavior of someone else in the past, found themselves applying the Twelve Steps to general problems of living. The shift in consciousness may also have been associated with the personal odysseys of many ACOA members. Some, for instance, moved on from the ACOA movement to AA as they became concerned about their own drinking, and then to Women Who Love Too Much or Sex and Love Addicts Anonymous (SLAA) as they moved to do something about their current pattern of relationships.

The emergence of a generalized 12-step consciousness has been marked by a loose but growing network of institutions. Connections between groups in different 12-step movements are often the natural results of sharing a common meeting space, as a single building may host a wide diversity of groups. For example, Dry Dock, a "recovery-oriented, non-profit membership club" in San Francisco, hosts 85 meetings serving 2,500 people each week, covering "Alcoholics, Cocaine, Debtors, Narcotics, Overeaters, Sex and Love Addicts, Smokers, and Workaholics Anonymous, as well as A.R.T.S. (Artists Recovering in the Twelve Steps) Anonymous, Addicted Parents, Adult Children of Alcoholics, Al-Anon, Cocanon, Codependents Anonymous, Parents Anonymous, and Women Who Love Too Much" (Taylor, 1988). The logistical organization of such shared space throws members from different 12-step groups together; hence each of the sixty 12-step groups meeting each week at a Seattle United Church of Christ sends a representative to a 12-step council, which "deals with the day-to-day problems of storage space, scheduling conflicts, and space allocation" (Doherty, 1991). Sometimes a generalized 12-step consciousness takes over the host organization itself. A Baptist church in San Francisco reorganized itself as a community center in recognition of the fact that, while its Sunday services attracted about two dozen people, a total of five hundred attended the fifteen different 12-step meetings held six nights a week at the church (Lattin, 1990).

An eager ancillary to the growth of a generalized 12-step consciousness has been the publishing industry, with the "virtual explosion of 'recovery' publishing" (Zedaker, 1989). Hazelden, long established as a distributor and publisher of AA-oriented books, broadened its scope and expanded its operations in the 1980s, marketing its publications for bookstore distribution through Harper, a main-line publisher; by 1989 it was publishing twenty books a year on recovery. Health Communications established more recently and specializing in books for adult children of alcoholics, was publishing thirty new titles in 1989, along with three monthly periodicals. "The big boom" came in about 1987, in one distributor's opinion, "when just about everybody started getting into what is now called stage two recovery. . . . More and more people want to get totally into their recovery—not just deal with the symptoms" (Zedaker, 1989).

Popular expert literature is more important for the new 12-step movements than for the older ones. There are still only a few titles published by AA and approved by the General Service Conference of AA, while Hazelden and other publishers connected with the treatment industry pour out a steady flow of pamphlets and books. The important difference is that where traditional AA literature is mainly built on the accumulated experience of individual members, the new recovery literature is based on therapeutic expertise. Recovery literature and professional 12-step treatment combine to strengthen the role of expert knowledge at the expense of the oral tradition and model learning of AA.

In AA, the speaker circuit is made up of unpaid old-timers of the movement. In the newer 12-step movements, paid expert speakers and expensive workshops play a much greater role. John Bradshaw, one of the gurus of codependency, gives two hundred speeches a year, and his fee is U.S.$ 5,000 for an all-day session (Hollandsworth, 1990).

The fruits of the publishing boom can now be seen in most general bookstores in the United States. Ten years ago a bookstore might have had, at most, a few books in a small alcoholism and drug addiction section. These days it will have a substantial recovery section, occupying several shelves and often a whole bookcase or more. In 1990, responding to the flood tide of new titles, a book distributor broke a recovery category out of its psychology/self-help category; 45 percent of the 367 titles in the recovery category had been published within the year (M. Jones, 1990). Alongside the general bookstores, a whole new category of stores specifically devoted to the recovery market has emerged, stocking not only books but also movement-related cards, tapes, sweatshirts, buttons, jewelry, and talking bears. The first of these stores, appearing in the mid-1980s, "started out selling the few toys and tokens and literature available from the 12-Step groups at the time," whereas now they carry "a lot of other self-help material that doesn't necessarily relate to alcoholism or drug addiction" (J. Smith, 1990). According to the owner of what is now a chain of three stores in San Diego, "the old concept of a 12-Step shop as being primarily a drug and alcohol recovery shop is vanishing. . . . More people want to find out what's wrong with them, and they no longer have to be alcoholics or drug addicts" (Zedaker, 1989). The primary customer base of the stores is reported to be college-educated between the ages of thirty and fifty (Rivkin, 1990).

Sober Times is an example of another general 12-step institution, the generalized recovery newspaper or magazine that usually appears on a monthly basis. By 1990, there were at least eleven such publications in the United States (M. Jones, 1990). The earliest of these, the *Phoenix* of Minneapolis, got under way in 1981. Some, like *Recovering* of San Francisco, aim at a limited geographical area. Others, like *Sober Times* or the new, Toronto-based magazine *Pathways,* are interested in broader distribution. The newsprint periodicals are generally distributed free, depending on advertisements for their survival, particularly advertisements from treatment centers, psychotherapists, recovery stores, and mail-order houses for movement books, tapes, and paraphernalia.

The institutions specifically serving the recovery movements are enmeshed in a wider network of friendly institutions. One profile of this network can be seen in the listing of places where *Recovery* is distributed without charge in Berkeley (a city of about 110,000). Included are nine therapy centers, five health and service institutions, seven bookstores, two bakeries, four other retail stores, and three other public agencies ("Berkeley distribution sites," *Recovering,* March 1991).

In San Francisco and other American strongholds of 12-step groups, the 12-step program is just one ingredient in a culture interested in personal transformation and spiritual growth, one competing and coexisting with shamanism, Eastern religions, psychodynamic therapies, and New Age ideology. The amalgamation of different traditions is clearly visible in therapeutic textbook spirituality. One important feature of the new American spirituality is the belief that spiritual, emotional, and physical aspects of well-being are fundamentally interconnected (McGuire, 1993). A corollary of this basic belief is the sanctification of health and physical enjoyment. Spirituality entails the harmony of body and soul, keeping fit is a spiritual commitment, and sexual fulfillment becomes one aspect of spiritual growth.

C. L. Whitfield teaches courses in "Stress management and spirituality during recovery" and has published a book on the topic (Corrington, 1989). Spirituality is defined as involving one's relationships with one's self, with other people and with the universe. The following are typical items in Whitfield's Spirituality Self-Assessment Scale. Few of the items are even remotely related to anything supernatural, and most seem to describe the stereotypically healthy and happy American.

I enjoy even my most menial tasks such as cleaning the toilet.

I turn the negative things in my life into the positive.

I exercise regularly.

I feel sexually fulfilled.

I live in the Here and Now.

I have a sense of being able to differentiate my mind (or ego) from my spirit (or higher self).

I see the paradoxes in my life, i.e., life's opposites, as compatible with each other.

I feel accepting and accepted.

I regularly take time off for myself for relaxation and recreation.

Relations between 12-Step Movements: Fragmentation and Holism

In the beginning was AA, and AA's seniority clearly still carries great weight in the recovery community. Those coming into the community, even if they themselves are not alcoholics, are nevertheless routinely encouraged to go to AA meetings, to make their pilgrimage to the heartland of the community. But this extra weight can sometimes become a burden both on AA and on other 12-step movements. The influx of people that are not addicted to alcohol threatens AA's "singleness of purpose." On the other side of the coin, members of other 12-step movements occasionally criticize the dominance of AA.

The proliferation of 12-step organizations reflects not only the precedent set by AA's single-minded focus on alcoholism, but also the continuing aspirations on the part of participants for singleness of purpose in a group and in the movement with which it is affiliated. Ironically, the search for singleness of purpose has led many to multiple memberships in 12-step organizations, as they find one life problem after another coming to the fore.

"Recently I've heard a lot of people introduce themselves at meetings this way: 'My name is John and I'm powerless over everything.' . . . 'my name is Sue and I'm just plain screwed up.' . . . Is AA in danger of becoming an Ellis Island for the ailing?"

Jim N., 1993, pp. 35–36

"My dog is codependent. He'd likely starve if I didn't feed him. But he doesn't belong at AA meetings."

Jack F., 1993, p. 29

"So many AA members have taken over service positions as secretaries of NA meetings that from 60 to 90 percent and more of the speakers they are bringing in . . . are carrying the message of Alcoholics Anonymous. . . . This gross overabundance of AA speakers is giving out the message that NA is a secondary, less-than program."

A.R.A., 1991, pp. 3, 16

The conventional response to perceived multiple dependencies has been to attend a different 12-step meeting for each problem, often tackling the problems one at a time, so that the individual's group membership is serial or cumulative, but for some the result of this is an increasing sense of fragmentation. It is reported that "there are unofficial 'All Anonymous' meetings where sharing on any addiction is allowed. There are unofficial Twelve Step meetings where those from many programs gather for step study and don't discuss individual diseases" (V.R.M., 1991).

"AA is not just people dealing with their alcoholism. It's a lot of people like me. I'm a victim of sexual abuse and rape. I'm the adult child of alcoholics, I qualify for Al-Anon, I'm a co-dependent and the list goes on and on. I have met people in AA with a list like that."

L. W., 1991, p. 3

Even in the absence of formal general 12-step organizations, the heightened belief in the possibility of multiple personal addictions, along with the growth of a generalized 12-step consciousness, is raising the threshold of what is expected of persons in recovery. In its early decades, AA differed fundamentally from previous spiritual approaches to inebriety in that it did not ask its members to give up anything except their drinking. A haze of tobacco smoke hung over the typical AA meeting, and the meeting coffeepot took on totemic significance. Now, instead of having a master status as an alcoholic or overeater, and organizing oneself around recovering from that addiction, movement members increasingly feel accountable for a wide variety of behaviors.

"Recovery today often means juggling programs. I belong to several programs because I see how one addiction balances another."

V.R.M., 1991, p. 1

"If I deal with my codependency at one meeting, my addiction at another, my abuse issues at yet another, where, when and how do I put it all together? When am I just me and not my issues?"

Mary W., 1991, p. 13

The proliferation of generic 12-step groups may change the nature of the 12-step program as a subcultural ideology. Traditional AA is different from most other subcultures with tight networks and strong ideology. Children of practicing Christians or of political militants may revolt against their parents, but they may also become acculturated to the subculture from their early childhood onward. Children of AA members may accept or revolt against the basic tenets of AA, but they cannot become full members of the subculture if they do not become (or define themselves as) alcoholics. In Alateen you may discuss your problems as a child of an alcoholic; in this case, however, you are not learning to become a permanent adult member of the AA subculture. It is not enough to be born in an AA family, you have to qualify on your own. In a generic 12-step culture, however, the program may be translated into a general lifestyle and worldview.

Codependency Consciousness and 12-Step Culture

As its name denotes, the 12-step culture is founded on a worldview and a set of practices derived from AA. Increasingly, however, its ideology and practices draw on other sources also. One major stream of influence has been the ideology of codependence and associated ideas. The term "coalcoholism," denoting that a family member (initially the wife) of an alcoholic was herself suffering from a disease that needed treatment, first arose among alcohol treatment professionals in the early 1970s, providing a justification for treatment of the alcoholic's family member in the absence of the alcoholic. In its identification of family members as having a disabling condition, the coalcoholism concept fell well outside the ideology of Al-Anon, the 12-step organization for the family of the alcoholic. As diagnostic terminology shifted from alcoholism to alcohol dependence, co-alcoholism was replaced by codependence (D. Martin, 1988). The latter term also had the advantages of broadening the concept to include family members of those with other addictions, and drawing on connotations from general psychotherapeutic usages of dependence in the sense of overdependence in personal relationships.

"An example is the OA person telling the recovering alcoholic that he or she is not really sober if they still drink coffee, eat sugar, or smoke. The flip side is the alcoholic bashing the OA or Al-Anon member for having a drink or smoking a joint. Love addicts bash sex addicts for being low-down sleazers. Sex addicts intimate that if only love addicts would get over that romantic hogwash and honor the more animal side of their natures, all would be well! Finally, the total judgement from the generic addicts: If you are not working all 12-step programs perfectly, you are a failure."

P.G., 1991, p. 4

Codependence has played a central role in the thought of the ACOA movement. In a further development, codependence is now often generalized beyond family processes, into "a general tendency toward being too other-directed." Alongside the various strands of the ACOA movement, Co-Dependents Anonymous, which began at the end of 1986, had grown to 1,600 meetings by mid-1990, and an observer wondered: "Is CoDA what we've all been waiting for, an opening to the general population, the 12-step program for everybody?" (Chuck W., 1990, p. 9).

The ideology of codependency tends to conflict with AA's original ideology in that it emphasizes external explanations of one's own behavior (Katz, 1993, pp. 54–55). Where AA members are taught to be suspicious of any rationalizations of their behavior ("your best thinking got you here"), the approach of the "co-" movements is to begin with a rationalization and interpretation in terms of external factors—the behavior of others. In emphasizing the effects on one's current life of patterns in one's childhood family, the ACOA movement also chooses a psychodynamic view of life problems, akin to the psychoanalytic views of the 1930s, as opposed to AA's more phenomenological view (Roizen, 1977). Hand in hand with this epistemology, the thinking of the "co-" movements is more heavily dominated by professional therapists. The central texts of the movements are not anonymously compiled, but are written by therapists who have acquired a celebrity status. Some movements, such as Robin Norwood's Women Who Love Too Much groups, are organized explicitly around the writings of a particular therapist. Quite a few "co-" groups have deviated from 12-step practice in having a professional-led structure.

Potentially the most crucial divergence between the original 12-step precepts and the ideology of codependency, from the viewpoint of the future of 12-step movements, is the contrast between the individualistic emphasis of codependency thinking and AA's emphasis on mutual support and building community. "Our primary responsibility is to ourselves, rather than to others" sums up an ACOA member's adaptation of the AA Twelve Steps (Peter W., 1991). Putting such an ideology into practice tends to put in question any altruistic or community-building behavior. Indeed, some participants have noticed signs of a breakdown in volunteering for service functions and even in the ethic of mutual support in 12-step groups.

"One woman, an AA member, summed up the response I got from many. 'The meetings have changed,' she said. 'I'm not sure when it happened. There used to be a core group holding everything together. Now we're more like individuals.' A fellow therapist, active in AA and CODA said simply, 'People don't reach out as much anymore. I don't know why.' "

Mary W., 1991, p. 13

Existential Identity, Organizational Continuity, and the Rules of 12-Step Speech

AA presents an amazing organizational continuity, but this may not be a necessary requirement for future 12-step groups. In principle, the format of a 12-step meeting and rules of AA discourse can be applied to the discussion of any existential or interpersonal problems. The same meeting format should be equally adaptable to a discussion of the existential destiny of being a woman or a man or of being afraid or insane. No complicated service structure is required for organizing weekly meetings, and the literature can be made available through commercial channels.

We may speculate that AA represents the first generation of mutual-help movements. Membership is no longer based on social position, as in the old social movements, but on the permanent identity of being an alcoholic for life. Even in AA, some members stop going to meetings after a few years of sobriety, and their proportion may be growing because of high-bottom newcomers. Still, old-timers having done a "regular" program and a "regular" AA career are of crucial importance for AA as a social movement. In 12-step movements of the second generation, people are free to choose and change their existential identities as they wander from one movement to the next.

"I like to see people drop the label or use it as only one part of their self-description. 'I'm Cathy, a sacred child of the Universe, recovering from addiction to alcohol.' I hate to see people reducing themselves to being an addiction."

Kasl, 1992, p. 159

No permanent identity is necessary for a person to be able to profit from 12-step meetings. On the other hand, it can be argued that some basic but at the same time partial existential sameness is required to keep intact the rules of 12-step speech and their particular combination of positive and negative politeness (Mäkelä, 1992b).

Even at AA meetings, the rules of discourse are constantly threatened by an intrusion of outside rules of speech in the form of, on the one hand, personal quarreling and emotional escalation, and, on the other, religious or doctrinal dispute. AA meetings are flexible in the sense that blatant transgressions of the rules of discourse do not necessarily disturb the main line of the meeting. At the same time, there is always the possibility that outside rules of discourse will be allowed to intensify any deviations. To take one example, cross talk is not a problem if other participants simply ignore it, but it may escalate into a problem if, instead, it is met with further cross talk.

The likelihood of outside rules of discourse taking over a 12-step meeting depends on how the meeting is able to regulate its social connections to the outside world. In one sense, what is at stake is how the distinction presented in the Serenity Prayer is drawn between things we can and cannot change. Twelve-step rules of discourse can be applied to existential issues related to being a woman only as long as the outside patriarchy is classified among the things members cannot change. As soon as members aim at changing the outside world, theoretical debate, faction formation, and the disruption related to variations in social status and life experiences will follow.

It may be symptomatic that, judging from published descriptions, the workshops and courses sponsored by the newer 12-step movements are much more confrontational and directive than traditional 12-step meetings (Hollandsworth, 1990).

Recovery Consciousness and Political Ideology

As noted in chapter 14, individual members of AA and organizations closely connected to AA have had a profound impact on professional treatment systems and treatment legislation in the United States. Until recently, however, individual members of AA have not been active in the field of alcohol control policies. As an organization founded at the high point of the backlash against American Prohibition, AA was always careful to distinguish itself from a temperance organization, and to insist that it had no position on general alcohol policies (Room, 1989). For many years, this predilection carried over to the National Council on Alcoholism and to fellow-traveling politicians. In part, this reflected the anti-temperance sentiments of a class and generation; it may also have reflected the tendency for the push for public alcoholism treatment to serve as a "cultural alibi" (Mäkelä et al., 1981) for the dismantling of alcohol controls. In general, beverage industry interests supported the National Council on Alcoholism (NCA), and until the late 1970s served on its board. Around 1980, the NCA made a decisive break from this tradition, dropping its beverage-industry board members and moving toward an activist role on general alcohol policy (Cahalan, 1987). This shift by NCA undoubtedly reflected a change in the public mood on alcohol issues in the United States, as alcohol consumption levels began a sustained fall. But this move seems not to have signaled any clear change in the orientation of politicians who have been AA-oriented: by and large, such politicians have not been in the forefront of efforts to increase alcohol controls or to crack down on drunk drivers. AA has made a point of stressing that alcohol is not bad as such, but that there are individuals who simply cannot drink moderately. In *A.A. Grapevine*, also, little attention has been paid to the production and distribution of alcohol.

The old temperance organizations also started as movements for individual reform. Only later were goals set concerning legislation and social policy. In the 1840s, the Washingtonians recruited large numbers of reformed alcoholics who related their stories to large public audiences (Maxwell, 1950). Eriksen's (1991) study of the membership records of a temperance society in a small Danish town in the 1880s and 1890s also indicates that, particularly among the earliest members, drunkenness was not an uncommon reason for joining the society. G. Phillips (1991) similarly stresses the nature of the nineteenth-century temperance movement as a coalition of reformers and reformed. He also points out that the reformed drunkards were more than obedient rank and file, for, following their conversion, they sometimes became vocal and celebrated exponents of abstinence.

There is a difference between the old temperance movement as a coalition of reformers and reformed and AA as a fellowship of members in recovery. For most of the members of the temperance societies, joining was not a necessity but the rational choice for a new lifestyle of thrift, respectability, and rational husbanding that could open an avenue of social advancement. For low-bottom members of AA, by contrast, membership is the only way out of a desperate life situation. This difference may help to explain how AA has so successfully resisted the adoption of a broader political agenda.

The growth of a general 12-step culture may change this situation. Joining a 12-step group may now become more of a value choice and the choice of a lifestyle than the only way out from intolerable pain. Signs are already visible that this may change the relationships of 12-step movements to public policy.

Besides articles on recovery, *Sober Times* regularly carries articles on the production and distribution of alcohol and drugs. The June 1991 issue reported, for example, that the land space used for tobacco growing in third-world nations could feed ten to twenty million people. Another news item reports that "an alarming proportion of high school seniors get high regularly." The issue also contains an article in which the author expresses anger at the military for the way it has promoted alcohol abuse through subsidized prices.

Signs like these indicate that membership in 12-step movements may develop into an ideological subculture and, perhaps, even into a political constituency having an influence on alcohol and drug legislation. But the ideological influence of 12-step thinking may extend beyond special fields of legislation. Social critics have long charged that

AA and other mutual-help groups are "a psychologically focused diversion from societal criticism and structural change" (Riessman, 1990). Not uncommonly, members do look at working on a 12-step program as the opposite of political activism. Phillip Z., the author of *A Skeptic's Guide to the Twelve Steps* (1991) tells (Kahn, 1991, p. 35) of how he now counsels several former major political activists. "These people went through the upheavals of the sixties and the seventies and are now in twelve-step programs and going through profound spiritual experiences. They say, 'God, I didn't understand it, what we were doing. It was spiritual, but it was being acted out in a political way.' " But reading the pages of 12-step newspapers like *Recovering* suggests that the relation between 12-step consciousness and political ideology can be quite complicated.

"As a nation we . . . suffer a disease far more insidious than any mere substance addiction—the United States is a power and control addict.

I urge Americans to accept the fact that our nation is the biggest addict the world has known and to insist that we begin the process of withdrawal. . . . If we are to survive and flourish, America must come into recovery."

Martinovic, 1990, p. 4

In recent years, 12-step language and conceptualizations have increasingly been put to the service of political analyses of a new type. The general political framing is anti-war and ecologically minded, with occasionally some recognition of class and poverty issues. Alongside the specific political content, a strong note of evangelism and even millenarianism can be detected in some of the writing. When people begin to talk about "the community as coalcoholic" (as treatment providers were in California by the beginning of the 1980s), the concept is on its way to serving general ideological functions. The book *When Society Becomes an Addict* (Schaef, 1987) completes the transformation in an idiosyncratic melding of feminist and codependency ideologies: for Schaef, addiction is the White Male System of the society, and codependency the Reactive Female System. Another telling book title is *My Name is Chellis, and I'm in Recovery from Western Civilization* (Glendinning, 1994). Writers such as those quoted above give further evidence of how 12-step movement disease concepts are being transformed into general ideological arguments. It remains to be seen what kinds of repercussions 12-step

Table 16.3 Selected 12-Step Groups in Study Countries That Were Active in 1990

Date founded	Name	Mexico	Austria	Sweden	French-speaking Switzerland	Finland	Iceland	German-speaking Switzerland	Poland
1951	Al-Anon Family Groups	+	+	+	+	+	+	+	+
1957	Alateen	+	+	+	+	+	+	+	+
1976	Adult Children of Alcoholics	+	+	+	+	+	+	+	+
1953	Narcotics Anonymous	+	+	+	+	+	+	+	–
1960	Overeaters Anonymous	+	+	+	+	+	+	–	–
1971	Emotions Anonymous	+	+	+	+	–	–	–	–
1985	Nicotine Anonymous	+	–	–	–	–	–	–	–
1957	Gamblers Anonymous	–	–[a]	–	–	–	–	–	–
1976	Sex and Love Addicts Anonymous	–	–	–	–	–	–	+	–
1976	Debtors Anonymous	–	–	–	–	–	–	+	–
1980	Incest Survivors Anonymous	–	–	–	–	–	–	–	–
1982	Cocaine Anonymous	–	–	–	–	–	–	–	–
1986	Co-Dependents Anonymous	–	–	–	–	–	–	–	–

[a]There are groups in Austria using the name "Gamblers Anonymous," but these groups do not apply the 12-step program.

evangelism and millenarianism may in the future have on political life in North America.

"The 12-Step programs, with their emphasis on a spiritual way of life, on process not product, and on equality, not hierarchy, are our best hope for healing ourselves and our planet. Now that we are no longer ignored or ridiculed, but publicized and respected, let's hope we can meet the challenge of our success."

V.R.M., 1991, p. 9

"1990 marks the beginning of the third stage [of the recovery movement] as we focus on the healing of the planet."

Jed Diamond, 1991, p. 6

Twelve-Step Movements outside the United States and Canada

As of the early 1990s, the diffusion of the 12-step program to general life problems was limited to English-speaking North America. Table 16.3 shows the extent to which selected 12-step movements had diffused to the sites of the present study by 1990. Overeaters Anonymous and Emotions Anonymous were the only movements not addressing alcohol or drug problems that had spread to more than one of the study countries. It is particularly noteworthy that Co-Dependents Anonymous had not taken root in any of the study countries. More recently, however, there have been some signs of a diffusion of generalized 12-step thinking to Iceland, Mexico, and Sweden. In all these countries, translations of general American recovery books have been published, and professional 12-step treatment is expanding to treat problems other than alcohol and drugs. It remains an open question, however, whether the dispersion of the 12-step program to general life problems will proceed outside the United States and Canada.

Part Six
Conclusions

17

The AA Movement in Perspective

Diversity and Commonalities in AA

In studying Alcoholics Anonymous in eight societies, we found both diversity and unity. The movement's history differs substantially in different societies. Founded in the United States, and with its headquarters still located there, AA spread first to other English-speaking societies, and to societies that had a strong Protestant-oriented temperance tradition. Among our study countries, Finland, Sweden, and Iceland were included in this first wave of diffusion of AA, although the growth of AA in Sweden was slowed until recently by the presence of a competing indigenous movement. AA was established later and has grown more gradually in other European societies, particularly in the wine-drinking cultures of southern Europe. It was essentially impossible to establish AA in Eastern Europe during the Soviet-bloc era. The spectacular growth of AA in Poland in the 1980s came in step with the disintegration of the socialist system.

In developing countries, the first AA groups were usually centered around English-speaking expatriates. But in many such societies, the membership base is now predominantly indigenous. This is certainly the case in Mexico, whose membership is the largest among non-English speaking countries.

There are important variations in AA practices in different societies. To some extent, these differences reflect the surrounding culture and society, in ways both small and large, and in ways that are both taken for granted and consciously recognized. Not surprisingly, we have found that cultural differences in interaction styles and personal expressiveness influence what goes on in and around AA meetings in different places. The ritualized greetings, hand-holding, and hugging that are taken for granted in a California environment do not occur in Finnish meetings, where such practices would make many participants uncomfortable. Some variations in membership characteristics—for instance, the fact that more members in Mexico than in Sweden believe in a Christian God—can be seen as expressions of general patterns in the society. There are also differences in the AA movement that reflect the society's institutional environment. Rental arrangements for meeting space, for instance, are strongly affected by general societal arrangements concerning meeting space for voluntary organizations.

But we would advise against interpreting all cross-national variability in AA as emanating directly from variations in the surrounding culture and society. Sometimes the variability can best be understood in terms of historical coincidences and the internal history of AA in each country. Differences in membership composition, for instance, seem to be partly related to what demographic groups the early members happened to represent. In addition, the internal dynamics of AA are also affected by external factors. The advent of institutional 12-step treatment may, for example, be of crucial significance for the national AA movement, but this and other external influences often cannot be understood as direct reflections of basic structural or cultural characteristics of the surrounding society.

AA also varies considerably within each society. At many levels, we found that diversification appears to have proceeded furthest in the United States. Certainly, none of the other places included in our study matched California in the proliferation of special groups for subdivisions of the population, defined by such criteria as gender, age, and sexual orientation. Outside the United States, many AA members would in fact disapprove of such special interest groups, regarding them as undermining the principle that differences between members are transcended by the unity derived from the common affliction of alcoholism.

Except in Mexico, AA has maintained its organizational unity. And even in Mexico (if the 24-hour movements are classified as outside AA), the organizational split does not appear to make much difference in the daily life of meetings and members. Within the general organizational unity, however, a very substantial diversity exists in each society with respect to the practices, tone, and composition of different AA groups. The AA proverb which has it that "all you need to start your own AA meeting is a resentment and a coffee-pot" (Pittman, 1988b, p. 236), expresses the reality that the origin of many groups is another group. This characteristic of AA turns the organizational weakness, which might result from conflicts of personality or principle, into a source of organizational growth and strength. Since a new group resulting from intragroup differences is also likely to ensure that its practices rectify what it sees as the deficiencies in the parent group's practices, the fissiparous nature of AA tends to increase the diversity within it. Thus the groups in a given area will often have highly differentiated reputations among AA members, on such dimensions as membership composition, the degree of "Big Book fundamentalism," and the degree of regimentation exercised by sponsors.

Yet, our study also found substantial unity in AA organizationally, and in terms of beliefs and practices. This relative unity has made it possible for us to describe characteristics of AA as a movement that are broadly applicable in each of our study sites. In each of the societies studied, we found a basic pattern of AA meetings at a regular time or times each week, with each meeting composed of relatively brief periods of recitations and announcements framing a core activity of participants taking turns in sharing their experiences. In each society, we found an adherence to the Twelve Steps, the Twelve Traditions, movement-sanctioned literature as the basic texts and approaches of the movement, and a bottom-up structure of governance based on autonomous groups. We also found that in some ways AA in different societies has converged over the years. This has sometimes been the result of better and more complete translations of AA materials, and sometimes of a deliberate action by a national AA movement to bring its practices into closer conformity with North American practice.

But the patterns of international influence still appear to be largely one-directional; we have not found any examples of North American practice changing in the light of experience elsewhere. And this one-way flow of influence is still built into the international structure of AA; the North American General Service Conference is still de facto the governing body of the international movement, with no formal provision for input from other national bodies.

Against this pattern of international influence must be set the fact that in some ways AA in North America has changed more than AA elsewhere. On a number of dimensions, we have found AA in the United States to be unique among our eight societies—and unique in ways that represent changes from earlier traditions in AA. As we have mentioned, the diversification of special groups by gender, age, and sexual preference has proceeded much further in the United States than elsewhere. Only in the United States, among our study sites, do AA groups generally cooperate with the courts by certifying mandated attendance at meetings. And, with the proliferation of other 12-step groups in North America, AA there finds itself more than elsewhere serving as a kind of "home church" for a generalized 12-step movement.

Despite the one-way flow of influence, these changes from the original practice or situation in North America seem so far to have had little effect in AA elsewhere. Internationally, AA seems to be following the pattern of change at the core and conservatism at the periphery, which is common in the diffusion of ideas and cultural practices. A conservatism with respect to change is supported by AA's bottom-up structure of local and national autonomy, and a preference for decisions by consensus at every level of decision-making.

AA as a Movement: A Unique Organizational Form

Any continuing organization must make a series of choices about its internal organization and its relation to the outside world. How is membership in the organization to be defined, and to what extent inclusively or exclusively? Is the basic unit of organization the individual, a face-to-face group, or some larger group? Are the forms of relation within the organization, both between individuals and between groups, egalitarian, hierarchical, a client/professional relation, or some mixture of these? Where in the organization are its assets held, and who controls them—the face-to-face group, the organization as a whole, an oligarchic committee of trustees, or some other party? Does the organization approach the outside world evangelically, seeking alliances, or with a stance of splendid isolation?

AA's organizational principles steer a clear path through these questions. Membership is defined inclusively; on the other hand, the stance to the outside world is isolationist, neither accepting nor seeking outside influence. Power resides at the base, in the "group conscience" of the face-to-face group; all superstructures are defined as responsible to the base-group level. Forms of relation are egalitarian, both within the group and between groups. Thus group officers and delegates are elected by group members, and incumbency is expected to rotate between members. Groups are autonomous and cannot be subject to control either by other groups or by some superior body. The problem of where assets are held is solved in large part by a prohibition on owning property or holding substantial assets (other than publication rights). As we have noted, nuances and even exceptions to these general choices exist, but their general direction is clear.

The normal development of long-lasting social movements, and also of mutual-help groups on the grassroots level, is that they are slowly transformed from their often charismatic beginnings and become more bureaucratic and professional (Bales, 1944; Kramer, 1981). The movement often seeks to be accepted by the public bureaucracy as a representative, or the sole representative, for a constituency. In the course of this the movement is itself absorbed into the bureaucratic system. This process has been described by Back and Taylor (1976) as "inchoate desires of a part of the population" to organize and form "social 'institutions' that sometimes supersede the accepted institutional set-up" (p. 296).

Usually one major aim of such movements or associations is to procure more resources, including economic support and subsidies. If they are successful, these subsidies are followed by increasing public control and demands for supervision. While movements commonly start with one specific interest, concentrating their efforts on one question or problem, their scope of interest often widens as they grow and their aims become more universal (Zald & Denton, 1963). Often they become political movements (Back & Taylor, 1976).

AA is unusual among movements in how long it has survived without fundamental alterations of ideology or program. To an unprecedented extent, AA has also succeeded in creating an organization that breaks the "iron law of oligarchy" (Michels, 1958) by building in structures and principles that minimize the professionalization of leadership and keep effective organizational power at the level of egalitarian face-to-face interaction (Helmersson, 1989). From another perspective, Bufe (1991) has remarked how well AA has carried into practice the organizational ideals of classical anarchist thought.

Conventional social science thinking tends to equate organizational efficacy with bureaucratic structure. Organizations lacking centralized structure and a clear division of work and power are regarded as embryos of a formal organization. Gerlach (1983) argues, however, that segmented cell structures can be very efficient organizations in modern societies. The success of AA strongly supports Gerlach's argument.

AA is based on a cell structure. All groups are autonomous and economically independent, at the same time being open to anyone wishing to stop drinking. Groups grow and die, proliferate and contract, divide and fuse spontaneously. The entire movement is financed by voluntary contributions and literature sales, and groups decide among themselves to what extent and for which purposes they wish to support national activities.

AA is also a polycephalous organization. There is an almost total lack of centralized decision-making structures. On the other hand, it has many influential people competing for leadership, but leadership does not predominantly rest on the individual's position in the formal structure. In all organizations, an informal network exists alongside the formal structure, but in AA the informal prestige structure is particularly important. An individual's prestige in AA has little to do with his or her social standing in the outside society. Members enjoy prestige because of their wisdom, life experience, work with people still having drinking problems, previous service engagements, and oratorical skills. Personality clashes often cause groups to split, but this forms no threat to the organization as a whole because AA grows by ramification.

AA is by no means only an amorphous collection of cells; they are bound together to form a complex network. Individuals visit groups in their own locality or elsewhere, groups arrange joint activities, and there are well-known traveling orators who attract more participants than ordinary meetings. Regional and national conferences provide a platform for prominent members and further strengthen the social network.

A polycephalous cell structure of this kind has many advantages. The risk of a member starting to drink is seen by AA as ever-present and as making it impossible to build the organization around individual members in powerful positions. By its nature, a polycephalous structure enables the organization to avoid the potential dysfunctions caused by leadership senescence or malfeasance, or of the ossification of hierarchical structures. It also prevents governments from easily suppressing the movement by attacking its leaders—although AA has not in fact been subjected to substantial political oppression anywhere. The cell structure also facilitates the task of reaching different population groups; in large communities, there is a great variety of groups for newcomers to choose from, allowing them to join groups that suit their social background, ideology, and personality.

At the same time, the cell structure increases the adaptability of the movement to diverse forms of activity. Maladapted variants simply vanish without endangering the movement as a whole. If a group splits or fails, the members are absorbed by other groups whose efforts have proven successful.

AA's stability, unity, and polycephalous character are enhanced by several features of its organization. The principle of decision by consensus rather than by majority vote tends to prevent division into factions. The principle of rotation is another factor preventing cleavages. An individual can be elected to serve on the national level for only one term, and this means that conflicts usually do not coincide with individual disagreements. That AA accepts no economic help from the outside contributes to keeping the group membership as the primary locus of decision-making. And, finally, the rule that AA as an organization takes no position on matters outside the movement, not even on questions pertaining to the care of alcoholics or matters directly related to the activities of the movement, diminishes the need for mechanisms for centralized decision-making.

In addition to its longevity and size, AA is perhaps pointed to as the model mutual-help group precisely because of the structural and organizational attributes just described. And although AA stands out as a model, these attributes actually render it exceptional among the whole range of mutual-help groups and organizations. In fact, that AA has been able to maintain its fundamental non-bureaucratic and non-heirarchic structure for almost sixty years through such principles is what makes AA most interesting as a movement.

AA as a Belief System

The newcomer to AA is introduced quickly to the main features of AA's system of thought and belief. The Serenity Prayer, which the newcomer is almost certain to hear or see at the first meeting attended, encapsulates two central values: of serenity as a transcendent life goal, and of action rather than contemplation as the means to this goal. The orientation to action is reinforced by the slogans the newcomer is likely to see on the walls of the meeting room. Both the prayer and the slogans also convey the fact that AA has a spiritual orientation. The term "alcoholic," likely to be uttered among the very first words of the meeting, carries with it important connotations. One is that the movement is concerned with a sickness, in turn implying a condition that one suffers from and that cannot be cured by pure unaided self-will. A second is that AA members share a common status, a democracy of the derogated, as alcoholics. In the course of the first meeting, the newcomer will almost certainly also hear that a prerequisite for the alcoholic's recovery is refraining from drinking, an action to be carried out "one day at a time" (Pittman, 1988b, p. 221), and that coming back to AA meetings is an important part of the program.

These first impressions will be immediately reinforced in a number of ways. The newcomer will quickly be introduced to the Twelve Steps, a spiritually oriented program of action that starts with naming the experience at the heart of AA's concept of alcoholism—the double loss of control, of one's drinking and one's life because of drinking. In the meeting, he or she will hear a succession of speakers share their own stories, with the stories very likely keyed to AA's main beliefs and ways of thinking. As the meeting breaks up, those in attendance will probably be encouraged to take movement literature home and to read AA's

Big Book, which lays out and explicates the 12-step program, and illustrates its promise with further stories from people's life experiences.

In themselves, the Twelve Steps are literally a program. They do not formulate a code of conduct but a series of tasks and problems to be solved. Despite the importance of the basic texts, the program and the methods of work are mainly transmitted orally, and learning by example plays an important role in the AA process.

The fundamentals of AA's ways of thinking and of its belief system are relatively few, and are quickly communicated. Since "the only requirement for membership is a desire to stop drinking," AA is in literal terms a non-creedal spiritual movement: there is no creed of beliefs to which members have to subscribe. Even for the small cluster of normative beliefs we have outlined, there is an expectation and often an encouragement for members to differ in their interpretations. As we have seen, there are large differences in what members would define as a spiritual approach, and in the relative weight given to the spiritual and the pragmatic sides of the AA program. Views will differ on what can be said more specifically about the nature of alcoholism. Some members adhere to particular theories about alcoholism, whereas others focus on their existential powerlessness with respect to alcohol.

Nevertheless, there is a normative element in the adherence to the core AA beliefs. The newcomer may challenge or reject any one of them, usually without so much as a remonstrance. He or she may be told sympathetically to "take what you can use, and leave the rest" (Pittman, 1988b, p. 224). At the same time, many—but not all—experienced members will tend to regard such views as temporary aberrations, expecting the newcomer in the fullness of time to fall in line.

Most elements of AA's belief system can pass through cultural barriers in the industrialized world, and in much of the developing world, without serious challenge. The most problematic element has been and will continue to be AA's spiritual approach. The difficulties with this come from two sides. On the one hand, an emphasis on the spiritual tends to offend the various offspring of the European Enlightenment, particularly those with Marxist, scientific, or humanist perspectives. As we have noted, many of the sobriety groups that started from an adaptation of the AA program—for example, Links in Sweden, the Hudolin clubs in Croatia, and Rational Recovery in the United States—specifically distinguished themselves from AA by dropping the spiritual dimension.

AA has had long experience in dealing with these objections, which arose in its earliest years, and a chapter of the *Big Book* is devoted to this issue. AA's first line of defense here tends to be to distinguish between the religious and the spiritual, identifying itself only with the latter. Its second line of defense is to suggest that it is up to each individual to define a personal higher power.

On the other hand, those committed to the idea that God is the same for everyone are often offended by AA's formulation that each person defines their higher power for themselves. Such a formulation is a good solution for a spiritual movement which seeks to operate across denominational lines in a multifaith or secular society. But it is likely to be troubling for those who are convinced that their faith's God is the only true one. This is likely to remain a stumbling block for AA in Islamic societies, for instance, as it is among more traditional and fundamentalist Christians and orthodox Jews.

AA as a System of Interaction

The AA meeting is the core expression of AA as a movement. But a dense structure of other interactions is built up around the meeting, as we have described. Members may get together before the meeting, many will usually linger over refreshments after the meeting, and some may go on elsewhere to continue their interaction. Telephone numbers will often be exchanged. A sponsor/sponsee relationship will add another, often intense, cycle of dyadic interaction.

As a social network, AA represents an important special type. Membership in AA is based on life experiences that are not direct reflections of social position. Unlike professional networks, AA networks are not based on instrumental performance, but they also differ from networks based on gender, family ties, or ethnicity. They are based on individual life experiences and existential identities transgressing gender, kin, work, and ethnicity.

The mutuality of the AA experience and the self-disclosure involved in taking turns at a meeting mean that the relations between members often have an unusual intensity. To reveal the secret and private to others, and to carry knowledge of their secrets and their private life, requires a great deal of mutual trust. Through the meeting process and other AA interactions, members of an AA group have an unusually clear view of how other members think and feel and act in the world. The formal equality of status as alcoholics and co-members also contributes to the feelings of camaraderie many AA members experience.

These feelings greatly facilitate AA's function as a mutual support and assistance network on matters not directly connected with drinking. As we have noted, many AA members find jobs through their AA connections. Finding a new place to live is also a frequent priority for those moving out of the drinking life, and other AA members will often help find housing. Though romantic relationships are usually discouraged early in the recovery process, dating and courtship relationships often develop from acquaintance in AA.

In our analysis we have emphasized the special nature of the interaction order in the AA meeting itself. AA meetings are based on extended turns that exclude a discussion in the ordinary sense of the word. In an AA meeting, those choosing to speak will speak in turn, usually only once during a meeting. The unwritten rules require a speaker to focus on his or her own experience as a drinker or in trying to follow the AA program and not to openly challenge previous speakers. The lack of cross talk and negative feedback creates space for candid self-revelations that in other contexts would signify a total loss of face. At the same time, some newcomers feel uncomfortable about not receiving as much direct affirmation or comfort as hearers would be expected to offer in ordinary conversation.

The special rules of talk in AA meetings do not mean that no challenging feedback is offered by others to the AA speaker. But the feedback happens outside the meeting time itself. In these circumstances, the speaker's formulation may be directly challenged, and the advice is often direct and earthy.

Much specialized language has grown up around the AA movement, relating both to aspects of the program and to views of the world it entails. The verbal tradition of AA mottos and proverbs is particularly richly developed in English. In North America, more than elsewhere, some terms and phrases are now widely known outside AA, and have become part of the general culture.

The traditional language of AA reflects the movement's emphasis on the experiential and the pragmatic. As we have described above, Bill W. saw the active alcoholic as full of justifications and rationalizations, and traditional AA thinking has been suspicious of responses of this kind. Instead of a psychodynamic interpretation, or any other interpretation that would tend to assign responsibility elsewhere, the speaker in an AA meeting is encouraged to interpret past events in a way that attributes a causal role to his or her own drinking.

Many AA members nowadays, particularly in North America, have had some experience with professional or semiprofessional psychotherapy, and bring to their participation in AA both a familiarity with therapeutic terms and a taste for psychodynamic interpretations. The Adult Children of Alcoholics movement, through which many new members have come to AA, has contributed its share of popular psychology terminology to the mix, and yet another set of terms and ways of thinking is associated with the rise of professional 12-step treat-ment institutions. Unlike AA's own meeting process, 12-step treatment has a tradition of confrontation in therapy groups, with the therapeutic aim often being to "break down denial." Longstanding AA members in the United States, and increasingly elsewhere, often complain of the intrusion of "psychobabble," as they term it, from these various tradi-tions into AA meetings.

The Social and Cultural Role of AA

In societies where it is well established, AA plays a significant social and cultural role. Firstly, it is a significant aspect of the society's response to alcohol problems. As we have seen, 9 percent of U.S. adults have at-tended an AA meeting at some time in their life, with 3 percent attend-ing for help with an alcohol problem of their own.

In societies where AA is strong, a large proportion of former heavy drinkers will have had an experience with AA. Population estimates based on a Finnish national drinking survey of 1984 (Simpura, 1987) can be used to calculate the number of sober AA members as a propor-tion of all abstaining former frequent drinkers in Finland. In order to obtain a measure of the relative significance of AA, we selected the subgroup of abstainers who (a) answered positively to the statement "I am afraid that I cannot control my behavior when intoxicated" and who (b) earlier in their life were drinking at least twice a week. Projecting results from the survey to the national population, there were 15,400 persons in Finland fulfilling these criteria. If those reporting an earlier drinking frequency of once a week are included, the population esti-mate is 25,100. Finnish AA recorded 4,800 members with at least one year of sobriety in 1985. The membership of AA thus represents some-thing between one-third and one-fifth of all abstaining former fre-quent drinkers with concerns about losing control over their drinking behavior (Mäkelä, 1994). This calculation underestimates the signifi-cance of AA to the extent that the former drinking frequency of AA members was more than twice a week. The comparison also includes only totally abstinent former drinkers, leaving out those former heavy drinkers who presently drink moderately.

Secondly, in many societies the general public thinks first of AA when asked about treatment for alcohol problems. When survey re-spondents from the general population are asked what treatment they would recommend if a friend or relative asked their advice, AA is more likely to be named than any other resource. In the Lothian district of Scotland in 1977, 55 percent of the general population said they would recommend AA, with 48 percent suggesting a general practitioner and 28 percent a unit for treatment of alcoholism (Rootman & Moser, 1985, p. 62). In the same study, over four-fifths of respondents in the Tlalpan area of Mexico City said they would recommend AA (p. 96). In Contra Costa County, California, in 1987–1988, 92 percent of the respondents to this study said they would recommend AA if a friend or relative asked where they should seek help for an alcohol problem of their own, while 65 percent said they would recommend "a private hospital program for alcoholism such as Care Unit," and 60 percent would recommend "a public alcoholism program" (unpublished Alcohol Research Group data). In Ontario in 1993, among adults in the general population who had made a suggestion to a friend or relative in the last year to seek professional help or had helped them get assistance with their drinking, 58 percent had recommended or suggested "AA or another support group meeting," 29 percent had recommended or suggested "doctor or nurse," and only 8 percent had recommended or suggested an "alcohol or drug treatment agency" (Bondy, 1994). In such societies, AA has clearly captured the imagination of the general public as the first recourse for someone with alcohol problems.

Thirdly, AA has had a substantial influence on professional thinking about and treatment for alcohol problems in many societies. The choice of "alcoholism" as the scientifically and professionally preferred term in the 1950s, 1960s, and 1970s, and its predominance in popular thought to the present, owes a great deal to the thinking of AA, and to its having been part of "an approach that worked" (Keller, 1972; Room, 1978). From the 1940s on in North America, a leading source of staffing for the growing treatment systems for alcohol problems has been AA members. Twelve-step approaches are central to most professional alcohol treatment programs in the United States, and in recent years the U.S. treatment model of a mix of psychotherapeutic and 12-step approaches has been exported elsewhere. As we have described, this model has become an important ingredient in the treatment systems used in such countries as Iceland and Sweden.

Fourthly, AA has an increasing influence on the general culture, particularly in North America. Through American films and television shows, audiences in America and eventually in much of the world are exposed to AA perspectives and meetings (Room, 1989). In addition to the direct influence of AA, North American culture is also substantially affected by indirect influences through institutions and movements that have sprung from AA or which AA members have helped to found and guide. Included in this list would be the many other 12-step movements and much of the alcohol and drug treatment efforts. As we have

noted, concepts derived from 12-step movements have become suffi-
ciently a part of the popular culture to be joked about in newspaper
comic strips.

All movements eventually reach a saturation point, the point at
which they have exhausted the population pool from which they
draw. Usually, the high-water mark of a movement is still only a small
fraction of all those who are eligible. From this point of view, AA may
be approaching saturation in the United States. Comparing the 9 percent of the U.S. adult population who have at some time attended an
AA meeting with the one-fifth or so who have at some time drunk at
all heavily, we might guess that the upward curve of AA membership
in the United States cannot long continue. As a whole, the broad spectrum of 12-step groups must be seen as further from saturation, but it
is worth keeping in mind that already about as many U.S. adults have
attended 12-step groups in the last year as went to any kind of psycho-
therapist or counselor.

Against this, it must be noted that each stage in AA's growth in the
United States could hardly have been predicted before it occurred. It
would have been a brave observer of AA before 1939 who would have
predicted its takeoff in the early 1940s. Similarly, a commentator in the
1950s might well have concluded that AA was associated with a particular age-cohort, and would dwindle like, for example, the Women's
Christian Temperance Union did as its founding generations aged and
died (Gusfield, 1957). A social analyst in the 1970s might have predicted that AA's organizational vitality would be sapped by the growth
of public and private alcoholism treatment institutions, and an observer in the 1980s might have expected recruitment to AA to decline
in parallel with the fall in the United States per capita consumption of
alcohol after 1981. So far, however, AA has muddled all such predic-
tions, growing to become a pervasive influence in American life.

As we have documented, AA is a movement that in successive
stages has also outgrown the cultural milieu of its birth. Again, it
would have required a brave observer indeed to predict the extent
and pattern of its growth. In the context of 1980s Sweden, with a
strongly established homegrown mutual-help movement, Links, and a
dense network of government-funded professional treatment, it
would have been hard to predict the upsurge of AA in the wake of the
promotion of institutional 12-step treatment. Similarly, in Poland in
the 1980s, with existing abstainers' organizations sponsored both by
clinicians and by the Catholic church, and in the context of a national-
ist workers' movement, the explosive growth of AA would probably
not have been predicted.

The most likely areas for further growth for AA in the immediate future are eastern and southern Europe and Latin America. In eastern Europe, the collapse of the Soviet system has created a space for autonomous social movements. In the relatively "wet" cultures of eastern and southern Europe, AA's emphasis on help for the individual drinker is more acceptable, given the cultural politics of alcohol, than more collective approaches to reducing drinking problems. In Latin America, the individuated abstention of AA may fit well into prevailing ideologies of modernization. The fellowship also has established bridgeheads in some industrialized Asian countries. It remains to be seen whether AA will be able to spread all over the industrialized world, irrespective of religious and cultural traditions. As we have noted, however, AA remains a phenomenon of highly developed and wealthy societies. Self-help may seem to provide an inexpensive solution to many social and health problems in developing nations, but movements such as AA have remained alien to most non-industrialized countries.

When the history of the twentieth century is written, AA will merit discussion not only for its influence in the specific field of alcohol problems, because AA is also the prototype of a new kind of social movement. It has served, and will continue to serve, as a general organizational model—a model of how mutual-help efforts can be organized on a non-hierarchical, nonprofessionalized, and flexible basis. And its international diffusion is evidence that the globalization of ways of thinking and being has reached a new level—that a system of thought and a program of action developed in middle-class North America in the 1930s can be adapted and made relevant, while still maintaining its core features, in cultural environments as diverse as the slums of Mexico City, the factory towns of Poland, and the agricultural villages of Switzerland.

18
Implications for Professional Practice and Research Programming

Drawing on the evidence presented in this report as well as on our experiences of collaboration with AA members during the fieldwork, we would like to offer two sets of observations on the practical implications of our work. The first series deals with issues that may be of interest to treatment professionals and treatment administrators. The second series addresses issues related to research and research programming.

Implications for Professional Treatment Practices

1. In itself, AA is not a treatment modality but a mutual-help movement.

2. A clear analytic distinction should be kept between AA as a mutual-help movement and the professional treatment inspired by or oriented to AA's Twelve Steps. AA differs from "12-step treatment" in many ways besides the absence of a professional/client relationship. One of the fundamental differences is the difference between what goes on in the group process of an AA meeting and what goes on in a group therapy session.

3. AA is not the only mutual-help movement for alcohol problems. Treatment agencies and other public agencies should not give special preference to AA or any other mutual-help movement.

4. AA and other mutual-help movements should be seen as initiatives by people in pain, not as solutions to society's alcohol problems. The proliferation of mutual-help groups cannot provide an alibi for dismantling public welfare services for alcohol problems, and mechanical referral to AA should not be used as a substitute for public treatment services. Public treatment systems should offer a broad spectrum of professional programs based on different treatment ideologies.

5. Professional and public agencies should respect the autonomy and principles of mutual-help groups.

6. Professionals should be informed, and should inform their patients about mutual-help groups active in their community.

7. AA groups and meetings vary in social composition, tenor, and interpretations of the AA program. In advising clients, account should be taken of this variability.

8. Membership in AA is based on social identification and existential self-definition. There are narrow ethical limits as to how far outside professionals can go in bringing about these processes. Any element of compulsion in professional advice to attend AA tends to be contrary to AA's principle of attraction as the mode of recruitment of new members.

9. Mandatory referral to AA or any other mutual-help movement adhering to specific ideological principles violates civil liberties.

Implications for Research

1. Since AA and other mutual-help movements are an important part of the social response to alcohol problems in many countries, it is important to do research on these movements. Funding agencies should be willing to support a broad range of methodologies in such studies.

2. Any studies of AA should be mindful of the difference between AA and structured treatment programs based on the 12-step program of AA.

3. As a mutual-help movement, AA cannot be adequately studied with a treatment outcome protocol. What should be evaluated is not the movement itself but the actions taken by the public health and social control system with respect to the movement. If medical practitioners recommend that their patients attend AA meetings, controlled trials can be designed to evaluate this advice. If courts use mandatory attendance to AA as an alternative to other penalties, this sentencing practice can and should be evaluated.

4. When the Twelve Steps of AA are applied in professional inpatient or outpatient treatment, the efficacy of the treatment can and should be evaluated.

5. The program of AA and other mutual-help movements may also be used as a source of ideas for experimental studies of specific tools and methods commonly used within the movements.

6. Studies of AA and of referral to AA need to take into account the wide variation between AA groups and meetings, even in a given society or locality.

7. Great caution is required in any generalizations about which groups of drinkers feel at home in AA and which do not. Insofar as the

recruitment of new members is based on informal networks and on social identification, membership composition tends to perpetuate itself. Historical contingencies may, therefore, have a long-lasting influence on the nature of AA in each country, or, for that matter, of any particular AA group. Institutional 12-step programs may also have an important impact on the recruitment process and the composition of the membership.

8. Retrospective studies are of limited value for an understanding of affiliation with AA. Retrospective clinical studies are particularly uninformative, since the subgroups having had contact with AA consist of members who have failed. For a better understanding of the affiliation process, randomized prospective studies are required, but randomized referral cannot imitate the self-selection processes inherent in spontaneous recruitment to AA. Another promising, and less expensive, approach is to compare the membership of AA directly to clinical samples and to the membership of other mutual-help groups for drinking problems.

9. There is a lack of ethnographic and organizational studies of AA in particular settings. In the long run, such studies would provide the basis for a systematic analysis of the dimensions of variability within AA.

10. Randomized clinical trials could include as an important component ethnographic and organizational studies of the groups the clients are referred to.

11. One important topic for research is the study of interrelations of AA and professional treatment systems in different countries and communities.

12. It would be important to describe differences in opinion among members of AA as well as ongoing historical changes. Important issues include the following:

- How do AA groups react to court referrals and mandatory AA attendance?
- What is happening with 12th-step work and sponsorship?
- Is going to AA meetings becoming more of an isolated therapeutic event rather than part of a way of life?
- What are the relationships between special interest meetings and general AA meetings?
- Is the primary identification of members in special interest groups with their demographic or identity category or is it with AA in general?
- What are the interrelations of AA and other 12-step movements?

13. Much of the specificity of AA lies in AA meetings as speech events. To describe the dynamics of AA meetings and the AA rules of discourse, both detailed microanalytical studies in the tradition of conversation analysis and more global descriptions in the tradition of ethnography of speaking are needed.

14. As a matter of research ethics, the traditions and tacit understandings of AA and of AA meetings should be respected, as would be appropriate for any voluntary organization.

Appendices
References
Index of Personal Names
Subject Index

Appendix A
Organization and Methods of Work of the International Collaborative Study of Alcoholics Anonymous (ICSAA)

The following research institutes and groups participated in the International Collaborative Study of Alcoholics Anonymous (ICSAA).

Austria
Ludwig Boltzmann Institute for Addiction Research, Vienna
Finland
Finnish Foundation for Alcohol Studies, Helsinki
Iceland
Department of Psychiatry, National University Hospital, Reykjavik
Mexico
Division of Epidemiology and Social Studies, Mexican Institute of Psychiatry, Mexico City
Poland
Institute of Psychiatry and Neurology, Warsaw
Sweden
Department of Sociology, University of Stockholm, Stockholm
Switzerland
Swiss Institute for the Prevention of Alcohol and Drug Problems, Lausanne
United States of America
Alcohol Research Group, Medical Research Institute, Berkeley, California
Prevention Research Center, Berkeley, California

In addition to the researchers representing these institutes, the project group included participants working on an individual basis.

259

The project group functioned as a scientifically autonomous body, but it has greatly benefited from the collaboration and support of the WHO Regional Office for Europe, under an agreement between the Regional Office and the Finnish Foundation for Alcohol Studies. The study also had the advantage of functioning as a project group of the Kettil Bruun Society for Social and Epidemiological Research on Alcohol.

The national projects were carried out independently by the participating groups. Klaus Mäkelä was elected project director for the international aspect of the study.

The international collaboration was organized around a series of working meetings. The project originated from a planning meeting held in June 1987 in Aix-en-Provence, France. At the first working meeting in August 1988 in Helsinki, Finland, the participants agreed on the scope and purpose of the project. At the second working meeting, held in October 1989 in Zaborow, Poland, a first outline of the final report was adopted. A draft report was discussed at the third working meeting in January 1991 in San Rafael, California, and further amended at the fourth working meeting in October 1992 in Mexico City, Mexico. The report was finalized at the fifth working meeting in November 1993 in Vienna, Austria.

At the first working meeting, project participants adopted comprehensive guidelines for data collection and a number of specific research instruments, available upon request at the Finnish Foundation for Alcohol Studies. The report from the first working meeting specifically states that AA traditions, including the principle of anonymity, will be strictly respected at all stages of the project.

The national and cross-national aspects of the project were closely intertwined. The guidelines for data collection and the questionnaires provided a common frame to enhance comparability, but participant groups were to decide individually which aspects were most important to study in their particular society. At project meetings, a large number of working papers on selected aspects of AA in each society were presented and discussed. Equally important for the drafting process were papers on the conceptual terms under which AA could best be understood. The participants also wrote more general national case descriptions, to be published in a companion volume to this report (Eisenbach-Stangl & Rosenqvist, in press). In addition, selected papers have appeared in special issues of *Contemporary Drug Problems* (winter 1992), *Drogalkohol* (no. 3, 1992), and *Wiener Zeitschrift für Suchtforschung* (nos. 1–2, 1994).

Appendix B
Collection of Interviews, Observations, Life Stories, and Other Qualitative Data

Making Contact with AA

Initial contacts with AA were made in 1987 or 1988 by approaching local and national service offices and members of AA with whom the researchers were already acquainted. In Finland, a five-page presentation of the study was distributed to anybody interested. The presentation contained a detailed discussion of how the principle of anonymity would be safeguarded. In Sweden, a presentation of the project was published in the AA newsletter. In other countries, a similar function was fulfilled by the report from the First Working Meeting. The report also spelled out the endorsement of the WHO Regional Office for Europe, which proved very helpful.

In many field projects, researchers can increase their credibility by asking some formally representative body to endorse the study. In AA, there was no central bureaucracy that could open the way. Although in all countries we were allowed to represent the project at business meetings at various levels of the service structure, we also needed to gain the confidence of each individual separately. In the course of the fieldwork and after establishing good relationships with a few prestigious old-timers, this task became increasingly easy. Personal recommendations from one AA member to another were vital for obtaining informants. We soon noted that it was of no use to rush to specific questions before the informant was given space to present his or her general view of AA and key parts of his or her own story. In the beginning, the general presentation of AA tended to be rather long, but a few short questions and comments showing some familiarity with AA were enough to unintrusively shorten the general introduction. With every new informant, however, the researcher had to earn the right to ask questions by disclosing some comprehension of the program. More than most other studies we have been involved in, the AA project was an experience of two-way communication.

Based on our experience, the simplest and best advice to researchers approaching AA is to be completely honest. We were well received when we said that we as researchers were interested in learning about AA. We did not represent the study as benefiting AA or people with alcohol problems.

261

Talks and Interviews

Table B.1 gives an overview of written records of talks and interviews collected for the project. Interviews with experienced AA members were a major source of information. To complement the points of view of veterans active in the service structure, effort was made to contact a wide variety of members, including newcomers and dissidents. A sub-study in Finland included structured interviews with female AA members. The informants were usually located through recommendations from members with whom we were already in contact, and also through encounters at meetings. The majority of the interviews were conducted from 1988 to 1990, but the fieldwork continued through 1992.

In many countries, researchers had close contacts with a few key members with long experience in AA who often were a part of the national service board. In Sweden, for example, project participants had more than fifty talks with five AA members. In many instances, no written notes were preserved, and these talks are not included in Table B.1.

Informant interviews covered a broad range of topics, such as the early beginnings and present activities of AA in each country, translations of AA literature and their distribution, the interpretation of Steps and Traditions, issues related to special categories of members such as newcomers and women, issues of internal organization and finances, and relations to other movements and to public authorities.

In four countries, members of Al-Anon were contacted. In Finland and Mexico, a sub-study collected thematic interviews on pathways to Al-Anon, first contact experiences, the Al-Anon program, and relations with the AA movement. Included among our informants are also members of other mutual-help groups for alcoholics. The majority of these come from the Swedish Link movement. In Austria, Mexico, Poland, Sweden, and Switzerland, treatment professionals were interviewed about their relationships to mutual-help groups.

Observations at Meetings

At the first working meeting, observation guidelines for AA meetings were adopted. As taking detailed notes during AA meetings would have been intrusive, the guidelines were to be used as checklists for reports written after the meetings. Separate guidelines were formulated for large open meetings where notes could be taken.

In addition to ordinary open AA meetings, project participants attended meetings at higher levels of the service structure such as regional and national business meetings and conventions (Table B.2). Notes were also taken on special occasions such as birthday celebrations and Christmas parties, as well as on meetings of Al-Anon and the Links. Detailed descriptions of eleven AA meetings and groups were prepared in English for comparative discussions at the third working meeting.

Life Stories

In a sub-study of the project, systematic samples of AA life stories were collected in Finland, Mexico, Poland, and Switzerland (Table B.3). The samples

Table B.1 Written Records of Talks and Interviews with Members of Mutual-Help Groups and with Treatment Professionals

	Austria	Finland	Iceland	Mexico	Poland	Sweden	French-speaking Switzerland	German-speaking Switzerland
Talks and interviews with AA members in								
metropolitan regions	18	104	13	35	39	10	5	5
other parts of the country	13	6	—	—	5	2	12	13
Structured interviews with female AA members in								
metropolitan regions	—	14	—	5	15	—	—	1
other parts of the country	—	2	—	—	—	—	—	—
Talks and interviews with members of Al-Anon in								
metropolitan regions	2	11	1	50	—	—	—	—
other parts of the country	—	3	—	—	—	—	—	—
Talks and interviews with members of other alcohol-related mutual-aid groups in								
metropolitan regions	3	—	—	8	—	18	—	—
other parts of the country	—	2	—	—	—	11	—	—
Talks and interviews with treatment professionals about AA	15	—	—	9	39	8	5	4
Talks and interviews with managers of Links' resort homes	—	—	—	—	—	7	—	—

Note: All interview data were collected from 1988 through 1992.

Table B.2 Written Records of Meeting Observations

	Austria	Finland	Iceland	Mexico	Poland	Sweden	French-speaking Switzerland	German-speaking Switzerland
AA meetings in metropolitan regions	6	37	5	86	12	9	—	—
AA meetings in other parts of the country	—	2	—	—	—	—	2	—
Service meetings above the group level, public information meetings, conventions	9	6	—	10	5	13	—	1
Celebrations and special occasions	1	3	1	12	3	1	1	1
Meetings of Al-Anon	—	5	—	25	—	—	—	—
Meetings of Links regular meetings	—	—	—	—	—	14	—	—
other gatherings	—	—	—	—	—	12	—	—

Note: All observational data were collected from 1988 through 1992.

264

Table B.3 Number of Life Stories Collected, by Background Characteristics of Life-Story Tellers

| | | –2 years in AA | | | 2–7 years in AA | | | 7 + years in AA | | | Total |
| | | Socioeconomic status | | | Socioeconomic status | | | Socioeconomic status | | | |
		Low	High	Total	Low	High	Total	Low	High	Total	
Finland	Men	4	3	7	5	3	8	6	4	10	25
	Women	2	2	4	2	2	4	2	2	4	12
Mexico	Men	5	4	9	7	7	14	4	4	8	31
	Women	5	3	8	3	4	7	1	2	3	18
Poland	Men	3	2	5	10	5	15	2	1	3	23
	Women	1	3	4	4	2	6	—	1	1	11
French-speaking Switzerland	Men	—	—	2*	—	—	4*	—	—	4*	10
	Women	—	—	—	—	—	5*	—	—	4*	9
German-speaking Switzerland	Men	—	—	3*	—	—	5*	—	—	3*	11
	Women	—	—	—	—	—	4*	—	—	6*	10

*These life stories were not classified by socioeconomic status.

265

were stratified by sex, age, socioeconomic status, and time in AA. In all, 160 life stories (100 male and 60 female) were collected. Material from the life stories has been used in the present report; more detailed analyses will be reported separately (Arminen, 1991b).

The stories were collected in and around metropolitan areas. The first contacts with the respondents were made at open AA meetings. Further contacts were made either by using a snowball technique or by attending open meetings. The stories were taped in private interviews at the home or in the office of the respondent or in the office of the researcher. Respondents were instructed to tell their first-step story (how they understood that they were powerless over alcohol) and to continue by telling about their later life as an AA member. The definition of an AA life story in the *Big Book* was usually read to the respondent: "Our stories disclose in a general way what we used to be like, what happened, and what we are like now" (1955, p. 58). The respondent was also reminded to cover events of all the different life arenas he or she felt were important. The expected length of a story was stated to be somewhat more than half an hour. The stories were told in monologue, without interruptions from the researcher. Sometimes additional questions were asked after the story. The average length of the stories was a little more than forty minutes.

Other Qualitative Data Sources

Individual members of AA were most helpful in providing access to a wide variety of unpublished documents: newsletters, annual accounts and reports, reports from service conferences, speeches, working papers, diaries, tapes of meetings, and personal notes on the AA program and various AA activities. We also have used published and unpublished members' accounts of the history of particular AA groups or of AA in a particular community or region. Similar material about Al-Anon and the Links has also been available.

Documentation of Findings

Much of the information collected for the study exists only in oral form. No written records are available to document many important details about the history and present activities of AA in each of the countries. Painstaking efforts were made, however, to cross-check any claims based on oral information. Individual working papers provide more detailed documentation of the oral and written sources used as evidence.

Some of the entries in the tables describing the situation of AA in each of the countries are based on detailed operational criteria, but others express summary judgments based on the overall information available. Providing references to all individual pieces of information would have been unwieldy. References are mainly given to published material and to systematic data sets, and only selectively to unpublished materials and oral sources.

Appendix C
Group, Meeting, and
Membership Surveys

For purposes of cross-cultural comparisons, three surveys were designed. Two surveys collected data on the basic functional units of AA, the group and the meeting. The third survey was concerned with information about the individual member.

The nature of AA ruled out orthodox and strictly comparable surveys. The goal was simply to collect cross-cultural data that would be relatively independent of the initial contacts made by the research teams. Local considerations determined which surveys were carried out in each country (Table C.1).

All three questionnaires were written in English and translated to study languages. National AA members helped adapt the questionnaires to local circumstances. A few questions and response alternatives were readjusted or deleted and other questions were added to the national research instruments. Special efforts were made, however, to safeguard the international comparability of the questionnaires.

The target region varied from one country to another. The Finnish and Mexican studies were carried out in metropolitan communities. The Austrian, Californian, Icelandic, Polish, Swedish, and Swiss surveys include data from rural areas as well.

In all study countries, information about the surveys was disseminated at different levels of the service structure. In consideration of the autonomy of individual groups and members in AA, we tried to establish personal contacts with as many groups as possible.

In some countries, good directories of groups and meetings were available, sometimes including contact adresses that permitted a mail survey. In Finland and Iceland, information in the directories could be used to compare the final sample and the non-response. In other countries, no accurate lists were available. Because of the anonymity principle, lists of individual members were not available.

Table C.1 Target Area and Year of Data Collection in Group, Meeting, and
Membership Surveys

	Target area	Group survey	Meeting survey	Membership survey
Austria	Country as a whole	1991	1991	—
Finland	Helsinki and Vantaa	1989	1990	—
Iceland	Country as a whole	1989	1989	1990
Mexico	Mexico City metropolitan area	1989	1989–1990	1990–1991
Poland	Country as a whole	1989	1989	1991
Sweden	Eastern AA district, including Stockholm and the surrounding countryside	1989	—	1990
French-speaking Switzerland	Region as a whole	—	—	1992
German-speaking Switzerland	Region as a whole	1991	1991	1992
California	Contra Costa County	—	—	1989

Group Survey

The English questionnaire consisted of fifty questions covering seven topical
areas: the group's background, membership, types of meetings organized, officers and group business, finances, activities and practices, and collaboration
with other groups.

The questionnaires were either mailed to the groups or handed out at
meetings at different levels of the service structure (Table C.2).

Institutional groups were included in Austria, Mexico, Poland, Sweden,
and Switzerland but excluded in Finland and Iceland.

In Austria, the questionnaires were handed out by the researcher at district business meetings or mailed to the district chairperson who distributed
them to the groups.

In Finland, the questionnaire was mailed to every second group in Helsinki and Vantaa listed in the 1987–1988 national directory. A letter of reminder was sent to groups that had not responded within five weeks. Before
the mailings, personal contacts had been established with most groups.

In Mexico, the division in the service structure (Central Mexicana and
Sección Mexico) and the lack of reliable directories made it difficult to set up
the sample frame. Contact was made with the General Service Offices of both

Table C.2   Number of AA Groups in Target Area, and Sample, Mode of Distribution of Questionnaires, Number of Completed Questionnaires, and Response Rate in Group Survey

Country	Number of AA groups in target area	Number of AA groups in sample	Mode of distribution	Number of groups responding	Response rate, %
Austria	101	101	Handed out at business meetings	62	61
Finland	138	69	By mail	39	57
Iceland	196	196	Handed out at service conference	35	18
Mexico	1,616	185	Handed out to GSRs or other group representatives	155	84
Poland	314	314	Handed out at service conference	78	25
Sweden	73	73	Handed out at district meetings and by mail	33	45
German-speaking Switzerland	112	112	By mail	66	59

service structures. With help from district representatives, a systematic sample of one out of every ten groups in metropolitan Mexico City was selected to complete both the group and the meeting survey. Members of the research team made several visits to the groups in order to gain their confidence and collaboration.

In Iceland and Poland, national bodies of AA gave their endorsement to distribute the questionnaires at the general service conference.

In Sweden, the questionnaires were distributed at two district meetings and sent by mail to the groups not represented at the meetings. Before distributing the questionnaires, the Swedish researcher had made contact with a number of the group representatives.

In the German-speaking part of Switzerland, the General Service Office distributed the questionnaires to all groups. The groups had beforehand been informed about the project by a leaflet. An attempt was made to survey AA groups in the French- and Italian-speaking parts of Switzerland. Questionnaires were sent to the groups but only one group responded, since the General Service Office in this area did not approve of the questionnaire.

The possibilities of assessing the representativity of the responses received

are limited. A comparison of the final Finnish sample to the groups not responding shows that responding groups are generally more active and larger
than non-response groups. In Iceland the groups that sent back their responses
were more often groups with open meetings. In Iceland and Poland, the questionnaire was available only to groups attending the general service conference.

Meeting Survey

The meeting survey was carried out in Austria, Finland, Iceland, Mexico, Poland, and the German-speaking part of Switzerland (Table C.3).

The English questionnaire included thirty-four questions on the following
topics: framework of the meeting, participants, collection of money, meeting
functionaries and speakers, meeting rituals, topic of meeting and structure of
discussion, and activities after the meeting.

In Austria and Switzerland, each group usually has one weekly meeting,
and there is no clear distinction between groups and meetings. Therefore, it
was natural to carry out both surveys simultaneously. In Poland as well, group
and meeting survey data were collected at the same time.

The target population for the Finnish meeting survey was defined as scheduled weekly meetings sponsored by non-institutional AA groups in Vantaa and
Helsinki. Out of 69 groups in the group survey sample, 4 had discontinued
before April 1990, and questionnaires were sent to the remaining 65 groups.

In Iceland, meeting questionnaires were made available at the general service conference at the same time as the group questionnaires. Since meetings in
treatment facilities and in prisons do not send representatives to the general
service conference, contact was separately made with these meetings.

In Mexico, the meeting survey aimed at collecting information on two
meetings organized by each of the groups that had returned the group questionnaire.

The instructions were to fill in the questionnaire for each meeting during a
specified study week or to complete the questionnaire for the same meeting as
close to the study week as possible.

Open meetings and meetings in Reykjavík were slightly overrepresented
in the Icelandic survey. In Finland, the group's size did not influence the response rate in the meeting survey.

Membership Survey

The membership survey was carried out in Iceland, Mexico, Poland, Sweden,
and Switzerland (Table C.4).

The English questionnaire covered the following topics: demographic and
social background, drinking habits, drug use, problems related to drinking,
treatment experiences and attempts to control drinking, the process of coming
to AA, participation in AA activities, and interpretations of the AA program.
In California, the questionnaire did not include all the questions used in this
report.

In California, the study covered a sample of regular weekly meetings listed

Table C.3 Number of AA Meetings in Target Area, and Sample, Mode of Distribution of Questionnaires, Number of Completed Questionnaires, and Response Rate in Meeting Survey

Country	Number of AA meetings in target area	Number of AA meetings in sample	Mode of distribution	Number of questionnaires completed	Response rate, %
Austria	101	101	Handed out at business meetings	62	61
Finland	191	101	By mail	68	67
Mexico	Not known	324	Handed out to GSRs or other group representatives	238	73
Iceland	196	196	Handed out at service conference	44	22
Poland	336	336	Handed out at service conference	83	25
German-speaking Switzerland	112	112	By mail	66	59

in the directory, with questionnaires handed out at the door at the end of the meeting, usually by research staff but in some cases by the group's general service representative.

In Iceland, questionnaires were made available at the national service conference in May 1990. About 120 out of a total of 196 groups were represented at the conference. Each general service representative was asked to take back enough questionnaires for all members in his or her AA group. Additional questionnaires were distributed by the AA service office to groups not represented at the conference (mostly small ones in remote areas of the country).

The Mexican questionnaire was distributed among members of the groups that had participated in the group survey. An average of four members in each group, with at least three months of AA membership, were selected to complete the questionnaire. Selection of the respondents was designed to reflect the age and sex composition of each group.

In Poland, the questionnaires were sent to five of nine existing intergroups, and representatives of the intergroups distributed the questionnaires.

In Sweden, membership questionnaires were distributed by the researcher at two district meetings and at open meetings, and district representa-

Table C.4   Mode of Distribution of Questionnaires, and Number of Completed
Questionnaires in Membership Survey

| Target area | Mode of distribution | Number of question-naires completed | | |
		Men	Women	Total[a]
Iceland	Handed out at service conference to GSRs for distribution at meetings and kept available at the national service office	170	35	205
Mexico	Handed out to GSRs or other group representatives	581	66	647
Poland	Given to five inter-groups for distribution at meetings	297	65	362
Sweden	Handed out at district meetings and distrib-uted by mail	148	65	216
French-speaking Switzerland	Given personally to all members who delivered their life stories	7	8	15
German-speaking Switzerland	Given personally to all members who delivered their life stories	40	27	73
California	Handed out at sched-uled weekly meetings	184	161	355

[a]Information on gender is missing for 10 respondents in California, 3 in Sweden and 6 in the German-speaking part of Switzerland.

tives carried questionnaires back to their group. Questionnaires were also available at the district office.

In Iceland, Mexico, Sweden, and Poland, the membership survey was designed to reach the members of the same groups as the group and meeting surveys. In the German-speaking part of Switzerland, questionnaires were distributed among all members of the groups where life stories were collected (see Appendix B). In the French-speaking part of Switzerland, only the individuals who delivered their life stories were asked to fill in the membership questionnaire. Because of the small number of respondents, data from the membership survey of the French-speaking part of Switzerland have not been used in the present report.

Not much independent information is available to assess the representativity of the membership response. In Iceland, women are underrepresented in the membership survey compared to the results of the group survey.

The Swiss response was stratified according to the design of the life-story project and is not representative of the overall membership.

More generally, it is likely that active members with a high meeting frequency are overrepresented among the respondents. It should also be kept in mind that there are members who regard data collection at meetings as conflicting with AA principles.

General Usability of the Survey Data

Because of differences in target populations and methods of data collection, the surveys are not strictly comparable. The small number of observations prescribes additional caution in interpreting cross-cultural differences. Despite these defects, the data serve their original purpose of illustrating the overall variability of AA and providing rough comparisons between countries.

Appendix D
Basic AA Texts

The AA Preamble

Alcoholics Anonymous is a fellowship of men and women who share their experience, strength and hope with each other that they may solve their common problem and help others to recover from alcoholism.

The only requirement for membership is a desire to stop drinking. There are no dues or fees for A.A. membership; we are self-supporting through our own contributions.

A.A. is not allied with any sect, denomination, politics, organization or institution; does not wish to engage in any controversy; neither endorses nor opposes any causes.

Our primary purpose is to stay sober and help other alcoholics to achieve sobriety.

The Serenity Prayer

God grant me the serenity to accept the things I cannot change, courage to change the things I can, and wisdom to know the difference.

The Twelve Steps

1. We admitted we were powerless over alcohol—that our lives had become unmanageable.
2. Came to believe that a Power greater than ourselves could restore us to sanity.
3. Made a decision to turn our will and our lives over to the care of God *as we understood Him.*
4. Made a searching and fearless moral inventory of ourselves.
5. Admitted to God, to ourselves, and to another human being the exact nature of our wrongs.
6. Were entirely ready to have God remove all these defects of character.
7. Humbly asked Him to remove our shortcomings.
8. Made a list of all persons we had harmed and became willing to make amends to them all.

9. Made direct amends to such people wherever possible, except when to do so would injure them or others.
10. Continued to take personal inventory and when we were wrong promptly admitted it.
11. Sought through prayer and meditation to improve our conscious contact with God *as we understood Him,* praying only for knowledge of His will for us and the power to carry that out.
12. Having a spiritual awakening as the result of these Steps, we tried to carry this message to alcoholics and to practice these principles in all our affairs.

The Twelve Traditions
1. Our common welfare should come first; personal recovery depends upon A.A. unity.
2. For our group purpose there is but one ultimate authority—a loving God as He may express Himself in our group conscience. Our leaders are but trusted servants; they do not govern.
3. The only requirement for A.A. membership is a desire to stop drinking.
4. Each group should be autonomous except in matters affecting other groups or A.A. as a whole.
5. Each group has but one primary purpose—to carry its message to the alcoholic who still suffers.
6. An A.A. group ought never endorse, finance or lend the A.A. name to any related facility or outside enterprise, lest problems of money, property or prestige divert us from our primary purpose.
7. Every A.A. group ought to be fully self-supporting, declining outside contributions.
8. Alcoholics Anonymous should remain forever nonprofessional, but our service centers may employ special workers.
9. A.A., as such, ought never be organized; but we may create service boards or committees directly responsible to those they serve.
10. Alcoholics Anonymous has no opinion on outside issues; hence the A.A. name ought never be drawn into public controversy.
11. Our public relations policy is based on attraction rather than promotion; we need always maintain personal anonymity at the level of press, radio, and films.
12. Anonymity is the spiritual foundation of all our Traditions, ever reminding us to place principles before personalities.

References

12 + 12: Twelve steps and twelve traditions. 1986. New York: Alcoholics Anonymous World Services. (1953).

44 questions. 1990. New York: Alcoholics Anonymous World Services.

A.A. group, The. 1990. New York: Alcoholics Anonymous World Services.

A.A. service manual combined with twelve concepts for world service, 1986–1987 edition, The. 1986. New York: Alcoholics Anonymous World Services.

A.A. service manual combined with twelve concepts for world service, 1988–1989 edition, The. 1988. New York: Alcoholics Anonymous World Services.

Language of the heart, The. 1988. New York: Alcoholics Anonymous World Services.

A.R.A. 1991. Letter to the editor, no title. *Recovering,* July, pp. 3, 16.

Aaltonen, I. 1990. *AA-liikkeen suomalaisessa jäsenlehdessä julkaistujen naisten ja miesten kirjoitusten vertailua* (Comparison between men's and women's contributions in the magazine of Finnish AA). Master's thesis, University of Helsinki.

Aaltonen, I., & K. Mäkelä. 1994. Female and male life stories published in the Finnish Alcoholics Anonymous journal. *The International Journal of the Addictions* 29 (4): 485–495.

Ahlström, S. 1987. Women's use of alcohol. In J. Simpura, ed., *Finnish drinking habits: Results from interview surveys held in 1968, 1976 and 1984,* pp. 109–134. Helsinki: The Finnish Foundation for Alcohol Studies.

Alcoholics Anonymous comes of age. 1986. New York: Alcoholics Anonymous World Services.

Anderson, D. J. 1980. The Minnesota experience. In P. Golding, ed., *Alcoholism: A modern perspective,* pp. 3–19. Lancaster: MPT Press Limited.

Anderson, J., & F. S. Gilbert. 1989. Communication skills training with alcoholics for improving the performance of two of the Alcoholics Anonymous recovery steps. *Journal of Studies on Alcohol* 30 (4): 361–367.

Anonymous. 1986. The power of the purse. *Box 459* 32 (5): 6–7.

Anonymous. 1989a. A noisy distraction. *AA Grapevine,* January, pp. 20–21.

Anonymous. 1989b. Do A.A.-style trinkets or bumper stickers violate the spirit of anonymity? *Box 459* 35 (2): 9–10.

Anonymous. 1989c. Practicing the Seventh Tradition—are we "walking like we're talking?" *Box 459* 35 (5): 1–2.

Anonymous. 1990a. Enormous possibilities. *AA Grapevine,* March, pp. 21–23.

Anonymous. 1990b. *Staying clean: Living without drugs.* San Francisco: Harper and Row.

Anonymous. 1993. Whatever happened to the circle and triangle? *AA Grapevine,* December, pp. 40–42.

Antze, P. 1979. Role of ideologies in peer psychotherapy groups. In *Self-help groups for coping with crisis,* pp. 272–304. San Francisco: Jossey-Bass.

Appel, C. 1988. Competition for recovery: Self-help groups for the recovering alcoholic and professionals' response within the West German treatment field. Paper presented at the 14th Annual Alcohol Epidemiology Symposium of the Kettil Bruun Society for Social and Epidemiological Research on Alcohol, at Berkeley, California.

Appel, C. 1992. Anonyme Alkoholiker in der Bundesrepublik Deutschland. *Drogalkohol* 16 (3): 173–179.

Arminen, I. 1991a. Characteristic features of spirituality within A.A. in Finland. Paper presented at the Third Working Meeting of the International Collaborative Study of Alcoholics Anonymous, January–February, at San Rafael, California.

Arminen, I. 1991b. Outline for comparative analyses of AA life stories: A research note. *Contemporary Drug Problems* 18 (4): 499–523.

Arminen, I. 1992. Sponsorship with AA in Finland. Paper presented at the Fourth Working Meeting of the International Collaborative Study of Alcoholics Anonymous, October, at Mexico City, Mexico.

Arminen, I. 1994. Interaction order of the meetings of Alcoholics Anonymous. Paper presented at the Conference on Addiction and Mutual Help Movements in a Comparative Perspective, at Toronto, Canada.

As Bill sees it. 1967. New York: Alcoholics Anonymous World Services.

Aune. 1991. Tuntemuksia alkuajoiltani ja matkan varreltakin (Memories of my early experiences and adventures on the way). *Ratkaisu* 41 (4): 28–31.

B.L. 1989. Serious dependency. *AA Grapevine,* February, pp. 21–22.

Back, K. F., & R. C. Taylor. 1976. Self-help groups: tool or symbol? *Journal of Applied Behavioral Sciences* 12: 295–309.

Badwa, D., & I. Kickbusch, eds. 1991. *Health promotion research: Towards a new social epidemiology.* WHO Regional Publications, European Series no. 37. Copenhagen: WHO Regional Office for Europe.

Bales, R. F. 1944. The therapeutic role of Alcoholics Anonymous as seen by a sociologist. *Quarterly Journal of Studies on Alcohol* 5: 267–278.

Barath, A. 1991. Self-help in Europe 1979–1989: A critical review. *Health Promotion International* 6 (1): 73–80.

Barbara N. 1994. Whose father? This AA feels that the Lord's Prayer can create barriers for some. *AA Grapevine,* April, pp. 18–19.

Barnlund, D. C. 1975. *Public and private self in Japan and the United States.* Tokyo: simul.

Bateson, G. 1985. The cybernetics of "self": A theory of alcoholism. In G. Bateson, *Steps to an ecology of mind*, pp. 309–337. New York: Ballantine Books.

Baumohl, J. 1986. Dashaways and doctors: The treatment of habitual drunkards in San Francisco from the gold rush to prohibition. Ph.D. diss., University of California, Berkeley.

Bean, M. 1975. *Alcoholics Anonymous*. Psychiatric Annals reprint, February-March. New York: Insight Communications.

Beckford, J. A., & M. Levasseur. 1986. New religious movements in Western Europe. In J. A. Beckford, ed., *New religious movements and rapid social change*, pp. 29–54. Paris & London: Sage/UNESCO.

Beckman, L. J. 1993. Alcoholics Anonymous and gender issues. In B. S. McCrady & W. R. Miller, eds., *Research on Alcoholics Anonymous*, pp. 233–248. New Brunswick: Rutgers Center of Alcohol Studies.

Bender, E. I. 1986. The self-help movement seen in the context of social development. *Journal of Voluntary Action Research* 15 (2): 77–84.

Bennett, L. A. 1984. Treating alcoholism in a Yugoslav fashion. *East European Quarterly* 18: 495–519.

Berger, J. 1994. From alcoholics group, reports of two murders. *The New York Times*, June 7, p. A12.

Bericht der 11. Gemeinsamen Dienst-Konferenz. 1991. Munich: Anonyme Alkoholiker.

Bernie B. 1992. Are we loosing the personal touch? *AA Grapevine*, June, pp. 14–16.

Big Book. 1955. *Alcoholics Anonymous: The story of how many thousands of men and women have recovered from alcoholism*. New York: Alcoholics Anonymous Publishing.

Bill C. 1965. The growth and effectiveness of Alcoholics Anonymous in a Southwestern city, 1945–1962. *Quarterly Journal of Studies on Alcohol* 26: 279–284.

Blau, M. 1991. Recovery fever. *New York Times*, September 9.

Blocker, J., Jr. 1989. *American temperance movements: cycles of reform*. Boston: Twayne Publishers.

Bloomfield, K. 1990. Dimensions of spiritual practice among gay and lesbian members of Alcoholics Anonymous. Paper presented at the 16th Annual Alcohol Epidemiology Symposium of the Kettil Bruun Society for Social and Epidemiological Research on Alcohol, June, at Budapest, Hungary.

Bloomfield, K. 1994. Beyond sobriety: The cultural significance of Alcoholics Anonymous as a social movement. *Nonprofit and Voluntary Sector Quaterly* 23 (1): 21–40.

Blumberg, L. U., & W. L. Pittman. 1991. *Beware the first drink! The Washington temperance movement and Alcoholics Anonymous*. Seattle, Washington: Glen Abbey Books.

Bock, G. 1991. Challenging dichotomies: Perspectives on women's history. In K. Offen, R. Roach Pierson, & J. Rendall, eds., *Writing women's history: International perspectives*, pp. 1–23. London: Macmillan.

Bondy, S. 1994. *Report of the Ontario alcohol and other drug opinion survey* [*sic*] 1993. Toronto: Addiction Research Foundation.

Borkman, T. 1990. Self-help groups at the turning point: Emerging egalitarian alliances with the formal health care system? *American Journal of Community Psychology* 18 (2): 321–332.

Box 459. News and notes from the General Service Office of A.A. (published monthly since 1954).

Bradley, A. M. 1988. Keep coming back: The case for evaluation of Alcoholics Anonymous. *Alcohol Health & Research World* 12 (3): 192–199.

Brandsma, J. M., M. C. Maultsby, R. Welsh, & S. Heller. 1977. The court-probated alcoholic and outpatient treatment attrition. *British Journal of Addiction* 72: 23–30.

Brandsma, J. M., M. C. Maultsby, & R. J. Welsh. 1980. *Outpatient treatment of alcoholism.* Baltimore: University Park Press.

Braun, J., & A. Greiwe. 1989. *Kontaktstellen und Selbsthilfe.* Cologne: ISAB-Verlag.

Brill, K. E. 1987. Der zweite Versorgungsweg. *Sozial Extra,* April, pp. 35–38.

Brown, D. J. 1989. The professional ex-: An alternative for exiting the deviant career. Paper presented at the Annual Meeting of the Society for the Study of Social Problems, August, at Berkeley, California.

Brown, H. P., Jr., & J. H. Peterson, Jr. 1990. Values and recovery from alcoholism through Alcoholics Anonymous. *Counseling and Values* 35 : 63–68.

Brown, H. P., Jr., & J. H. Peterson, Jr. 1991. Assessing spirituality in addiction treatment and follow-up: Development of the Brown-Peterson Recovery Progress Inventory (B-PRPI). *Alcoholism Treatment Quarterly* 8 (2): 21–50.

Brown, P., & S. C. Levinson. 1987. *Politeness: Some universals in language usage.* Cambridge: Cambridge University Press.

Bruun, K. 1971. Finland: The non-medical approach. In C. G. Kiloh & D. S. Bell, eds., *Proceedings of the 29th International Congress on Alcohol,* pp. 545–555. Chatswood: Butterworths.

Bufe, C. 1991. *Cult or cure?* San Francisco: See Sharp Press.

Bulletinen–Mötet mellan mötena (The Bulletin—The Meeting between Meetings). Newsletter of the National Service Office of AA in Sweden (published four to six times a year since 1973).

C.C. 1981. Cooperation. *AA Grapevine,* May, pp. 26–28.

Cahalan, D. 1987. *Understanding America's drinking problem: How to combat the hazards of alcohol.* San Francisco: Jossey-Bass.

Cahn, S. 1970. *The treatment of alcoholics: An evaluative study.* New York: Oxford University Press.

Cain, C. 1991. Personal stories: Identity acquisition and self-understanding in Alcoholics Anonymous. *Ethos* 19 (2): 210–253.

Came to believe. 1973. New York: Alcoholics Anonymous World Services.

Casriel, D. 1963. *So fair a house: The story of Synanon.* Englewood Cliffs, New Jersey: Prentice-Hall.

Cerclé, A. 1985. *L'Analyse descriptive des mouvements d'anciens buveurs*. Rennes: Université Rennes II. ("Extraits de ma thèse de doctorat, 'L'identité de l'ancien malade alcoolique membre actif d'une association d'entraide: abstinence militante et restructuration identitaire.' ") Prix Robert Debré 1985, Paris: Haut Comité d'Études et d'Information sur l'Alcoolisme, 2 vols.

Chuck W. 1990. ACA vs. CoDA. *Changes*, May–June, p. 9.

Cohen, J. L. 1985. Strategy or identity: New theoretical paradigms and contemporary social movements. *Social Research* 52 (4): 663–716.

Comments on A.A.'s triennial surveys. Unpublished report, Alcoholics Anonymous World Services, New York.

Cook, C. C. H. 1988. The Minnesota model in the management of drug and alcohol dependency: Miracle, method or myth? Part I, The philosophy and the programme. *British Journal of Addiction* 83: 625–634.

Corrington, J. E. 1989. Spirituality and recovery: Relationships between levels of spirituality, contentment and stress during recovery from alcoholism in AA. *Alcoholism Treatment Quarterly* 6: 151–165.

D.E. 1993. Medallions. In *AA Grapevine*, January, pp. 44–45.

Dalton, R. J., & M. Kuechler, eds. 1990. *Challenging the political order: New social and political movements in Western democracies*. Cambridge: Polity.

David A. 1989. Talking the talk. *AA Grapevine*, August, pp. 8–9.

Dawson, D. A. 1994. Are men or women more likely to stop drinking because of alcohol problems? *Drug and Alcohol Dependence* 36: 57–64.

de la Fuente, R. 1992. Alcoholism and alcohol abuse in Mexico. In J. Cohén-Yáñez, J. L. Amezcua-Gastélum, J. Villareal, & L. Salazar Zavala, eds., *Drug dependence: From the molecular to the social level*, pp. 335–342. Elsevier: Amsterdam.

Denzin, N. K. 1987. *The recovering alcoholic*. Newbury Park: Sage.

Denzin, N. K. 1991. *Hollywood shot by shot: Alcoholism in American cinema*. New York: Aldine de Gruyter.

Diamond, Jed. 1991. Letter to the editor, no title. *Recovering* August, pp. 6, 11.

Diani, M. 1992. The concept of social movement. *The Sociological Review* 1: 1–25.

Die Struktur der Gemeinschaft der Anonymen Alkoholiker in der deutschsprachigen Schweiz. Grundlage für die Arbeit in den Diensten. 1986. Zürich: Anonyme Alkoholiker.

Ditman, K. S., G. G. Crawford, E. W. Forgy, H. Moskowitz, & C. MacAndrew. 1967. A controlled experiment on the use of court probation for drunk arrests. *American Journal of Psychiatry* 124 (2): 160–163.

Doherty, J. J. 1991. Seattle church and Twelve-Steppers live side by side but separate. *Sober Times*, May, p. 14.

Dolph, L. 1989. "Guys like Louie and me." *AA Grapevine*, August, pp. 2–3.

Don P. 1989. Experience, strength, and hope—a visit to the Soviet Union. *AA Grapevine*, July, pp. 28–35.

Dr. Bob and the good oldtimers. 1980. New York: Alcoholics Anonymous World Services.

Duckert, F. 1989. The treatment of female problem drinkers. In E. Haavio-Mannila, ed., *Women, alcohol and drugs in the Nordic countries.* NAD-publication no. 16, pp. 172–191. Helsinki: Nordic Council for Alcohol and Drug Research.

Durkheim, E. 1953. The determination of moral facts. In E. Durkheim, *Sociology and philosophy,* pp. 35–62. Glencoe, Illinois: The Free Press.

E.O. 1981. Service fanatic? *AA Grapevine,* August, pp. 5–6.

Edwards, G., C. Hensman, A. Hawker, & V. Williamson. 1966. Who goes to Alcoholics Anonymous? *The Lancet,* August, pp. 382–384.

Eisenbach-Stangl, I. 1986. Nüchterne Frauen—Berauschte Männer. Geschlechtsspezifischer Drogenbrauch in Österreich. *Österreichische Zeitschrift für Soziologie* 11 (4): 52–67.

Eisenbach-Stangl, I. 1991a. *Eine Gesellschaftsgeschichte des Alkohols: Produktion, Konsum und soziale Kontrolle alkoholischer Rausch- und Genussmittel in Österreich 1918–1984.* Frankfurt: Campus.

Eisenbach-Stangl, I. 1991b. Expertendiagnose—Laiendiagnose. *Wiener Zeitschrift für Suchtforschung* 14 (3–4): 69–72.

Eisenbach-Stangl, I. 1991c. Trunksucht und Menschenwürde. In *Materialien zur Kriminalpolitikforschung 1: Unvernunft und Menschenwürde,* pp. 17–28. Bremen: Wissenschaftliche Einheit Kriminalpolitikforschung, Universität Bremen.

Eisenbach-Stangl, I. 1992a. Eine gutmütige Anarchie: Geschichte und Struktur der Gemeinschaft der Anonymen Alkoholiker in Österreich. *Drogalkohol* 16 (3): 153–171.

Eisenbach-Stangl, I. 1992b. Die Gemeinschaft der Anonymen Alkoholiker in Österreich. *Wiener Zeitschrift für Suchtforschung* 15 (3): 27–34.

Eisenbach-Stangl, I. 1992c. Trunksucht und Selbstreform. *Drogalkohol* 16 (3): 181–191.

Eisenbach-Stangl, I. 1992d. Alcoholics Anonymous as a spiritual community. Paper presented at the Fourth Working Meeting of the International Collaborative Study of Alcoholics Anonymous, October, at Mexico City, Mexico.

Eisenbach-Stangl, I. 1993. "Mon monstre." Ein Programm für Steigerung der Lebensfreude. *Manuskripte* 33 (121): 16–26.

Eisenbach-Stangl, I. In press. How to live a sober life in a wet society. In I. Eisenbach-Stangl & P. Rosenquist, eds., *Diversity in unity: Studies of Alcoholics Anonymous in Eight Societies.*

Eisenbach-Stangl, I., & P. Rosenqvist, eds. In press. *Diversity in unity: Studies of Alcoholics Anonymous in eight societies.*

Emrick, C. D. 1987. Alcoholics Anonymous: Affiliation processes and effectiveness as treatment. *Alcoholism: Clinical and Experimental Research* 11 (5): 416–423.

Emrick, C. D. 1989. Alcoholics Anonymous: Membership characteristics and effectiveness as treatment. In M. Galanter, ed., *Recent developments in alcoholism: Vol. 7. Treatment research,* pp. 37–53. New York & London: Plenum.

Emrick, C. D. 1994. Alcoholics Anonymous and other twelve-step groups. In M. Galanter & H. D. Kleber, eds., *Textbook of substance abuse treatment*, pp. 351–358. Washington: American Psychiatric Press.

Emrick, C. D., J. S. Tonigan, H. Montgomery, & L. Little. 1993. Alcoholics Anonymous: What is currently known? In B. S. McCrady & W. R. Miller, eds., *Research on Alcoholics Anonymous: Opportunities and alternatives*, pp. 41–76. New Brunswick: Rutgers Center of Alcohol Studies.

Encuesta sobre los miembros de Alcohólicos Anónimos México. 1990. Mexico City: Central Mexicana de Servicios Generales de Alcohólicos Anónimos.

Eriksen, S. 1991. Thisted abstinence society as a local self-help organization. Paper presented at the conference International Perspectives on Self-Help. July, at the Centre for Social History, University of Lancaster, England.

Eyerman, R., & A. Jamison. 1991. *Social movements: A cognitive approach*. Cambridge: Polity.

Fahrenkrug, H., & R. Müller. 1989. *Alkohol und Gesundheit in der Schweiz. Bericht über eine Umfrage aus dem Jahre 1987. Mit Trenddaten zu Alkohol-, Tabak- und Arzneimittelkonsum aus den Jahren 1975, 1981 und 1987*. Arbeitsberichte der Forschungsabteilung, no. 20. Lausanne: Schweizerische Fachstelle für Alkoholprobleme.

Falk, G. 1975. Gesellschaftliche Definitionen des Trinkens und ihre Zuschreibungsbedingungen. *Österreichische Zeitschrift für Soziologie* 3 (1): 37–48.

Fichter, J. H. 1976. Parallel conversions: Charismatic and recovered alcoholics. *Christian Century* 93: 148–150.

Fillmore, K., & D. Kelso. 1987. Coercion into alcoholism treatment: Meanings for the disease concept of alcoholism. *The Journal of Drug Issues* 17 (3): 301–319.

Final report of the 9th World Service Meeting. 1987. New York: Alcoholics Anonymous World Services.

Final report of the 11th World Service Meeting. 1991. New York: Alcoholics Anonymous World Services.

Final report of the 12th World Service Meeting. 1993. New York: Alcoholics Anonymous World Services.

Final report of the Thirty-Ninth Annual Meeting of the General Service Conference of Alcoholics Anonymous. 1989. New York: Alcoholics Anonymous World Services.

Fingarette, H. 1988. *Heavy drinking: The myth of alcoholism as a disease*. Berkeley & Los Angeles: University of California Press.

Galanter, M. 1990. Cults and zealous self-help movements: A psychiatric perspective. *American Journal of Psychiatry* 147 (5): 543–551.

Galanter, M., S. Egelko, & H. Edwards. 1993. Rational Recovery: Alternative to AA for addiction? *The American Journal of Drug and Alcohol Abuse* 19 (4): 499–510.

Galanter, M., D. Talbott, K. Gallegos, & E. Rubenstone. 1990. Combined Alcoholics Anonymous and professional care for addicted physicians. *American Journal of Psychiatry* 147 (1): 64–68.

Garcia, A. 1991. Dispute resolution in mediation. *American Sociological Review* 56 (6): 818–835.

Garfinkel, H. 1967. *Studies in ethnomethodology.* Englewood Cliffs, New Jersey: Prentice-Hall.

Garrard, J. 1991. Friendly societies, the Poor Law and working class politics in Rochdale. Paper presented at the conference International Perspectives on Self-Help, July, at the Centre for Social History, University of Lancaster, England.

Gary R. 1989. Recovery feels better than "feeling good." *AA Grapevine,* August, pp. 4–5.

Gellman, I. P. 1964. *The sober alcoholic: An organizational analysis of Alcoholics Anonymous.* New Haven: College and University Press.

Gerlach, L. P. 1983. Movements of revolutionary change: Some structural characteristics. In J. Freeman, ed., *Social movements of the sixties and the seventies,* pp. 133–147. New York: Longman.

Giddens, A. 1990. *The consequences of modernity.* Cambridge: Polity Press.

Glaser, F. B. 1981. The origins of the drug-free therapeutic community. *British Journal of Addiction* 76: 13–25.

Glaser, F. B., & A. C. Ogborne. 1982. Does A.A. really work? *British Journal of Addiction* 77 (2): 123–129.

Glendinning, C. 1994. *My name is Chellis, & I'm in recovery from Western civilization.* Boston: Shambhala.

Grant, B. F. 1992. Prevalence of the proposed DSM IV alcohol use disorders: United States, 1988. *British Journal of Addiction* 87: 309–316.

Greil, A. L., & D. R. Rudy. 1983. Conversion to the world view of Alcoholics Anonymous: A refinement of conversion theory. *Qualitative Sociology* 6: 5–28.

Gusfield, J. 1957. The problem of generations in an organizational structure. *Social Forces* 35: 323–330.

H.B. 1981. I will always be an alcoholic. *AA Grapevine,* July, pp. 32–34.

Haaken, J. 1993. From Al-Anon to ACOA: Codependence and the reconstruction of caregiving. *Signs: Journal of Women in Culture and Society* 18 (2): 321–345.

Haavind, H. 1984. Love and power in marriage. In H. Holter, ed., *Patriarchy in a welfare society,* pp. 136–167. Oslo: Universitetsforlaget.

Haavisto, K. 1992. Vuori-ryhmä (The Mountain group). Master's thesis, University of Helsinki.

Habermas, J. 1981. *Theorie des kommunikativen Handelns 1–2.* Frankfurt am Main: Suhrkamp.

Hall, T. 1990. New way to treat alcoholism discards spiritualism of A.A. *New York Times* (national edition), December 24, pp. 1, 10.

Harry, F. 1993. Bursting the babble. *AA Grapevine,* June, p. 14.

Helgason, T. 1984. Alkoholmisbrugets epidemiologi (The epidemiology of alcohol abuse). *Nordisk medicin* 99: 290–293.

Helmersson, K. 1989. A.A.—an exception from the rule. Paper presented at the Second Working Meeting of the International Collaborative Study of Alcoholics Anonymous, October, at Zaborow, Poland.

Helmersson Bergmark, K. In press. AA in the welfare state of Sweden. In I. Eisenbach-Stangl & P. Rosenqvist, eds., *Diversity in unity: Studies of Alcoholics Anonymous in eight societies.*

History and recommendations of the World Service Meeting 1969–1988. Revised 3/90. 1990. Unpublished report, Alcoholics Anonymous World Services, New York.

Hoem, B., & J. M. Hoem. 1988. The Swedish family: Aspects of contemporary developments. *Journal of Family Issues* 9: 397–424.

Hoffman, F. 1994. Cultural adaptations of Alcoholics Anonymous to serve Hispanic populations. *The International Journal of the Addictions* 29 (4): 445–460.

Hoffman, J. 1994. Murder case damages faith in confidentiality of therapy. *New York Times,* June 15, pp. A1, A13.

Hollandsworth, S. 1990. The codependency conspiracy. *Texas Monthly* 18 (2): 110–137.

Hornik, E. L. 1977. *The drinking women.* New York: Association Press.

Hughes, H. E. 1988. Foreword. *Alcohol Health & Research World* 12: 234–235.

Hulac, K. 1991. AA's trademark lawsuit. *Recovering,* April, pp. 1, 13.

Humphreys, K. 1992. Stories and personal transformation in Alcoholics Anonymous. Paper presented at the Annual Meeting of the Midwestern Psychological Association, May.

Humphreys, K. 1993. Psychotherapy and the Twelve Step approach for substance abusers: The limits of integration. *Psychotherapy* 30 (2): 207–213.

Humphreys, K., & M. D. Woods. 1993. Researching mutual help group participation in a segregated society. *The Journal of Applied Behavioral Science* 29 (2): 181–201.

If you are a professional Alcoholics Anonymous wants to work with you. 1986. New York: Alcoholics Anonymous World Services.

J.M. 1989. Untitled. *AA Grapevine,* November, p. 42.

Jack F. 1993. Where does it lead? *AA Grapevine,* July, pp. 28–30.

Jack G. 1993. The basics stay the same. *AA Grapevine,* October pp. 16–18.

Jacobs, M. K., & G. Goodman. 1989. Psychology and self-help groups. *American Psychologist* 44 (3): 536–545.

James, W. 1903a. Is life worth living? In W. James, *The will to believe and other essays in popular philosophy,* pp. 32–62. New York: Longmans Green.

James, W. 1903b. *The varieties of religious experience: A study in human nature.* London, New York, & Bombay: Longmans Green.

Jellinek, E. M. 1952. Phases of alcohol addiction. *Quarterly Journal of Studies on Alcohol.* 13: 673–684.

Jilek-Aall, L. 1978. Alcohol and the Indian-White relationship: A study of the function of Alcoholics Anonymous among Coast Salish Indians. *Confinia psychiatrica* 22: 195–233.

Jim N. 1988. A toast to our future. *AA Grapevine,* August, pp. 2–4.

Jim N. 1993. And words will never hurt us! *AA Grapevine,* July, pp. 34–36.

Joan T. 1992. Somebody's got to do it! *AA Grapevine,* June, p. 36.

Johnson, B. H. 1973. The alcoholism movement in America: A study in cultural innovation. Ph.D. diss., University of Illinois, Champaign-Urbana.

Johnson, H. C. 1987. Alcoholics Anonymous in the 1980s: Variations on a theme. Ph.D. diss., University of California, Los Angeles.

Johnson, V. E. 1986. *Intervention: How to help someone who doesn't want help.* Minneapolis: Johnson Institute Books.

Jones, M. 1990. The rage for recovery. *Publishers Weekly,* November 23, pp. 16–24.

Jones, R. K. 1970. Secretarian characteristics of Alcoholics Anonymous. *Sociology* 4: 181–195.

Joyce H. 1975. An equal-opportunity disease. *AA Grapevine,* March, pp. 36–37.

Kahn, J. 1991. The skeptic's journey. *San Francisco Focus,* January, pp. 33–36.

Kaskutas, L. A. 1989a. *A Study of Alcoholics Anonymous in Marin County.* San Rafael: Marin Institute for the Prevention of Alcohol and Other Drug Problems.

Kaskutas, L. A. 1989b. Women for sobriety: A qualitative analysis. *Contemporary Drug Problems* 16 (2): 177–200.

Kaskutas, L. A. 1992a. An Analysis of "Women for Sobriety." Ph.D. diss., University of California, Berkeley.

Kaskutas, L. A. 1992b. Beliefs on the source of sobriety: Interactions of membership in Women for Sobriety and Alcoholics Anonymous. *Contemporary Drug Problems* 19 (4): 631–648.

Kaskutas, L. A. 1993. Study of Alcoholics Anonymous in Marin County. Paper presented at the Fifth Working Meeting of the International Collaborative Study of Alcoholics Anonymous, November, at Vienna, Austria.

Kaskutas, L. A. In press. What do women get out of self-help? Their reasons for attending Women for Sobriety and Alcoholics Anonymous. *Journal of Substance Abuse Treatment.*

Kasl, C. D. 1992. *Many roads, one journey: Moving beyond the 12 steps.* New York: Harper Perennial.

Kasper, G. 1990. Linguistic politeness: Current research issues. *Journal of Pragmatics* 14: 193–218.

Katz, A. H. 1981. Self-help and mutual aid: An emerging social movement? *Annual Review of Sociology* 7: 129–155.

Katz, A. H. 1986. Fellowship, helping and healing: The re-emergence of self-help groups. *Journal of Voluntary Action Research* 15 (2): 4–13.

Katz, A. H. 1993. *Self-help in America: A social movement perspective.* New York: Twayne Publishers.

Katz, A. H., & E. I. Bender. 1976. Self-help groups in Western society: History and prospects. *The Journal of Applied Behavioral Science* 12: 265–282.

Katz, A. H., H. L. Hedrick, D. H. Isenberg, L. M. Thompson, T. Goodrich, & A. H. Kutscher, eds. 1992. *Self-help: Concepts and applications.* Philadelphia: Charles Press.

Keller, M. 1972. On the loss of control phenomenon in alcoholism. *British Journal of Addiction* 67: 153–166.

Kennedy, M., & K. Humphreys. 1994. Understanding worldview transformation in members of mutual help groups. *Prevention in Human Services* 11: 181–198.

Kenta. 1992. Pånyttfödelsen (Rebirth). *Bulletinen* 6: 6–10.

Keso, L. 1988. *Inpatient treatment of employed alcoholics: A randomized clinical trial on Hazelden and traditional treatment.* Helsinki: Research Unit of Alcohol Diseases, Helsinki University Central Hospital.

Kickbusch, I., & S. Hatch, eds. 1983. *Self-help and health in Europe.* Copenhagen: WHO Regional Office for Europe.

Kiviranta, P. 1969. *Alcoholism syndrome in Finland.* Helsinki: The Finnish Foundation for Alcohol Studies.

Klandermans, B., H. Kriesi, & S. Tarrow, eds. 1988. *From structure to action: Comparing social movement research across cultures.* Greenwich & London: JAI Press.

Klee, L., C. Schmidt, & G. Ames. 1991. Indicators of women's alcohol problems: What women themselves report. *International Journal of the Addictions* 26 (8): 879–895.

Kolumbus. [Annotations on the history of AA in Finland, 1961–1971]. Unpublished manuscript, General Service Office of Alcoholics Anonymous in Finland, Helsinki.

Kramer, R. M. 1981. *Voluntary agencies in the welfare state.* Berkeley and Los Angeles: University of California Press.

Krogh, P. 1989. Alcoholics Anonymous in Norway. In *Proceedings of the 35th International Congress on Alcoholism and Drug Dependence,* vol. 2, pp. 671–677. Oslo: National Directorate for the Prevention of Alcohol and Drug Problems.

Kühlhorn, E., K. Helmersson, & N. Kurube. 1991. One idea and two realities: AA members and Links in Sweden. Paper presented at the Third Working Meeting of the International Collaborative Study of Alcoholics Anonymous, January–February, at San Rafael, California.

Kurtz, E. 1982. Why A.A. works: The intellectual significance of Alcoholics Anonymous. *Journal of Studies on Alcohol* 43 (1): 38–80.

Kurtz, E. 1991. *Not-God: A history of Alcoholics Anonymous.* Center City, Minnesota: Hazelden.

Kurtz, E. 1992. Commentary. In J. W. Langenbucher, B. S. McCrady, W. Frankenstein, & P. E. Nathan, eds., *Annual Review of Addictions Research and Treatment,* vol. 2, pp. 397–400. New York: Pergamon Press.

Kurube, N. 1991a. The Link movement: A historical overview. Paper presented at the Third Working Meeting of the International Collaborative Study of Alcoholics Anonymous, January–February, at San Rafael, California.

Kurube, N. 1991b. Organizations and activities of Links. Paper presented at the Third Working Meeting of the International Collaborative Study of Alcoholics Anonymous, January–February, at San Rafael, California.

Kurube, N. 1992a. The ideological and organizational development of the Swedish Links movement. *Contemporary Drug Problems* 19 (4): 649–676.

Kurube, N. 1992b. National models: Self-help groups for alcohol problems not applying the Twelve Steps. *Contemporary Drug Problems* 19: 689–715.

L.F. 1983. Are we forgetting twelfth step calls? *AA Grapevine*, March, pp. 2–5.

L.W. 1991. Letter to the editor, no title. *Recovering*, July, p. 3.

La Croix d'Or Française. 1989. Statuts (By-laws). Unpublished document.

Larimer, T. 1992. Dysfunction junction. *USA Weekend*, May 8–10, pp. 4–5.

Lattin, D. 1990. Going to church the 12-Step way. *San Francisco Chronicle*, December 17, pp. A1, A6.

Leach, B., J. L. Norris, T. Dancey, & B. LeClair. 1969. Dimensions of Alcoholics Anonymous: 1935–1965. *The International Journal of the Addictions* 4 (4): 507–541.

Leach, B., & J. L. Norris. 1977. Factors in the development of Alcoholics Anonymous (A.A.). In B. Kissin & H. Begleiter, eds. *The Biology of Alcoholism: Vol. 5. Treatment and Rehabilitation of the Chronic Alcoholic,* pp. 441–543. New York: Plenum Press.

Lehto, J. 1991. *Juoppojen professionaalinen auttaminen* (Professional help for drunkards). Helsinki: VAPK-kustannus.

Lender, M. E., & J. K. Martin. 1982. *Drinking in America: A history.* New York: The Free Press.

Levine, H. 1978. The discovery of addiction: Changing conceptions of habitual drunkenness in America. *Journal of Studies on Alcohol* 39 (1): 143–174.

Levine, H. 1992. Temperance cultures: Concern about alcohol problems in Nordic and English-speaking cultures. In M. Lader, G. Edwards, & D. C. Drummond, eds., *The nature of alcohol and drug related problems,* pp. 15–36. Oxford: Oxford University Press.

Levinson, S. C. (1983). *Pragmatics.* Cambridge University Press: Cambridge.

Lieberman, M. 1986. Self-help groups and psychiatry. In A. I. Frances, & R. E. Hales, eds., *American Psychiatric Association Annual Review,* vol. 5, pp. 744–760.

Little Red Book. 1987. New York: Harper/Hazelden.

Living sober. 1975. New York: Alcoholics Anonymous World Services.

Löfstedt, R. 1991. Kvinnor och missbruk (Women and alcohol and drug abuse). Unpublished memorandum, National Board of Social Affairs, Stockholm.

M.E. 1990. "The power of a pronoun." *AA Grapevine,* January, p. 39.

McCarthy, K. 1984. Early alcoholism treatment: The Emmanuel movement and Richard Peabody. *Journal of Studies on Alcohol.* 45 (1): 59–74.

McCrady, B. S., & S. Irvine. 1989. Self-help groups. In R. K. Hester & W. R. Miller, eds., *Handbook of alcoholism treatment approaches,* pp. 153–169. New York: Pergamon Press.

McGuire, M. B. 1993. Health and spirituality as contemporary concerns. *Annals, APPPS* 527: 144–154.

MacIntyre, A. 1984. *After virtue.* Notre Dame: University of Notre Dame Press.

Madsen, W. 1979. Alcoholics Anonymous as a crisis cult. In M. Marshall, ed., *Beliefs, behaviors, and alcoholic beverages,* pp. 382–388. Ann Arbor: University of Michigan Press.

Madsen, W. 1980. *The American alcoholic.* Springfield, Illnois: Charles C. Thomas.

Mäkelä, K. 1989. Service structure of Alcoholics Anonymous in Finland. Paper presented at the Second Working Meeting of the International Collaborative Study of Alcoholics Anonymous, October, at Zaborow, Poland.

Mäkelä, K. 1991. Social and cultural preconditions of Alcoholics Anonymous (AA) and factors associated with the strength of AA. *British Journal of Addiction* 86 (11): 1405–1413.

Mäkelä, K. 1992a. Episodes related to Finnish AA meetings as speech events: Excerpts from interviews and field notes. Paper presented at the Fourth Working Meeting of the International Collaborative Study of Alcoholics Anonymous, October, at Mexico City, Mexico.

Mäkelä, K. 1992b. The lay treatment community: Alcoholics Anonymous and the new self-help movement. In J. W. Langenbucher, B. S. McCrady, W. Frankenstein, & P. E. Nathan, eds., *Annual Review of Addictions Research and Treatment,* vol. 2, pp. 345–366. New York: Pergamon Press.

Mäkelä, K. 1993a. Implications for research of the cultural variability of Alcoholics Anonymous. In B. S. McCrady & W. R. Miller, eds., *Research on Alcoholics Anonymous,* pp. 189–208. New Brunswick: Rutgers Center of Alcohol Studies.

Mäkelä, K. 1993b. International comparisons of Alcoholics Anonymous. *Alcohol Health & Research World* 17 (3): 228–234.

Mäkelä, K. 1994. Rates of attrition among the membership of Alcoholics Anonymous in Finland. *Journal of Studies on Alcohol* 55 (1): 91–95.

Mäkelä, K. In Press. Alcoholics Anonymous in Finland. In I. Eisenbach-Stangl & P. Rosenqvist, eds., *Diversity in unity: Studies of Alcoholics Anonymous in eight societies.*

Mäkelä, K., R. Room, E. Single, P. Sulkunen, B. Walsh, R. Bunce, M. Cahannes, T. Cameron, N. Giesbrecht, J. de Lint, H. Mäkinen, P. Morgan, J. Mosher, J. Moskalewicz, R. Müller, E. Österberg, I. Wald, & D. Walsh. 1981. *Alcohol, society, and the state: 1. A comparative study of alcohol control.* Toronto: Addiction Research Foundation.

Mann, M. 1950. *Primer on alcoholism: How people drink, how to recognize alcoholics, and what to do about them.* New York: Rinehart.

Manual de servicios. 1990. México City: Grupos 24 Horas y Terapia Intensiva de Alcoholicos Anonimos.

Marge R. 1993. "Know thyself." *AA Grapevine,* October, p. 19.

Mariolini, N. 1992. Anonyme Alkoholiker und das professionelle Behandlungssystem in der französischsprachigen Schweiz. *Drogalkohol* 16 (3): 193–209.

Mariolini, N., J. Rehm, H. Klingemann, & J. Besson. 1993. AA self-help groups in French- and Italian-speaking parts of Switzerland. Paper presented at the Fifth Working Meeting of the International Collaborative Study of Alcoholics Anonymous, November, at Vienna, Austria.

Mariolini, N., & J. Rehm. In press. Alcoholics Anonymous and its finances: The relationship of the material and the spiritual. *Alcoholism Treatment Quarterly.*

Martin, D. 1988. A review of the popular literature on codependency. *Contemporary Drug Problems* 15: 383–398.

Martin, J. E. 1992. The evolution of Al-Anon: A content analysis of stories in two editions of its "Big Book." *Contemporary Drug Problems* 19 (4): 563–585.

Martinovic, L. 1990. America the addicted. *Recovering,* October, p. 4.

Mary, W. 1991. Left-handed non-smoking pagan AA meeting here tonight! *Recovering,* June, pp. 1, 13.

Marzahn, C., & H. Bossong. 1989. Selbsthilfe im Sozialstaat. In S. Scheerer & I. Vogt, eds., *Drogen und Drogenpolitik,* pp. 431–446. Frankfurt & New York: Campus.

Maton, K., G. Leventhal, E. Madara, & M. Julien. 1990. The birth and death of self-help groups: A population ecology perspective. In A. H. Katz & E. I. Bender, eds., *Helping one another: Self-help groups in a changing world,* pp. 105–122. Oakland: Third Party Publishing Company.

Maxwell, M. A. 1950. The Washingtonian movement. *Quarterly Journal of Studies on Alcohol* 11 (3): 410–451.

Maxwell, M. A. 1984. *The Alcoholics Anonymous experience.* New York: McGraw Hill.

Melucci, A. 1980. The new social movements: A theoretical approach. *Social Science Information* 19: 199–226.

Melucci, A. 1989. *Nomads of the present: Social movements and individual needs in contemporary society.* Philadelphia: Temple University Press.

Memorias de la VI Reunion Iberoamericana de AA. 1989.

Michels, R. 1958. *Political parties: A sociological study of the oligarchical tendencies of modern democracy.* Glencoe, Illinois: The Free Press.

Miller, W. R. 1983. Alcoholism American style: A view from abroad. *Bulletin of the Society of Psychologists in Addictive Behaviors* 2 (1): 11–17.

Miller, W. R. 1986. Haunted by the Zeitgeist: Reflections in contrasting treatment goals and concepts of alcoholism in Europe and the United States. In T. Babor, ed., *Alcohol and culture,* pp. 110–129. New York: Academy of Sciences.

Miller, W. R. 1990. Spirituality: The silent dimension of addiction research. The 1990 Leonard Ball oration. *Drug and Alcohol Review* 9: 259–266.

Miller, W. R., & E. Kurtz. 1994. Models of alcoholism used in treatment: Contrasting AA and other perspectives with which it is often confused. *Journal of Studies on Alcohol* 55 (2): 159–166.

Milofsky, C., C. Haun, T. Butto, & M. Gross. 1988. *In search of the safety net: The migration of urban substance abusers to North Central Pennsylvania.* Mimeographed report, December.

Moeller, M. L. 1978. *Selbsthilfegruppen.* Reinbek bei Hamburg: Rowohlt.

Montgomery, H. A., W. R. Miller, & S. J. Tonigan. 1993. Differences among AA groups: Implications for research. *Journal of Studies on Alcohol* 54: 502–504.

Moos, R. H. 1986. *Group environment scale manual,* 2nd ed. Palo Alto: Consulting Psychological Press.

Morawski, J. 1988. Self-help groups of alcoholics in Poland. Paper presented at the First Working Meeting of the International Collaborative Study of Alcoholics Anonymous, August, at Helsinki, Finland.

Morgan, P., K. Bloomfield, & M. Phillips. 1989. Description of initial study sites for the U.S. component of the International Collaborative Study of Alcoholics Anonymous. Paper presented at the Second Working Meeting of the International Collaborative Study of Alcoholics Anonymous, October, at Zaborow, Poland.

Morisaki, S., & W. B. Gudykunst. 1994. Face in Japan and the United States. In S. Ting-Toomey, ed., *The challenge of facework: Cross-cultural and interpersonal issues,* pp. 47–93. New York: State University of New York Press.

Mossé, P. 1992. The rise of alcohology in France: A monopolistic competition. In H. Klingemann, J.-P. Takala, & G. Hunt, eds., *Cure, care, or control: Alcoholism treatment in sixteen countries,* pp. 205–221. New York: State University of New York Press.

Murken, S. 1994. *Religiosität, Kontrollüberzeugung und seelische Gesundheit bei Anonymen Alkoholikern.* Frankfurt am Main: Peter Lang.

Offe, C. 1985. The "New Social Movements": Challenging the boundaries of institutional politics. *Social Research* 52: 817–868.

Ogborne, A. C. 1989. Some limitations of Alcoholics Anonymous. In M. Galanter, ed., *Recent developments in alcoholism: Vol. 7. Treatment research,* pp. 55–65. New York & London: Plenum.

Ogborne, A. C., & F. B. Glaser. 1981. Characteristics of affiliates of Alcoholics Anonymous. *Journal of Studies of Alcohol* 42 (7): 661–675.

Oka, T. 1994. Self-help groups of Japanese alcoholics. Paper presented at the International Conference on Addiction and Mutual Help Movements in a Comparative Perspective, September, at Toronto, Ontario.

Ólafsdóttir, H. 1988. Lekmenn, alkoholisme og behandling (Laymen, alcoholism, and treatment). *Alkoholpolitik* 5: 83–90.

Ólafsdóttir, H. 1991. Working notes on the interaction of the Icelandic AA and the treatment system over time. Paper presented at the Third Working Meeting of the International Collaborative Study of Alcoholics Anonymous, January–February, at San Rafael, California.

Ólafsdóttir, H. 1992. Comparison of A.A. groups in seven countries. Paper presented at the 18th Annual Alcohol Epidemiology Symposium of the Kettil Bruun Society for Social and Epidemiological Research on Alcohol, June, at Toronto, Canada.

Ólafsdóttir, H. In press. The fluctuating boundaries between Alcoholics Anonymous, alcoholism treatment and the Icelandic society. In I. Eisenbach-Stangl & P. Rosenqvist, eds., *Diversity in unity: Studies of Alcoholics Anonymous in eight societies.*

Österling, A., M. Berglund, L.-H. Nilsson, and H. Kristenson. 1993. Sex differences in response style to two self-report screening tests on alcoholism. *Scandinavian Journal of Social Medicine* 21 (2): 83–89.

P.G. 1991. Letter to the editor, no title. *Recovering,* September, p. 4.

Pass it on. 1984. New York: Alcoholics Anonymous World Services.

Peele, S. 1989. *The diseasing of America: Addiction treatment out of control.* Lexington, Massachusetts: Lexington Books.

Peter, W. 1991. Review of Tony A., *The Laundry List. Recovering,* August, pp. 16–17.

Peterson, J. H. 1992. The international origins of Alcoholics Anonymous. *Contemporary Drug Problems* 19 (1): 53–74.

Petrunik, M. G. 1972. Seeing the light: A study of conversion to Alcoholics Anonymous. *Journal of Voluntary Action Research* 1: 30–38.

Phillip, Z. 1991. *A skeptic's guide to the Twelve Steps.* New York: HarperCollins.

Phillips, G. 1991. Becoming sober: Temperance in England in the nineteenth century. Paper presented at the conference International Perspectives on Self-Help. July, at the Centre for Social History, University of Lancaster, England.

Phillips, M. 1988. The American criminal justice system and mandates to alcohol treatment: The role of Alcoholics Anonymous. Paper presented at the First Working Meeting of the International Collaborative Study of Alcoholics Anonymous, August, at Helsinki, Finland.

Phillips, M. 1991. An introduction to a glossary of words about not drinking. Paper presented at the Third Working Meeting of the International Collaborative Study of Alcoholics Anonymous, January–February, at San Rafael, California.

Pike, T. 1988. Hearing room dreams and the birth of NIAAA. *Alcohol Health and Research World* 12: 268–269.

Pittman, B. 1988a. *AA, the way it began.* Seattle: Glen Abbey.

Pittman, B. 1988b. *Stepping stones to recovery.* Seattle: Glen Abbey.

Polich, J. M., D. J. Armor, & H. B. Braiker. 1981. *The course of alcoholism: Four years after treatment.* New York: John Wiley & Sons.

Pomerantz, A. 1984. Agreeing and disagreeing with assessments. In J. M. Atkinson & J. Heritage, eds., *Structures of social action,* pp. 57–101. Cambridge: Cambridge University Press.

Population Crisis Committee. 1988. Country rankings of the status of women: Poor, powerless and pregnant. Population Briefing Paper, no. 20. Washington, D.C.

Prestwich, P. E. 1988. *Drink and the politics of social reform: Anti-alcoholism in France since 1870.* Palo Alto, California: The Society for the Promotion of Science and Scholarship.

Questions and answers on sponsorship. 1983. New York: Alcoholics Anonymous World Services.

Ramirez, B. M. 1987. *Comunidad sin fronteras.* México: Diana.

Rappaport, J. 1993. Narrative studies, personal stories, and identity transformation in the mutual help context. *The Journal of Applied Behavioral Science* 29 (2): 239–256.

Régie fédérale des alcools. 1963–1988. *Rapports cantonaux sur la part des cantons au bénéfice net de la Régie fédérale des alcools.* Berne: Régie fédérale des alcools.

Rehm, J. 1993. Don't drink: Believe and act! The derivation from philosophical pragmatism of the principles of Alcoholics Anonymous. *Addiction Research* 1: 109–118.

Rehm, J., N. Mariolini, M. Huber, H. Klingemann, & B. Besson. 1992. Die Selbsthilfeorganisation der AA in der deutschsprachigen Schweiz. *Drogalkohol* 16 (3): 141–152.

Rehm, J., & N. Mariolini. In press. AA in Switzerland: Different organization for different cultural traditions? In I. Eisenbach-Stangl & P. Rosenqvist, eds., *Diversity in unity: Studies of Alcoholics Anonymous in eight societies.*

Rehm, J., & R. Room. 1992. Mutual help for alcohol-related problems: Studies of Al-Anon and alternatives to Alcoholics Anonymous. *Contemporary Drug Problems* 19 (4): 555–562.

Report of the Literature/Publishing Committee, 10th World Service Meeting. Unpublished report, Alcoholics Anonymous World Services, New York.

Riessman, F. 1990. Bashing self-help. *Self-Help Reporter,* summer/fall, pp. 1–2.

Riessman, F, & A. Gardner. 1987. The Surgeon General and the self-help ethos. *Social Policy* 18: 23–25.

Rivkin, J. 1990. Recovery stores: A sense of mission. *Publishers Weekly,* November, 23 pp. 26–27.

Robertson, N. 1988. *Getting better: Inside Alcoholics Anonymous.* New York: Morrow.

Robertson, R. 1970. *The sociological interpretation of religion.* New York: Schocken.

Robinson, D. 1979. *Talking out of alcoholism: The self-help process of Alcoholics Anonymous.* London: Croom Helm.

Roizen, R. 1977. A note on alcoholism treatment goals and paradigms of deviant drinking. *Drinking and Drug Practices Surveyor* 13: 13–16.

Roizen, R. 1987. The great controlled drinking controversy. In M. Galanter, ed., *Recent developments in alcoholism: Vol. 5. Memory deficits, sociology of treatment, ion channels, early problem drinking,* pp. 245–279. New York & London: Plenum.

Room, R. 1978. Governing images of alcohol and drug problems: The structure, sources and sequels of conceptualizations of intractable problems. Ph.D. diss., University of California, Berkeley.

Room, R. 1983. Sociological aspects of the disease concept of alcoholism. In R. G. Smart, F. B. Glaser, Y. Israel, H. Kalant, R. E. Popham, & W. Schmidt, eds., *Research Advances in Alcohol and Drug Problems,* vol. 7, pp. 47–91. New York: Plenum Press.

Room, R. 1989. Alcoholism and Alcoholics Anonymous in U.S. films, 1945–1962: The party ends for the "Wet Generations." *Journal of Studies on Alcohol* 50: 368–383.

Room, R. 1992. "Healing ourselves and our planet": The emergence and nature of a generalized twelve-step consciousness. *Contemporary Drug Problems* 19 (4): 717–740.

Room, R. 1993. Alcoholics Anonymous as a social movement. In B. S. McCrady & W. R. Miller, eds., *Research on Alcoholics Anonymous*, pp. 167–187. New Brunswick: Rutgers Center of Alcohol Studies.

Room, R., & T. Greenfield. 1993. Alcoholics Anonymous, other twelve-step movements and psychotherapy in the US population, 1990. *Addiction* 88: 555–562.

Rootman, I., & J. Moser. 1985. *Community response to alcohol-related problems* (DHEW publication no. ADM 85-1371). Washington, D.C.: USGPO.

Rosenqvist, P. 1991. AA, Al-Anon and gender. *Contemporary Drug Problems* 18 (4): 687–705.

Rosenqvist, P. 1992a. Common experiences, common identity? Women and men in the AA movement. Paper presented at the 18th Annual Alcohol Epidemiology Symposium of the Kettil Bruun Society for Social and Epidemiological Research on Alcohol, June, at Toronto, Canada.

Rosenqvist, P. 1992b. From the rib of AA: Al-Anon in Finland. *Contemporary Drug Problems* 19 (4): 605–629.

Rosenqvist, P., & N. Kurube. 1992. Dissolving the Swedish alcohol-treatment system. In H. Klingemann, J.-P. Takala, & G. Hunt, eds., *Cure, care, or control: Alcoholism treatment in sixteen countries*, pp. 65–86. New York: State University of New York Press.

Rosovsky, H. 1991. Qualitative aspects of AA in Mexico. Paper presented at the Third Working Meeting of the International Collaborative Study of Alcoholics Anonymous, January–February, at San Rafael, California.

Rosovsky, H. 1992. What Mexican males get in AA. Paper presented at the Fourth Working Meeting of the International Collaborative Study of Alcoholics Anonymous, October, at Mexico City, Mexico.

Rosovsky, H. In press. AA in Mexico: A strong but fragmented movement. In I. Eisenbach-Stangl & P. Rosenqvist, eds., *Diversity in unity: Studies of Alcoholics Anonymous in eight societies*.

Rosovsky, H., L. Casanova, C. Perez-Lopez, & A. Narvaez. 1992. Alcoholics Anonymous in Mexico. In J. Cohén-Yáñez, J. L. Amezcua-Gastélum, J. Villareal, & L. Salazar Zavala, eds., *Drug dependence: From the molecular to the social level*, pp. 343–352. Amsterdam: Elsevier.

Rosovsky, H., G. Guadalupe, R. Gutierrez, & L. Casanova. 1992. Al-Anon groups in Mexico. *Contemporary Drug Problems* 19 (4): 587–603.

Rucht, D., ed. 1991. *Research on social movements: The state of the art in Western Europe and the USA*. Frankfurt am Main & Boulder: Campus & Westview.

Rudy, D. R. 1986. *Becoming alcoholic: Alcoholics Anonymous and the reality of alcoholism*. Carbondale & Edwardsville: Southern Illinois University Press.

Rudy, D. R., & A. L. Greil. 1989. Is Alcoholics Anonymous a religious organization? Meditations on marginality. *Sociological Analysis* 50 (1): 41–51.

Ryhmäkäsikirja (The AA Group Handbook). 1983. Helsinki: AA-kustannus.

Sacks, H., E. A. Schegloff, & G. Jefferson. 1974. A simplest systematics for the organization of turn-taking for conversation. *Language* 50 (4): 696–735.

Sadler, P. O. 1979. The "crisis cult" as a voluntary association: An interactional approach to Alcoholics Anonymous. In M. Marshall, ed., *Beliefs, behaviors and alcoholic beverages*, pp. 388–394. Ann Arbor: University of Michigan Press.

SAKRAM (Schweizerische Arbeitsgemeinschaft der Kliniken und Rehabilitationszentren für Alkohol- und Medikamentabhängige). 1991. *Das spezialisierte Behandlungssystem für Alkoholabhängige: Statiozionäre Therapie und Rehabilitation 1984 bis 1990*. Lausanne: Schweizerische Fachstelle für Alkoholprobleme.

Schaef, A. W. 1987. *When society becomes an addict*. San Francisco: Harper and Row.

Schmidt, C., L. Klee, & G. Ames. 1990. Review and analysis of literature on indicators of women's drinking problems. *British Journal of Addiction* 85: 179–182.

Scollon, R., & S. B. K. Scollon. 1981. *Narrative, literacy and face in interethnic communication*. Norwood: Ablex.

Scott, A. 1990. *Ideology and the new social movements*. London: Unwin Hyman.

Seija. 1992. Elämäni löytö (The discovery of my life). *Ratkaisu* 42 (7): 29–33.

Sex and Love Addicts Anonymous. 1986. Boston: The Augustine Fellowship, Sex and Love Addicts Anonymous, Fellowship-Wide Services, Inc.

SFA (Schweizerische Fachstelle für Alkoholprobleme). 1993. *Zahlen und Fakten zu Alkohol und anderen Drogen*. Lausanne: Schweizerische Fachstelle für Alkohol- und anderen Drogenprobleme.

Shimanoff, S. B. 1994. Gender perspectives on facework: Simplistic stereotypes vs. complex realities. In S. Ting-Toomey, ed., *The challenge of facework: Cross-cultural and interpersonal issues*, pp. 159–207. New York: State University of New York Press.

Simpura, J., ed. 1987. *Finnish drinking habits: Results from interview surveys held in 1968, 1976 and 1984*. Helsinki: The Finnish Foundation for Alcohol Studies.

Smith, A. R. 1993. The social construction of group dependency in Alcoholics Anonymous. *The Journal of Drug Issues* 23 (4): 689–704.

Smith, D. H., & K. Pillemer. 1983. Self-help groups as social movement organizations: Social structure and social change. *Research in Social Movements, Conflicts and Social Change* 5: 203–233.

Smith, J. 1990. Setting store by personal recovery. *San Francisco Examiner*, December 16, pp. F1, F4.

Smith, L. N. 1993. A descriptive study of alcohol-dependent women attending Alcoholics Anonymous, a regional council of alcoholism and alcohol treatment unit. *Alcohol & Alcoholism* 27 (6): 667–676.

Smithers, R. B. 1988. Making it happen: Advocacy for the Hughes Act. *Alcohol Health and Research World* 12: 271–272.

Speiglman, R. 1994. Mandated AA attendance for recidivist drinking drivers: Ideology, organization and California criminal justice practices. *Addiction* 89 (7): 859–868.

Stafford, R. 1979. Alcoholics Anonymous and the woman alcoholic. In V. Burtle, ed., *Women who drink*, pp. 248–270. Springfield, Illinois: Charles C. Thomas.

Steffen, V. 1993. *Minnesota-modellen i Danmark* (The Minnesota model in Denmark). Holte, Denmark: Socpol.

Stein, J., ed. 1967. *The Random House dictionary of the English language*. New York: Random House.

Steinman, R., & D. M. Traustein. 1976. Redefining deviance: The self-help challenge to the human services. *Journal of Applied Behavioral Science* 12: 347–361.

Stenius, K. 1991. "The most successful treatment model in the world": Introduction of the Minnesota model in the Nordic countries. *Contemporary Drug Problems* 18: 151–179.

Stenius, K. 1994. AA und das spezielle Behandlungssystem für Alkoholkranke. *Wiener Zeitschrift für Suchtforschung* 17 (1/2): 69–80.

Stewart, C. 1986. *A reference guide to the Big Book of Alcoholics Anonymous*. Seattle: Recovery Press.

Sue, W. 1991. Letter to the editor, no title. *Recovering*, June, p. 3.

Suler, J. 1984. The role of ideology in self-help groups. *Social Policy* 14 (1): 29–36.

Suomen AA-palvelun ja toimikuntien suosituksia 1961–1986 (Recommendations 1961–1986 by the General Service and Committees of Finnish AA). 1986. Unpublished report, General Service Office of Alcoholics Anonymous in Finland, Helsinki.

Sutro, L. D. 1989. Alcoholics Anonymous in a Mexican peasant-Indian village. *Human Organization* 48 (2): 180–186.

Suurla, L., ed. 1989. *Nainen, alkoholi, elämä* (Woman, alcohol, life). Helsinki: Kirjapaja.

Świątkiewicz, G. 1991. Alcoholics Anonymous conferences in Poland. Paper presented at the Third Working Meeting of the International Collaborative Study of Alcoholics Anonymous, January–February, at San Rafael, California.

Świątkiewicz, G. 1992a. Others in AA life stories. Paper presented at the Fourth Working Meeting of the International Collaborative Study of Alcoholics Anonymous, October, at Mexico City, Mexico.

Świątkiewicz, G. 1992b. Self-help abstainer clubs in Poland. *Contemporary Drug Problems* 19 (4): 677–687.

Świątkiewicz, G., & A. Zieliński. In press. Alcoholics Anonymous in Poland. In I. Eisenbach-Stangl & P. Rosenqvist, eds., *Diversity in unity: Studies of Alcoholics Anonymous in eight societies*.

Taipale, I. 1979. *Poikkeavien alkoholin käyttäjien nimitykset ja määrittelyt Suomessa* (Terms applied to deviant drinkers in Finland). Report no. 124. Helsinki: The Social Research Institute of Alcohol Studies.

Takala, J.-P., H. Klingemann, & G. Hunt. 1992. Afterword: Common directions and remaining divergences. In H. Klingemann, J.-P. Takala, & G. Hunt, eds., *Cure, care, or control: Alcoholism treatment in sixteen countries*, pp. 285–304. New York: State University of New York Press.

Takala, J.-P., & J. Lehto. 1992. Finland: The non-medical case reconsidered. In H. Klingemann, J.-P. Takala, & G. Hunt, eds., *Cure, care, or control: Alcoholism treatment in sixteen countries*, pp. 87–109. New York: State University of New York Press.

Taylor, E.P. 1988. The New Watering Holes. *Recovering* (October/November), p. 18.

Taylor, M. C. 1977. Alcoholics Anonymous: How it works—recovery processes in a self-help group. Ph.D. diss., University of California, San Francisco.

Tervetuloa palvelemaan (Welcome to serve). 1989. Helsinki: Suomen AA-kustannus.

Thom, B. 1986. Sex differences in help-seeking for alcohol problems—1. The barriers to help-seeking. *British Journal of Addiction* 81: 777–788.

Thompson, E. P. 1979. *The making of the English working class.* Harmondsworth: Penguin.

Thune, C. 1977. Alcoholism and the archetypal past. *Journal of Studies on Alcohol.* 38: 75–88.

Touraine, A. 1978. *La voix et le regard.* Paris: Seuil.

Trevino, A. J. 1992. Alcoholics Anonymous as Durkheimian religion. *Research in the Social Scientific Sudy of Religion* 4: 183–208.

Trice, H. M., & P. M. Roman. 1970a. Sociopsychological predictors of affiliation with Alcoholics Anonymous. *Social Psychiatry* 5 (1): 51–59.

Trice, H. M., & P. M. Roman. 1970b. Delabeling, relabeling, and Alcoholics Anonymous. *Social Problems* 17 (4): 538–546.

Turner, B. S. 1986. Personhood and citizenship. *Theory, Culture & Society* 3 (1): 1–16.

Uffe. 1992. Mitt farväl till flaskan (My farewell to the bottle). *Bulletinen* no. 2, p. 30.

V.R.M. 1991. The Twelve Steps: Meeting the challenge of our success. *Recovering,* January, pp. 1, 9.

Vilmar, F., & B. Runge. 1986. *Auf dem Weg zum Selbshilfegesellschaft.* Essen: Klartext.

Vourakis, C. 1989. The process of recovery for women in Alcoholics Anonymous: Seeking groups "like me." Ph.D. diss., University of California, San Francisco.

Walsh, D. C., R. W. Hingson, D. M. Merrigan, S. M. Levenson, L. A. Cupples, T. Heeren, G. A. Coffman, C. A. Becker, T. A. Barker, S. K. Hamilton, T. G. McGuire, & C. A. Kelly. 1991. A randomized trial of treatment options for alcohol-abusing workers. *The New England Journal of Medicine* 325 (11): 775–782.

Weisner, C., & L. Schmidt. 1992. Gender disparities in treatment for alcohol problems. *Journal of American Medical Association* 268: 1872–1876.

Weiss, S. 1990. Characteristics of the Alcoholics Anonymous movement in Israel. *British Journal of Addiction* 85: 1351–1354.

Westerman, R. C. 1978. The structure of formal and informal situations. Ph.D. diss., University of California, Los Angeles.

White, B. J., & E. J. Madara, eds. 1992. *The self-help sourcebook*, 4th ed. Denville: American Self-Help Clearinghouse.

Whitley, O. R. 1977. Life with Alcoholics Anonymous: The Methodist class meeting as a paradigm. *Journal of Studies on Alcohol* 38: 831–848.

Wolf/Altschul/Callahan, Inc. 1990. *1990 Al-Anon/Alateen membership survey*. New York: Al-Anon Family Groups Headquarters.

World Health Organization. 1981. *Self-help and health: Report on a WHO consultation*. Copenhagen: WHO Regional Office for Europe.

Woronowicz, B., & A. Zieliński. 1992. Alcoholics Anonymous meetings in Poland. Paper presented at the Fourth Working Meeting of the International Collaborative Study of Alcoholics Anonymous, October, at Mexico City, Mexico.

Woronowicz, B. T. 1992. Abstainer clubs in Poland and their relationship to the Alcoholics Anonymous community. Paper presented at the Fourth Working Meeting of the International Collaborative Study of Alcoholics Anonymous, October, at Mexico City, Mexico.

Yinger, J. M. 1970. *The scientific study of religion*. New York: Macmillan.

Zald, M. N. 1988. The trajectory of social movements in America. *Research in Social Movements, Conflicts and Change* 10: 19–41.

Zald, M. N., & P. Denton. 1963. From evangelism to general service: The transformation of the YMCA. *Administrative Science Quarterly* 8: 214–234.

Zedaker, L. D. 1989. Booming new industries serve millions in recovery. *Sober Times*, October, pp. 23–24.

Zieliński, A. 1992. Dynamics of establishment of new groups in Poland. Paper presented at the Fourth Working Meeting of the International Collaborative Study of Alcoholics Anonymous, October, at Mexico City, Mexico.

Zieliński, A. 1993. The rules of discourse at AA meetings in Poland. Paper presented at the Fifth Working Meeting of the International Collaborative Study of Alcoholics Anonymous, November, at Vienna, Austria.

Zimmerman, D., & M. Polner. 1970. The everyday world as a phenomenon. In J. Douglas, ed., *Understanding everyday life*, pp. 80–104. Chicago: Aldine.

Zink, M. 1990. The story of creating a sober world. *Sobriety/Трезвость News*, July/August, pp. 1–3.

Index of Personal Names

Subject Index

DATE DUE